ONE YEAR WITHOUT SOCIAL MEDIA

Ben Wilson is a journalist and former editor of *Official PlayStation Magazine* and a number of successful websites. He was born in South London and now lives near Bath with his family, juggling the responsibilities of being a full-time dad with freelance writing commitments. His work has featured in *The Guardian, The Telegraph, The Independent,* and many more. This is his first book.

ONE YEAR WITHOUT SOCIAL MEDIA

BEN WILSON

ONE YEAR WITHOUT SOCIAL MEDIA

Copyright © 2021 Ben Wilson

First published in Great Britain by KDP 2021

All rights reserved

Ben Wilson has asserted his right under the Copyright, Designs and Patent Acts 1988 to be identified as the author of this work.

No part of this book may be reproduced, or stored in a retrieval system, or transmitted in any form or by any means, electronic, mechanical, photocopying, recording, or otherwise, without express written permission of the publisher. Under no circumstances may any part of this book be photocopied for resale.

Some names and identifying details have been changed to protect the privacy of individuals.

Paperback ISBN 9798724728157
eBook ASIN B08ZJDWYMS

Cover design by Andrew Leung

For Lady S and Little Blue
And Olivia, for convincing me that I could

CONTENTS

Prologue	1
1. January	13
2. February	35
3. March	55
4. April	75
5. May	95
6. June	117
7. July	143
8. August	163
9. September	183
10. October	201
11. November	221
12. December	241
Epilogue	261
Acknowledgements	267
Source Notes	271

PROLOGUE

This cannot be real. This definitely, categorically, emphatically cannot be real.

I read the magic words for the 733rd time. Just to be sure.

'Dear Mr Benjamin Wilson.

Glastonbury Deposit Booking Confirmation.

You have booked to attend Glastonbury 2020 at Worthy Farm, Pilton-Somerset on 26–28 June 2020. Gates open Wednesday 24th June.'

Flash back 25 minutes or so. It's a sorry Sunday in October. Like two million other desperadoes I've been breathlessly refreshing my way across a spaghetti junction of wires and electronics in the hope of scoring tickets to the world's most storied music festival, marking its 50th anniversary. To little avail. My laptop's reaction to this critical task is a repeated 'could not process your request' error. My phone isn't even that kind, refusing to so much as try to load the necessary webpage. Adhering to a public request from organisers Michael and Emily Eavis to avoid server overload, I've not even bothered with my iPad, which remains out of sight and mind in another room.

I've never done Glastonbury before, but know that recent years took 30–45 minutes to sell out. At the 20-minute mark, halfway to crushing disappointment, my refreshing becomes less obsessive and I instead bring up Twitter, entering 'Glasto tickets' as a search term and whirring through responses. Most of those sharing their thoughts are in a similar position to myself, dismayed at their festival aspirations fading. Yet I spot one trend: almost all of those reporting to have secured tickets claim to have done so using an iPad.

Superstition? Pot luck? Destiny? Whatever the reasoning, I figure I have nothing to lose. I retrieve the iPad from the living room, wince at its 17% battery life, and find a space for it amid the tangle of extension leads on the dining room table. I paste the link I've been refreshing on the laptop into an email, send it to myself, and click on it in my iPad's mail client.

The most ridiculous thing occurs.

The link works first time.

Hands trembling, stomach churning, I enter the details of my four-strong travelling party as swiftly yet meticulously as possible. There's a disheartening pause as I click through to the payment page, but it loads fine and I input bank digits with similarly speedy, if nerve-fraying, diligence. One more click. A few more agonising seconds. Then a very real, off-the-charts-exciting confirmation page.

I'm going to Glastonbury.

I'm going to bloody Glastonbury.

I'm going to bloody Glastonbury, for the first time in my life, as the most ridiculous 40th birthday celebration.

I send a WhatsApp group message to my three travelling buddies, mainly consisting of happy swears. They send various messages back, also mainly consisting of happy swears.

And then I...

You'd like to say I rejoice, right? Do a little dance around the kitchen? Knock back a celebratory gin or seven despite the early hour? Run through the streets of my tiny West Country village chanting Taylor Swift songs in contented delirium?

I'd like to say that too.

I do precisely none of these things.

Instead, I panic like I've seldom panicked before.

Not about the prospective line-up. Swift has been the rumoured headliner for months, and – with two daughters aged six and four – long been our family's prime in-car listening choice. Other artists I like will be a bonus.

Nor is my panic about a longstanding fear of perennially overflowing portaloos, or a constitution that collapses in on itself at the merest whiff of gluten, or how I'll survive five days without my kids. The reaction to that last one is the opposite of panic.

Nope, instead of all of those very real concerns, I panic about... how I'm going to charge my mobile phone while camping for five days in England's most legendary of pastures green.

And did those feet in ancient time not think about the need for USB sockets?

27 minutes after discovering that I'm going to Glastonbury, I'm having a preposterous hissy fit about battery life.

Because it's the most social-media friendly festival in the world, isn't it? And I am a bona fide social media addict. King of the overshare. Prince of the annoying selfie. I treasure my Twitter blue tick as if it were a third child. My Facebook account is updated daily with stories of parenting mishaps and career achievements which friends kindly 'Like' in the internet world while almost certainly rolling their eyes in the real one. When not writing articles in exchange for pounds and pence, I spend my hours on forums debating my football team (Crystal Palace), or political views (let's maybe not go there), or wrestling obsession (let's absolutely not go there).

Photographic abilities best described as blurrier than Damon Albarn mean my Instagram account is less utilised, but Glastonbury is a chance to rectify that. Idyllic snaps of glowing faces happily knocking back cider, of Swift owning the Pyramid Stage, of secret acoustic sets and 10 trillion flags and flawless sunsets. All glorious imagery, all requiring day-long battery life in order for me to snap and post (and tweet and Facebook bleat).

Panic, panic, panic.

I'm researching myriad options now, from taking a bank of pre-loaded chargers, to borrowing a second phone, to accommodation choices that include some form of electricity for overnight charging. Most tempting is a scheme offered by the phone network EE. For a £20 fee you collect a fully loaded power bar upon arrival which can be swapped out for a fresh one once per day. Couple that with two or three of my own pre-purchased electro-bricks and I should be good for the whole festival.

Hysterical plan after hysterical plan. Just not in the amusing sense.

I stop, and breathe, and realise how absurd I'm being. Then I lurch in the other direction.

Glastonbury is the most social-media-savvy festival around – but it's also the most hippie. Eco-friendly and chilled and all about enjoying the vibe. What if I go the other way completely, and commit to staying off social media for the entire thing? No more concerns about lithium, unless Swift busts out a surprise Nirvana cover. No need to get flustered about my god-awful snapshot skills. Just me, three friends, five days of music, and an abundance of smiles and alcohol and memories. And more alcohol.

Half my panic is gone. With the immediacy of a Thanos finger snap. To alleviate the rest, a further idea blooms.

What if I extend this premise to the entire calendar year? What if, for all of 2020, I bid farewell to Facebook, and Twitter, and Instagram, and instead devote it to my children, friends, family, to enjoying life? Without the chase for the next gurning selfie, or the quest for the perfect 280-character summary of a football match or political mishap?

What if I go one year without social media?

It's an idea I've kicked around in the past. From offices to pubs, football matches to baby groups, I've lost count of the number of times I've heard friends say, "I need a break from social media." Often, in those moments, I've agreed – yet never taken the idea seriously because of my profession. I'm a freelance journalist. My specialist fields are sports, wrestling, and videogames. Open interaction is a key factor in writing for those audiences so, bolstered by that blue tick, I've repeatedly convinced myself that I need to be on Twitter, and Facebook, and all those forums. The 70%-sensible, WWE-addicted alternative to Piers Morgan. With 7.1 million fewer followers.

Yet in the weeks after securing Glastonbury tickets the reasons for taking an extended break crystallise. They are fourfold, and stem from an incident on Twitter two years prior. I'd made a glib comment about the Chelsea footballer Eden Hazard's predilection for tumbling in the penalty area, and had been met with some direct, expectedly unkind responses from the Stamford Bridge faithful. One set of comments went too far, with a series of foul threats made towards my then-four-year-old, who was visible in my profile picture. The culprit was swiftly banned, but a report to local police amounted to nothing, and the experience damaged me. I needed to use social media for work, but felt tattooed with a deep unease about doing so. My already fragile mental health spiralled, to the point of requiring one-to-one treatment.

Fast forward to the December 2019 UK general election. During its build-up I became embroiled in a series of political discussions on our village's Facebook forum. As an opinionated, but hopefully open-minded, liberal living in old-fashioned Conservative Jacob Rees-Mogg's constituency, I anticipated blowback to every post, and got it. But the level of grudge-laden fury and personal insult, from people I recognised from the local chippy or branch of Tesco, felt shocking.

I'd post what I intended to be a logical, considered opinion on the area's Liberal Democrat candidate, or a few sentences trying to offer balance on Labour leader Jeremy Corbyn, and be met with abuse and C-words and, on one occasion, a revelation that I needed "a slap" from someone I knew to live two roads away. Passion was expected. Nastiness was the norm.

Reason three was tied to my 40th birthday – packed with stress which had nothing to do with passing a landmark number. Instead, it was using Facebook to arrange a party which played further mental health havoc. Three months' notice was given to hand-picked friends, yet many ignored polite group nudges to RSVP. The event came and went with two-dozen choosing to take the Ronan Keating route and say nothing at all. I had an excellent evening, but the no-word no-shows lingered. 24 needle pricks to the heart, induced by social media.

All of which makes me sound like a needy man-toddler. Guilty as charged, but apparently I'm not alone. US website The Verge ran a feature on this phenomenon, revealing that the hurt comes from the same place as "read receipt pain" – knowing someone has seen a text or WhatsApp message and chosen to get on with their day. "What people do typically in this situation is they see that someone has seen [the event invite]," says former Facebook senior product manager Aditya Koolwal, "and then they just directly message them and say, 'hey, can you let me know?'" In response journalist Ashley Carman confesses, "I've just taken to not opening events. Because I don't want [the creator] to know that I saw it." Foolishly I didn't follow up on an individual basis, and instead let self-pity reign.

The deal-sealer came days later. For many years I'd suffered from the skin condition psoriasis, monitored by a thorough dermatologist. In late December I attended a routine appointment and was stunned to learn that one patch of skin had changed appearance dramatically, and would require an immediate biopsy to check for cancer. "Sign this form and come back in an hour," requested the doc. I signed the form. I then sat in a waiting room for that hour in a state of all-consuming fear.

My Facebook friends list was populated by 838 contacts from schools, uni, jobs, and toddler groups. All good, caring people, who'd been phenomenally supportive when I posted about completing my cognitive behavioural therapy (CBT). Yet fearful I was dying, desperate to tell *anyone* on a one-to-one basis, the list drew a blank. Thanks to a sense of social anxiety which became debilitating in my thirties, I'd drifted out of real-life, day-to-day contact with almost every single one, maintaining relations via status updates like winning a football match, or cute pics of our kids, or thoughts on favourite Pot Noodle flavours. (Sweet & Sour, although I've still not forgiven them for ditching Sausage Casserole.) I didn't want to worry family members. I didn't want to panic the mother of my children.

I froze.

838 Facebook friends. Yet, in that wait to have a square of epidermis lopped off to be tested for the big C, I felt truly alone.

In that moment, extending the Glasto plan became something I had to do. It was a chance to re-establish friendships using conversation rather than a Like button. The opportunity to take a break from Twitter abuse every time I tried to offer balanced analysis of a football transfer or videogame. 12 months to get to grips with constructing Insta posts superior to a reception-class Crayola project.

A fortnight later I received good news. The biopsy showed a lichenoid eruption, but no cancer. The ensuing wave of relief strengthened my will power to push ahead, and threw up some questions I'm keen to see answered from 12 months of social-media silence. Will it make me healthier, mentally and/or physically? Will focussing on friendships and family put me in a better mindset to receive future news of a similarly troubling vein? Will anyone notice my absence, or care? Once the 12 months are up will I commit to staying away?

On a personal level I'm entirely devoted to a year without social media. But there are two complications: one professional, one school-related. You're going to roll your eyes at the next bit. You might even consider drawing an asterisk on the cover. Or Asterix, taking his stubby sword to my name. Ow! Right in the second N! Do what you must, but please stick with me if you can.

Right, ready? Here's the thing. As sports editor of a large gaming website I still require strictly limited Twitter access for work, or this will also turn into a year without food and a roof over our heads. I've also just taken over as chair of my daughter's school PTA, so will have to make relevant announcements on its Facebook group occasionally. But I don't want these caveats to infringe upon the spirit of the project. I *definitely* don't want you getting dizzy from all the eye-rolling and asterisk-doodling you're contemplating right now.

So we're going to need to establish some ground rules, aren't we? Come on then…

1. I can use Twitter for work purposes where strictly relevant. For instance, much of my freelancing pertains to football sim *FIFA 20*, for which publisher EA reveals content and screenshots on Twitter at 6pm most Fridays. It's imperative that I access that. But I can't use my usual, blue-tick @BenjiWilson account. Instead, I'll access one I've not signed into for years: @wrestlingquiz, set up in 2014 to promote an app my wife built. I'm still forbidden to tweet anything from that account, and can only use it to check pertinent feeds.

2. I must leave all Facebook groups other than the school PTA one. This can be accessed for essential reasons – to flag up committee decisions, confirm upcoming events, and disclose meeting minutes.

3. I can log into Twitter, Facebook and Instagram once per month – on the 15th – to check notifications such as direct messages and @ replies, as a housekeeping measure. For instance, if a family member gets in touch on Facebook, or potential work contact makes an enquiry on Twitter, I can direct them to email or text message to continue the conversation. I cannot post anything public myself.

4. WhatsApp doesn't count. Because we all know it's just free text messaging.

5. The use of sports app Strava is permitted. I'm aware that sounds arbitrary, but this is the one social media form which has changed my life for the better, levelling-up once-comedic running skills and upgrading my mental health as a direct result. I can already say, with certainty, that deleting it would be detrimental. Plus I need it in order to track my monthly tarmac totals.

Ah yes, the monthly tracker. The sixth rule is that I will monitor quantifiable elements of the challenge in order to figure out whether staying off social media has enabled a degree of self-improvement. These include my nightly sleep, monthly weight, cumulative running distance, and number of books read. I'm hoping to go old school and replace the many digital words digested each month with papyrus ones.

I'll also track how many friends and followers I drop, to judge whether my failure to post affects social media numbers. I've often figured that the best way to sustain a Twitter following once you reach a certain level – 5,000 followers, for me – is to avoid upsetting anyone by saying the sum total of zero.

Onward to 31 December. Before deleting the necessary apps from phone and iPad, I need to purge my Facebook group subscriptions. A cautionary check shows that I've signed up to more than 50 over the years, and all must be detached if this project is going to have any value. It's an arduous process. Some, like Vauxhall Zafira Car Fires – related to a vehicle type we owned years back – are of zero relevance and easy to bin.

Others are tough to cut ties with. Funko Pop UK has been vital to expanding my uber-geeky vinyl-figure collection, and the thought of going a year without browsing it feels like a genuine wrench. Shit London is a brilliant source of photographic amusement pertaining to my city of origin, from entertaining shop names, to sex toys stranded on park benches, to a refrigerator abandoned in a busy street today with 'Happy New Year' graffitied onto it. Hitting the 'leave group' button proves a bind.

Goodbye to the local village group, source of pre-election squabbling but also helpful information for events related to Halloween, or Christmas, or World War III breaking out when someone sets off fireworks on a date other than 5 November. Adios, sales groups where I've picked up bargains and cleared tat in recent times. Laters, forums dedicated to my old secondary school, and Sega Everything Sega, Cornwall Holiday Homes, even Glasto Goers – I'll have to work out my own way at the festival now.

Also out are some 'classic' groups from Facebook's experimental early days, such as Prawn Vindaloo Appreciation Society, Room To Let In Tooting and – I kid you not – Phone Numbers All Gone Coz Nokia Are Twats. [Last post: April 2011. Should survive okay.]

The year without social media hasn't even started and I feel bereft. As though I'm walking away from a group of carousing friends, certain they're going to have the jolliest time without me. It takes an hour to remove all trace of my old network, and the blank canvas I was hoping to be faced with looks more like an impassable brick wall. One of my motivations behind the project was some kind of catharsis. In this moment, it isn't forthcoming. I feel glum.

Still, I press on. My mood is lifted by the swift decisiveness of culling social media from mobile devices. Grab iPad, bring up the little 'cross' symbols required to remove apps, tap the ones for Facebook, Twitter, and Instagram. Then do the same on mobile. Extricating myself from Facebook groups felt cumbersome and isolating; this process is much more liberating. Goodbye, ya brick-shaped blighters.

All that remains is to provide some kind of non-flouncy, cryptic farewell Facebook message on the stroke of midnight. Having passed that milestone birthday, gone through an amicable separation from my ex-wife, and successfully completed CBT, I opt to end 2019 with something positive and a touch romantic: the lyrics to 1968 hit This Will Be Our Year, by The Zombies. I do have a particular individual in mind, which we'll get to, but it's also a sentiment I hope rings true for all 838 people on that bloated friends list – even if my role in their version of 2020 is now likely to be minimal.

End of month stats: December 2019

Weight: 15st 5lb
Twitter followers: 5,033
Facebook friends: 838
Instagram followers: 223
Average sleep: 6h 4min
Books read: 2 – Harry Redknapp: Always Managing, *Simon Hughes:* And God Created Cricket
Distance run: 25.1km
Time running: 2h 24min
Best 5K time: 27min 52s
Best 10K time: N/A

Note from the author: The upcoming chapter contains a reference to Chadwick Boseman penned in advance of his sad passing in August 2020. Due to it being written as a diary in real time, I've chosen to retain it in unedited form, and hope this is not considered poor taste.

JANUARY

Wednesday 1 January

This is it. One year without social media is underway. It takes two nanoseconds for my mettle to be tested, as the peace in our village is obliterated by a cacophonous fireworks display. Despite New Year's Day being a traditional cause for celebration I know the Facebook forum will already be a den of squabbling, and am tempted to log in and referee. However, that's no longer my business, so I divert my attentions to watching the London sparks fly on TV.

The capital's light show is accompanied by football anthems Three Lions and Nessun Dorma, as a prelude to the Euro 2020 final being played at Wembley in the summer. It's a game I have tickets for, and experiencing the build-up and match itself with zero access to social media will be a seismic change from my norms.

There's an inevitable urge to sign back into devices and cycle through 'Happy New Year' posts, but I resist.

12:15am brings bedtime. 900 seconds survived. Just another 365 days, 23 hours and 45 minutes to go. [Trust me to take this on in a leap year.]

I awake at 6.44am. As a rule, the first thing I do on any given day is reach down the side of the bed, grab my phone, and spend five minutes scrolling through Facebook, then Twitter, then Insta – before I've even considered what my two kids are doing. That gravitational pull of bedside electronics remains in place. Yet no sooner have I picked up my phone, I recall that ties to the outside world have been cut and it's relegated back to the floor. Then a peculiar thing happens: I nod off.

This is uncharted territory. I am an atrocious sleeper, fortunate if my head hits hay before midnight, prone to 3am wake-ups which keep me alert until morning. On the occasions I do sleep through, any time past 7am feels like a lie-in with two small blonde fidgets pole-vaulting onto my ribs at daybreak. Yet this morning, with my ex-wife Mrs E kindly looking after the tiny ones, I drift into a contented slumber all the way to 8.26am.

86 whole minutes of bonus kip. It's a New Year's miracle of sorts. The project has been a success! Maybe I'll just stop here and quit while ahead.

That would make for a rubbish book though, so better to press on.

As the day progresses my temptation to sign back into everything is a minute-by-minute nuisance, so I gather up the family for a half-hour drive to Trowbridge and a spot of lunch. Even then I find myself on autopilot, grasping for the internet's familiar embrace. As Mrs E takes the kids to the loo, I pick up my phone and instinctively type cpfc.org [a Crystal Palace supporters' site] into the browser – then, remembering the rules, stroppily launch it across the table. Thankfully, my daughters have selected a dining booth with sofas.

Sports wise, I'm in at the deep end. Palace are playing Norwich City at 5.30pm. I attempt to ignore the fixture, focussing on blissful domesticity. I load the dishwasher. Throw some pots and pans into lukewarm water. Run a sponge over them. Bathe the children. Pretend that there is no football match occurring at Carrow Road, and if there were no one in the world would be discussing it on Twitter or Facebook.

At 7.15pm, nippers in bed, I take a tentative peep at the Sky Sports Score Centre app. Crystal Palace are losing 0-1. Of course they are! At some point of most weekends, Crystal Palace are losing 0-1.

Within seconds, an update: Palace have had a goal ruled out for offside. Or have they? There's a VAR (Video Assistant Referee) check.

I squint at the tiny screen. Under normal circumstances Twitter would be feeding me live reactions, setting me up for glory or sadness, but all I have today is a pregnant pause. It's agony. Then the app updates, and agony becomes ecstasy. A goal! An 86th minute goal, scored by Connor Wickham, assisted by VAR.

A goal I have no one to celebrate with.

It's an odd, unaccustomed feeling. I can text mates, but in terms of a live reaction the moment will be gone. It makes the equaliser, and resulting 1-1 draw, feel hollow, although there are 40-odd matches to come across the year. So while there's a mild sense of solitude following the final whistle, it's not something I dwell on.

To end the day, I pour a beer and watch the Daniel Radcliffe movie *What If*. The operative word being 'watch'. Usually this is shorthand for selecting a movie, then letting it play out to an audience of none as I spend 90 minutes cycling between Insta, Twitter, Facebook, and bulletin-board forums. Tonight there are no distractions. I really do *watch*. The beer (Brakspear Oxford Gold) is distinctively honey-like and the film enjoyable too, if grown-up Harry Potter chasing an unattainable girl while being a bumbling oaf but still getting lucky in the end is your jam.

Apparently it is my jam. Though maybe for the best that I can't admit it publicly for another 365 days.

Thursday 2 January

The polar opposite of yesterday, sleep wise. Insomnia surging through every axon, I'm up at 4am, and awake – in the loosest sense – for the rest of the day.

In addition to being a freelance writer I'm a full-time dad, so there's no option other than to suck it up and crack on. I drop our youngest, Little Blue, at nursery for 9am and head into Bath with our eldest, Lady S, for breakfast – partly to keep my eyes open, chiefly to avoid social media temptations. Even then I find myself automatically grabbing my mobile every 90 seconds, searching for an app to open, then putting it down again. This reflex behaviour is annoying the hell out of me, and it's only been 24 hours since I realised I did it. What's it been like for my friends in pubs or at sporting events for the last decade?

I know the guy to ask – and so invite a dad-mate for a man-date at the weekend, under the pretence of watching *Avengers: Endgame*. Bearded, surfer-haired, super-chilled parenting pal Steve is a fellow manchild, and therefore regular visitor for nights of wrestling and American sports and Chris Hemsworth movies. As such, he knows exactly how much time I spend interacting with blue screens when I should be socialising. So it's appropriate that he's the first to be informed about this project.

Saturday 4 January

Steve has barely poured his first beer when I assault him with the news.

"Mate, I'm giving up social media for a year. And I'm going to write a book about it."

"Really?"

I nod.

"Wow."

Time, and conversation, freezes. I attribute this on Steve's part to three quarters disbelief, one quarter really, really wanting to make a start on his pint of Doom Bar. If you've ever so much as sipped Doom Bar, you'll understand his quandary.

Finger of Cornish ale quaffed, he continues.

"Nice one mate. Good luck! You're, er, coming from quite an intense place on that front…"

He lets those words hang out of politeness, but I know what he means. Steve doesn't do social media outside of running app Strava, and last used Facebook before I met him five years ago. He still has a 'friend request' pending from yours truly which was sent in 2016.

"Once you get into the swing of it you'll find you don't have the pull," he continues. "But going by your past use it'll take you a few months."

"What do you think I'll find most difficult?" I ask.

"The habit of it. When we're out in town or watching stuff here you grab your phone and scroll every 10 minutes. You're generally pretty good at multitasking: you'll have your laptop up looking at Twitter and be chuntering to me at the same time. But you do sometimes zone out when I'm responding. That's when I know you've gone back into Twitter world."

I apologise. Steve laughs. Embarrassed, I change the subject and explain that my main fear is missing out on important news regarding family and friends.

"Mate, that depends what you think news is," he responds. "Someone putting something on Facebook generally isn't news to me. From past experience on there it was usually someone showing off or gloating. Someone's on holiday here, someone else has a new car, someone else has a new house, someone's had a baby. It fascinates me that people trawl through all that, because they come away feeling worse."

"So how do you get your news?"

"I'm old school. I text or phone someone," says Steve.

"Reckon you feel happier now than you were in the days of having a cheeky gander at Facebook during your lunch hour?" I ask.

"I don't know, as it's so long since I used Facebook," he says. "Some people seem to crave knowing what everyone else is doing. I prefer to do that catching up in person. I'd rather sit here and have you talk for three hours about what you've been up to, than scroll through endless pics of you at Avon Valley Wildlife Park. That way we get to talk about the stuff that interests us both."

My addiction to social media is so powerful that my phone is effectively a tiny fifth limb. I have to have it attached to me at all times. It's by my laptop when working, in my pocket when doing housework, on the bedroom floor next to me when I doze off while getting the girls to sleep. I ask Steve how he compares, and the answer is like some kind of fever dream.

"I hardly use any devices once home from work," he says. "I can easily get in, put my phone down, and then struggle to remember where I've left it when it gets to bedtime and I need to set my alarm for the next day. If it's to hand I might spend half an hour looking at the Sky Sports app or checking Strava but generally Bethan [Steve's wife] and I chill out and chat, or read, or watch TV. Without second screens."

I'm a long way off such relaxation. But it's something to aim for in 11 months' time. Steve is finally permitted to continue his Doom Bar and watch Chris Hemsworth smash things with a giant hammer. And for *Endgame's* entire 181-minute duration, neither of us touches a mobile phone.

Wednesday 8 January

Half a decade ago, I gave up my day job editing a national magazine to look after our one-year-old daughter, enable Mrs E to return to her career, and do some freelance writing on the side.

I was blasé about it, much like Ewan McGregor's character in *Salmon Fishing in the Yemen* when he suggests resigning in order to raise a baby with Emily Blunt: "I could take him to the park and to school, I could take him fishing." There would be no fishing for me. In its place I would play a ton of *FIFA*, develop a *Homes Under the Hammer* addiction, and occasionally change a dirty nappy. Easy.

The reality wasn't close. I had no idea how all-consuming childcare could be. Indeed I soon felt embarrassed about the occasions when I'd got in from work and enquired as to why the dishwasher hadn't been emptied, or the hallway looked like a nuclear disaster zone. Turns out, safeguarding a tiny creature requires superhuman attention, saintly patience and Olympian reaction times. Every single second of every single day. It is utterly exhausting.

As such, toddler groups became my salvation. They offered a chance to occasionally make new friends, or sit scrolling through Facebook while my firstborn gnawed at a wooden train or pawed at a bowl of dismembered grapes and regurgitated banana.

Lady S is now six, and at school, but Little Blue is four, and not. Meaning today is my first ever toddler group without the luxury of Facebook.

No get-out. No mobile phone escape route. I'm going to have to… socialise.

I'm the only dad present, but I'm fairly used to that. The West Country is not a hotbed of stay-at-home fathers. Thankfully there's a welcoming face in the form of mummy mate Amber, a kind-hearted hippie with exemplary TV and reading tastes, who I last saw on my 40th. We catch up on Christmas and New Year happenings, and she recommends her latest page-turner: *Eleanor Oliphant is Completely Fine* by Gail Honeyman. In that moment, I realise that without social media promptings it's going to be a sterile year for entertainment. So I tell Amber I'll read the book and establish a seventh ground rule: real-life friendships will be used to steer my year.

If a mate recommends a film, I'll watch it. If I'm invited on an impromptu night out, childcare permitting, I'll go. If an old pal commands me to visit for a weekend, same again. Time to get out more and reconnect. And, given the hours hopefully freed up by avoiding social media, read stuff I'd never have previously considered. Bring on the Oliphant.

The morning is thoroughly enjoyable, making a mockery of those pre-group nerves. My day feels buoyed by having had uninterrupted interaction with real humans experiencing the same parenting challenges as I am. Sibling warfare. Sleepless nights. Potty-training fails. Knocking back a morning glass of orange juice without adding a shot of vodka. Or – on the days where the eldest's left glove, the youngest's right shoe and the car keys all go AWOL precisely 51.8 seconds before you need to be out of the door for the school run – just drinking it neat from the bottle.

Friday 10 January

Unthinkably, I've finished my first book of the year inside 10 days. It's the light, informative *Still Friends* by Saul Austerlitz, looking back at 25 years of Ross, Rachel, Chandler and co. I've always been a bookworm but the time-melting blend of childcare and freelance writing has turned my reading speed glacial. I'm lucky if I finish one book in a single month. That's already changed, and it's clear that eschewing social media is giving me some welcome free time.

Sadly, nights provide unwelcome free time. The wonder of that New Year's Day lie-in has evaporated, replaced by regular wake-ups between 3am and 5am. It's the one period when this experiment is punishingly lonely. There's not the option to log into apps and surround myself with friends, and no point texting anyone in the dead of night. The project is into double figures in terms of days passed, with encouraging signs – but clearly giving up social media is no immediate insomnia cure.

Saturday 11 January

For the first time in 2020 I've been out drinking heavily, discussing the past, present, and future with two close friends. Hazel is an always-smiling bundle of energy and fun, Lindo an affectionate, straight-talking, mischief-making whirlwind: "I mean, it's not a proper night out if we don't do one cheeky Jägerbomb." It's unplanned entertainment of the type I'd committed to earlier in the week. Mrs E and I are still cohabiting, so the subjects were biggies. Divorce. Selling a house. Finding two new ones. The hilarious concept of a 40-year-old dude joining dating apps after two decades 'out of the game'. I couldn't tell them just yet that I may have already met someone. *This will be our year…*

Last night, with strawberry-and-lime Kopparberg coursing through every vein, it all seemed comical and throwaway, but I wake with a monster hangover and sense of impending doom. I've always had anxious tendencies – for four years editing that national magazine I was taking an antidepressant called amitriptyline every evening, to cope with the pressure – and tackling today's alcohol-fumed wobbles without my social media umbilical cord feels impossible.

I've long struggled to negotiate the white noise of Facebook: all the achievements and look-where-I-am-now overshares that Steve mentioned on *Avengers: Endgame* night, even though I'm notoriously guilty of humblebrags and braggadocio. Today I register that this white noise is a little like a Big Mac: mildly nauseating when swallowed sober, but the ideal stomach-settler when you've had a few too many the night before, and are wallowing in a mix of self-pity and cider sweat. I'd love to immerse myself in my cousins' family pics, or updates from mates going to this afternoon's Crystal Palace match. This is a lonely, lonely morning.

That Palace game is against Arsenal, and I'm still not ready to sit through a live match without Twitter – so I escape the house and take the kids swimming. It refreshes the brain, at least when I'm not being half-drowned by dive-bombing teenagers, and I return home to find we've drawn 1-1. The urge to offset hangover blues by checking in with friends has subsided. I get through the afternoon and evening by looking forward to *Match of the Day*. A simple goal, rewarded with the viewing of complex and uproarious ones.

Sunday 12 January

Still feeling the depressive fallout from Friday, and unable to search for salvation from Twitter and Facebook, I emerge from my pit at 5am and run, and run, and run. Run until my lungs feel like they're burning, and my calves like they're about to burst, and I get pins and needles in the top of my neck for 30 seconds. That part possibly isn't healthy.

It's transformative for my mood. I fly past the 10km mark – as opposed to my standard habit of crawling past the 5km mark – and the instant I do so, the heavens open. A steady, driving rain that simultaneously invigorates and relaxes: I know I'm 500 metres from my first-ever quarter marathon, and bound the necessary final steps.

The next part sounds so Hallmark movie that I'm tempted to avoid mentioning it, but you'll have to trust my word. Among the Britpop band Suede's best-kept secrets is a soothing album track called When The Rain Falls. Upon finishing that quarter marathon, it shuffles onto my iPod. The timing couldn't be more apt. Especially when I slow to a contented walk through our local park, look up, and see a rainbow above me.

Told you it felt fictional. Cub Scout's honour, it really happened. There's a photo on Strava if you need proof.

Mad coincidence, or sign that I need to trust in the universe to carry me forward through 2020? I choose to interpret it as the latter. This is already my fourth run of the year, and I'm taking to the bumpy village pavements with a clearer head than during my fixated-by-Facebook days.

I'm intrigued to see how this plays out across the year. I've always wanted to build up to doing an official half marathon, and considered signing up to March's Bath Half, but bottled it. Instead the Bristol version, in September, feels like an achievable target. Even if typing that caused both hamstrings to tighten up like violin strings.

Tuesday 14 January

Attend the local village committee meeting on behalf of the school PTA. Old me would have mined such an occasion for nonsensical local nuggets to amplify – and mock – on Twitter. Inter-village dog-poo wars. The bolted-down picnic tables in the local park vanishing overnight. A black panther being spotted on the loose. Preposterous as these examples may sound, only one is made up. Happily – because I'd love to randomly bump into Chadwick Boseman down the local Co-op – it isn't the panther tale.

Tonight is different. I take the event seriously, and every one of the seven locals present is friendly and talkative. In this kind of scenario, I would usually whip out my phone after 20 minutes, then sneakily check Facebook while pretending to note down an important date. Tonight that temptation isn't there. I'm enjoying it. Other than the lack of big-cat updates.

After 90 light-hearted minutes, most participants get up to leave. "Staying for a drink with me and Cathy, Ben?" asks Mel, a committee member who I know as my predecessor on the school PTA. My brain searches for excuses, not out of rudeness, but because under normal circumstances I'd be silently lamenting all the sports updates I was missing on Twitter. Yet before I can find a believable excuse, an excitable "yes" has departed my lips.

The next hour is smashing. I've come to the meeting with my journalistic radar for quirky stories switched off, yet ended up hearing some of the funniest of my career. Mel, it transpires, is a former nanny to the stars, and in her lifetime has crossed paths with a number of celebrities whose identities can't be shared here. With one and only exception.

In the early '90s, Mel and her flatmate Sue – there's a name pairing that would work for a comedy double act – lived in south-west London, and for two years Sue commuted to Kings Cross on the same bus as Chesney Hawkes. Sue suffered from cystic fibrosis, and contacted a wish foundation about meeting

Hawkes as she felt it inappropriate to accost him without warning, but was told that, at 23, she was over the age limit to have a 'wish' come true.

Unfazed by the challenge of dealing with celebs, Mel stepped in. During a boozy night with an estate agent friend she was able to coax out Hawkes' address – but, in the days before mobiles and Notes apps, had to commit it to memory. Hazy memory, by the next morning. She knew the address contained a '3' and a '6', and a 'Victoria' in the street name, so called Directory Enquiries to request phone numbers for every house with that combination in Mortlake. Only one was ex-directory. It had to be Chez.

Mel penned a letter explaining Sue's condition, and his status as her unwitting bus buddy, and posted it through Hawkes' door. It contained her number, and an invite to come around for dinner, for which she would cook any meal of his choice.

He called Mel a couple of days later to say that he would love to meet Sue, and enquire as to whether he could bring a friend, and request his exotic dinner choice. Sure enough, he showed up as planned on time, and buzzed the doorbell of their flat.

Sue answered the intercom.

"Hi! It's Chesney Hawkes…"

"Yeah, right. Fuck off."

Thankfully, he saw the funny side when eventually allowed in.

As for that bohemian meal choice, would it be oysters and champagne, or a white truffle pizza? Caramelised quail and sweetbreads? Perhaps some wagyu beef in a light teriyaki sauce?

None of the above. It was, quite magnificently, shepherd's pie.

Wednesday 15 January

Time for my first housekeeping check of @ replies and direct messages. Instagram and Facebook check-ins are drama-free, but signing into Twitter fills me with dread. There are a couple of direct messages which need following up, but I'm in and out again in under two minutes. Even so, the anxiety is palpable, and I spend a while afterwards pondering just how much stress I'd been putting myself under for years by willingly challenging my mental health in this way. Blue tick or not, I've a hard decision to make regarding Twitter on 31 December.

Thursday 16 January

Motivated by having survived two weeks of the project, I load up Strava and power off for a morning run at a pace that seemed impossible when I started two years ago: four minutes 20 seconds per km. I expect to burn out inside 2km, but there's a feeling of rocket fuel in my veins and somehow, I sustain it for the entire distance to clock a time of 23 minutes and 22 seconds.

It's a minute speedier than my previous PB (personal best), four minutes faster than my quickest time of the year, and a world apart from my first-ever 5K two years previously, which came in at almost 40 minutes.

It would be rash to put the running improvement down to my social media exit alone, but it's another example of the positive effect it's having, even through the depressive blips that leave me craving a quick Facebook fix. Extra spare time and reduced stress is enabling me to run more often, with a mostly upbeat mindset – while Strava's live tracking, and virtual medals for best times and segments, drive me on.

Friday 17 January

Invited for an impromptu cafe breakfast with two PTA members, Anna and Camilla, who are celebrating their birthday today. Say yes. Invited out again for a journalist friend's birthday drinks in the evening. Again say yes.

The evening event is notable for friends expressing surprise at me "being allowed out to play". They're right to do so. Since having kids I've built up a reputation as the guy who only ever attends social occasions if given three weeks' notice – I can't recall the last time I went 'out out' two Fridays running. It's nothing to do with supposed permissions; rather, my depressive years have been accompanied by crippling social anxiety, a condition exacerbated by that daily need to keep up with the Zuckerbergs. Without that pressure I already feel more relaxed about saying yes to stuff, and less obsessed with masking personal insecurities by acting like a character from of *The Inbetweeners* when I do go out.

Tuesday 21 January

Another book completed: Gail Honeyman's *Eleanor Oliphant is Completely Fine*, as recommended by Amber at toddler group. It's a likeable tale of a twenty-something lady with mental health issues trying to heal and overcome a fractured relationship with her mother, featuring some outstanding observational writing – the awkwardness of having a makeover in the middle of a busy department store, the agony of going for a lady wax. Information which I'd have once deemed impertinent, but may ultimately come in useful as my daughters advance towards adulthood. Gulp.

Thursday 23 January

It's taken a little over three weeks to note a discernible change, but the instincts I wrote about at the month's onset are waning. I no longer reach down the side of the bed to grab my phone in the mornings. I can take Little Blue on playdates, or the girls out for food, without constantly feeling the urge to open an app and check something. Mrs E tells me this is the most relaxed she's seen me since we got married. 12 years ago!

99% of the time this is a very good thing.

At 5.05pm today this is not a good thing.

I collect Little Blue from nursery and notice three missed calls from Steve. Missed because, being the new chilled out Benjamin who no longer requires constant mobile access, I've not looked at my phone since mid-afternoon.

Curious.

There's also one WhatsApp message waiting. It's from Steve.

"Hey dude. You on your way to the party?"

Party? Is he throwing me a celebratory, you've-done-it-mate-I'm-so-bloody-proud bash to mark my successful disconnection from social media? Whatta man! It's 344 days premature, but nonetheless an astonishing vote of confidence from a dear friend. I can already taste the Doom Bar. My mouth waters.

Then… the taste sours.

H-Buzz's birthday party. Oh no.

H-Buzz is Steve's daughter, and Little Blue's best friend. Knowing that I was no longer on social media, Steve informed me multiple times over the past fortnight, both in person and via text message, that Little Blue is invited to her birthday party.

Thursday 23 January, 4.30pm.

Thursday 23 January, 4.30pm.

Thursday 23 January, 4.30pm.

It is Thursday 23 January, 5.05pm. We are very much not at H-Buzz's birthday party. Hence missed calls and WhatsApp messages.

It's another 20 minutes before we arrive. Bedraggled and present-less, with the girls still in the clothes they wore to school and nursery. We are just in time for pass the parcel, which they both refuse to get involved in, irate at being the only two attendees not wearing princess-themed attire. The opportunity to go wild on an unattended play kitchen is turned down. An entire table of party food is met with apathy and seething looks. You know you've really upset your kids when they turn down complimentary pizza.

We stay later than the official end to make up time, but I know I've let both the girls down – not to mention a good friend and his family. Steve laughs off such suggestions, aware of the irony that my quest to follow his social-media-free example has bounced back to wallop us both in the face, on today of all days.

For all my complaining about ignored Facebook event invites, I'm guilty of letting that same tech guide my social calendar. It's a habit I have to snap out of, fast. This project was in part inspired by feeling let down by friends on a big occasion. It has little value if I spend its duration doing the exact same thing in reverse.

Saturday 25 January

An alarming BBC news story reports on a new virus originating in the Chinese city of Wuhan, that's brought about 1,200 confirmed cases and 41 deaths. With people travelling in and out of the nation to mark Lunar New Year, there's concern that it may already have spread beyond borders. The UK is said to be tracing anyone who recently visited Hubei province. A story to monitor.

Sunday 26 January

An evening where TV and internet are dominated by the death of basketball megastar Kobe Bryant.

After seeing the headline on the BBC homepage, I instinctively prepare to leap on Twitter. Without wishing to be morbid, it can be a very good news resource where events such as this are concerned. Most of the useful information pertaining to the death of Michael Jackson in 2009 emerged there. For any reputable journalist, filtering through the mix of genuine grief and mawkish attention-seeking to dig out facts, and report them delicately and accurately, is a crucial skill.

However, Bryant's death is only loosely related to my field of journalism, so that Twitter instinct is turned back. Instead my attentions turn to TMZ, a site infamous for clickbait tabloid headlines, but also a critical resource for incidents such as this. The site broke the story of Bryant's death, the 41-year-old's helicopter coming down in Calabasas, California, killing all on board. The death count stands at five.

Bryant's stats are astonishing. 18 All-Star teams, five NBA championships, a host of individual accolades. Sky News reports that his final tweet was directed at fellow b-ball legend LeBron James, congratulating him for surpassing his total career points of 33,643 the previous day.

The hardest part to digest is a photo of James, again on TMZ, sharing a court-side hug with his 13-year-old daughter Gianna, herself an upcoming star of the sport. Gianna is presumed to be one of four daughters left behind by Bryant's death, alongside Natalia, Bianka, and Capri. The latter is just seven months old, and will grow up with no memories of her father.

Bryant's ability and fame make this a story that resonates the world over. But that part, the baby girl who'll never be able to hug or hold her daddy, or even remember doing so, is the one that breaks me.

Monday 27 January

Another tough day, where my isolation from social media is anything but splendid.

First, from the real world, news that Gianna Bryant perished alongside her father in the Calabasas helicopter crash. Not only that, but also the death count has risen overnight to nine. On this front, I have no desire to dip back into the Twitter-sphere. It's dispiriting enough without additional details.

Then a hammer strike of my own to deal with, albeit trivial compared to events in California. Late last year I'd been set up for an evening's drinks – very much not a date – with a friend of a friend in a similar situation to mine. Divorcee, two daughters the same age as my pair, lots in common.

The drinks turned out better than either of us anticipated, with us talking and bonding non-stop from 7pm to 1am. We'd gone on to arrange a series of playdates with our children, who got on fantastically, and we texted each other hourly – most waking minutes, in fact – since. A bit of flirting, a lot of chemistry, discussions of summer night-out plans and dream holiday destinations. We'd even tactfully yet seriously gone over provisional ideas for the distant future, including how mad it might be to co-parent four mini princesses with Maleficent tendencies. Conclusion: fine, so long as we co-owned a large car, an even larger TV, and an entire distillery of gin.

When I mentioned not telling my friends about having met someone, this was the lady.

This will be our year...

All of which leaves me shell-shocked by a WhatsApp request to cool things off: an incredibly apologetic 'it's not you, it's me' romance death knell. It's delivered with utmost respect and affection, and an explanation that my new friend feels things are moving too fast, and she needs to prioritise her kids over her love life in the immediate term. Totally understandable, particularly with the complexity of my ex-wife [who'd kindly given us her blessing] still being under the same roof. The heartbreak emojis from both ends are sufficient to make every teenager in the land cringe – but while such niceties are appreciated and reciprocated, it's the first time I've been friend-zoned in 20 years, and a Tyson-Fury-heavy blow.

Seriously, I'm crushed. Like a 10-tonne weight is pressing on my chest. Calves rendered gelatinous, stomach performing gold-medal somersaults, burning pinpricks behind the eyes. (If you're expecting this to be an alpha-male tome I'm afraid I have bad news.) Not only at the loss of a potential other-half, but also – after agreeing that a spell of non-contact is the best method of letting us both heal – the sudden farewell to an unexpected close friend.

Since our not-a-date night, January Girl has been a massive inspiration for this project, texting sunrise messages of support, and curating the soundtrack to my working afternoons. To carry on without her feels like being told that tomorrow I have to climb Everest. On stilts. Blindfolded.

Depression has been a constant nuisance in my life, and its cold grip encloses again. I know not to beg: I can tell January Girl's decision has been a burdensome one. Grovelling would be undignified and only serve to make her feel unjustly guilty. But for the first time this year I do feel a compelling desire to get onto Facebook and bellow some sort of a cry for help, after meeting the perfect lady at an imperfect time.

Last May, upon completion of 20 weeks' cognitive behaviour therapy, I'd shared my issues for the first time via an unfiltered Facebook post. The response – 230 Likes, more than fifty supportive comments – carried me through the summer. It's exactly the type of lift I need right now. This is the lowest I've felt since starting CBT.

Somehow, I resist. Is it stubbornness? Bloody minded idiocy? A fear of admitting failure? All three, actually. Yet, at least for tonight, it's also down to an ability to place the last 24 hours in context, in a way that wasn't possible in my days of racing to find the next Twitter titbit, the next Facebook overshare. Even with the black dog yapping at my Achilles, I'm still here. I still have my kids. I can't do anything to change events 5,370 miles away, but I can use them to be grateful for my own health, and my children's.

I only hope I'm able to maintain this sense of perspective in the Facebook-free months ahead.

Tuesday 28 January

Spend the day tempted to rip out yesterday's entry and never make mention of it again. I suspect books in which male divorcees lament their love-life failures are not big sellers in Waterstones.

In the end, it's that conclusion which drives me to leaving it in. Hollywood may paint greying men of a certain vintage as responsibility-free lotharios, but in reality turning 40 doesn't suddenly stop you seeking authentic long-term companionship. I feel heartbroken, and in need of help. What seems trivial to one person can feel life-destroying to another. I know from CBT that my best chances of halting the spiral are sharing emotions, rather than bottling them up. With social media unavailable, I take the step of confiding in a couple of friends by text message. Even before they've replied it is a burden lifted.

Friday 31 January

The end of a wallowing week. Sleep continues to prove fitful. Any notion of running has been abandoned. Yet there's reason to celebrate: even with the lows of the last few days I've restrained myself from blurting everything out to Facebook. This project has made it through a month.

A primary objective was to reconnect with close friends, and it's one of those who pulls me back from the metaphorical precipice. Andy S is a fellow Palace fan and former journalist who I lost touch with after his move to Abu Dhabi in 2012. We've been speaking again regularly since my axing of social media channels, and in response to my Tuesday message he offers just the words to lift my spirits.

"Look at a pic of yourself as a kid," he writes. "Would you ever be mean to that kid? The answer is, of course, no. So don't be mean to yourself now. If in six days, months, or years this lovely lady is still single and keen then you can have a go at a relationship. But don't settle. People should be all in, or not at all. You've got a busy freelance career and two kids. Keep life simple."

It's more personal, tailored advice than I'd have got by playing woe-is-me to a social-media hive mind, and it really does lift my mood, and reinforce my drive to keep this up.

I'm 8.33% of the way there, although it's hard to conclude anything definitive from January. The running stats show promise, aided by my sense of having more time, but they're yet to translate into a restful night's shuteye. Twitter followers have dropped as forecast, but on Facebook and Insta they've bizarrely gone up. (My Instagram account is unprotected, so anyone can add me, while on Facebook I've made a judgement call to accept friend requests from school parents during my monthly check, because of the PTA role.)

Mid-afternoon two of my Glastonbury travel buddies send texts inviting me out in Bristol for 'Farewell EU' drinks. Lauren is a bubbly, iron-willed former journalist whose Lancastrian directness once terrified this Southern pansy, but has become an essential presence since CBT: her "seize the day, you've bloody well got this" missives rescuing me from many a downward spiral. Her partner Andy H is an ex-colleague. I barely knew him when we worked together, yet the kindred challenges of parenting and divorce and turning 40 have forged a strong bond. After that promise made at toddler group to broaden my horizons, I can only say yes to a third Friday night out in four weeks. It's so very un-me. Yet a thoroughly enjoyable evening pub-crawling King Street ensues.

Boozer of the night is the Famous Royal Navy Volunteer, a converted 17th-century townhouse where we sample a selection of novel craft beers and more traditional, yet still sublime, gin. Four hours of Glastonbury planning – and a belly full of ale – alleviate the January Girl sadness for now, and at the stroke of midnight I am in a cab halfway home, thanking Lauren and Andy for a spectacular evening, and feeling temporarily triumphant.

Month down, but not man down. 11 to go.

End of month stats: January 2020

Weight: 15st 1lb
Twitter followers: 5,022 (-11)
Facebook friends: 839 (+1)
Instagram followers: 225 (+2)
Average sleep: 5h 34min
Books read: 3 – Saul Austerlitz: Still Friends, *Gail Honeyman:* Eleanor Oliphant is Completely Fine, *Nasser Hussain:* Playing With Fire
Distance run: 61km
Time running: 5h 31min
Best 5K time: 23min 29s
Best 10K time: 55min 48s

FEBRUARY

Saturday 1 February

Apologies. I've been frightfully rude.

You and I have known one another for 31 days now. 32, if you include the last day of December. Two entire book chapters. Yet, unless you've spent the last two decades immersed in videogaming magazines, you have no idea who I am. Other than some dude inspired to give up social media by the acquisition of Glastonbury Festival tickets.

Thank you for getting this far on that information alone.

Let's fill in some gaps with a quick rewind. To 19 December 1979. The day I was born in the Tesco Superstore opposite Clapham South tube station, with a protruding belly and a lazy eye – the root of many of my depressive tendencies.

Mercifully, the building wasn't a Tesco then. Instead it was South London Hospital for Women and Children. My mum already had a nine-year-old daughter from her first marriage. My father relocated to Dubai for work in 1982. Mum's next long-term relationship added three more boys to her noisy, sports-obsessed, bowl-haircutted brood. We grew up on South London council estates, squeezed into box rooms and bunk beds, first in Clapham, then Streatham, then Carshalton.

Our dads weren't around often. We were taught the value of money, of a hot dinner, of charity shop clothing, of jumble sale toys. Sunday morning boot sales were a weekly highlight which I've resurrected with my own daughters. My mum was on benefits but made every penny count and strove for us to better ourselves. It's one of the reasons I bristle when families on benefits are casually labelled as scroungers. Perhaps some are. A great many want to pull themselves upwards but have no means of doing so.

I was fascinated with words from an early age. I loved trying to find unconventional rhymes, unusual turns of phrase, attempting to make every sentence count. I attended state schools – Bonneville in Clapham, Fenstanton in Tulse Hill – but my mum was convinced I had something 'extra' (don't all mums?) and lobbied hard for prep school bursaries. I'd write stories and poems and reports of football matches and she'd bundle them up with schoolwork cuttings and mail them off. All while juggling the needs of four other kids in a tiny council flat, as a single parent. I've no idea how.

When I was seven, mum's hard work paid off. I was granted a bursary to Dulwich Prep, a posh private school three miles away. (Name-dropping yet cool trivia note: Chiwetel Ejiofor, of *Love Actually* and *12 Years a Slave* fame, was in the year above me.) Three years later the same relentless mix of lobbying and letter-writing got me into Christ's Hospital, a boarding school in Sussex set up with the specific objective of assisting children from impoverished backgrounds. I spent seven mostly content years there.

That love of words never went away, other than a brief period where I wanted to become a bus driver and would regularly draw myself at the wheel of the 118 route from Brixton to Morden. Let's keep that our secret, yeah? I did a Journalism degree at City University, then went straight into writing for websites amid the dot-com boom. Alternative music editor, whereits.at. Sports editor, Nickelodeon. Website editor, Bliss. Website editor, More. Website editor, Zoo.

I spent four years launching and writing for websites but had grown up on magazines, and at 25 wanted to move into print. Plus I'd met my wife-to-be at university in London, but she was keen to move closer to home in the West Country – so I began looking at magazine jobs in Bath. I'd been a videogaming nerd since an Amstrad CPC 464+ took pride of place in one of those box rooms two decades earlier, and couldn't apply fast enough when a job as reviews editor for my favourite mag ever – *Official PlayStation Magazine* – came up in October 2005.

I got the job.

I was made deputy editor in 2007.

I was offered the big chair, over a chicken pitta in the Bath branch of Nando's, in December 2009, and stepped down in 2014 as the longest-serving editor in the magazine's history. It was an honour – a role I took absolute pride in every time I set foot in the office, collaborating with best-in-class writers and premier designers. I still own and treasure every single issue we made. It was also a time riddled with depression and anxiety and the very worst single moment of my professional life. Which we'll get to later, and is probably the point that I should have quit Twitter, years before the Eden Hazard fiasco.

Those are the basics. The rest – self-employment, raising two daughters, being a delicate flower when it comes to friends ignoring Facebook event invites, falling in love at the flutter of an eyelash – you already know. Don't worry, there won't be a test. Shall we grab an Oreo each and step on into February?

Sunday 2 February

Today marks the pinnacle of the United States' sporting calendar: Super Bowl Sunday. This year's NFL decider sees Kansas City Chiefs and San Francisco 49ers go branded-helmet-to-branded-helmet.

It's not only in the US that this fixture resonates. Traditionally I invite my middle brother down from London, and have a couple of friends over. While waiting for their arrival I spend the morning scouring Twitter to soak in the atmosphere: coach interviews, betting tips, highlights of the play-offs. In the afternoon I dash to a supermarket to pick up Stateside-themed treats. The wait for guests to arrive is then spent back in internet mode, sharing predictions for the big game. By 4pm I'm practically punching the walls in excitement.

Essentially, however old this shambling mass of bones and cartilage gets, the brain at its helm will forever belong to an over-testosteroned 12-year-old.

Time to grow up, though. No social media today. Therefore I'm going cold turkey: no family or friends, and no America-feast. The idea of this challenge is to snap longstanding habits – the good and the bad. So that's my approach to the entire day.

It works in the morning. Keen to escape the house rather than ponder what I'm missing from the build-up, I set off on a run at 7:40am and don't return for another 64 minutes. There's no grand plan: I just keep my feet motoring and cycle through some favourite songs. Swift and Suede are on the playlist, but so too the superb Scottish band Chvrches, and even a couple of Robbie Williams' numbers.

Don't roll your eyes! The Pet Shop Boys' backed No Regrets is five fantastic minutes of wrongs-righting motivation.

I span the village, disappearing up hills and down lanes I've never explored in nine years here, and by the time those 64 minutes are up I've covered 11.2km. It's the furthest I've ever run, and at a reasonable lick: 5.45 minutes per km. A fresh, uplifting start to Super Bowl Sunday which I'd never have considered without stepping away from Twitter.

Nonetheless, watching the game without company is deflating. I've always waved away claims that the NFL is stop-start, because the gaps in play are usually filled by conversation. That isn't the case tonight. I'm now acutely aware that the Super Bowl is drawn out further than necessary for the sake of gargantuan advertising dollars. Between 2am and 3am, eyes barely open and body exhausted by that morning run, I miss the Gridiron-focussed camaraderie of Twitter.

Still, the game itself is a good one: a 10-10 tie at half-time, with Kansas City coming out on top 31-20. To help pass the ad-break tedium, I read an entire book in one evening for the first time in two-and-a-half decades.

How to Change the World by Jean-Paul Flintoff is Amber's latest toddler group recommendation, patchy in places but best when keeping self-help advice to a local level. I particularly like its idea that change can be triggered via small acts of what Gandhi called "blessed monotony" – specifically, folding laundry as if it were the robes of Jesus or Buddha, but also applicable to litter picking, or planting trees, or – possibly – writing books about the health benefits of abandoning social media.

I also enjoy Flintoff's take on raising children. "We can impose a kind of grandeur on everyday parenting," he writes, "if we see it as the work of 'a good ancestor', striving to pass on the best of our distant forbears to people as yet unborn."

Yes! My kids are going to be really, really great at *FIFA 28*, remembering lyrics to unfashionable pop songs, and heating pasta.

Monday 3 February

An unspoken skill of journalism is speed-deleting non-pertinent press releases. This became habit long ago, but with no Twitter to distract me, I've found myself spending the first 15 minutes of each working day cycling through these desperate pleas delivered to my inbox, just to see what I've been missing out on.

Today's surprising answer is Super Bowl self-service statistics. The first email I open is less 49ers, more 69ers: a missive from the Pornhub press office, mostly related to the half-time show. Performing artists Shakira and Jennifer Lopez received 1401% and 381% boosts in traffic respectively, while a spike in searches for 'Latina MILF' also occurred. Even the national anthem apparently gets Yankees yanking, with show-opener Demi Lovato securing a 270% search traffic boost.

As for the winning team, it's a relief to see that Kansas City fans were paying attention to oval rather than shrivelled balls, with Pornhub traffic falling by 30% across Missouri while the game was on. That was the biggest drop of any state, narrowly ahead of Connecticut, on -27%. This changed after the game, with Kansas City residents recording a 22% rise in their dirty action as the real-life champagne corks popped.

The only two Pornhub search terms to outrank Shakira across the day? 'Super Bowl' (5921%) and 'touchdown' (1664%). Not sure I ever wanted to know what the latter meant in a bedroom context. Having just looked it up on Urban Dictionary, I can confirm that neither do you.

Tuesday 4 February

An amusing social-media related story emerges from parliament. It's funny not for its subject matter – Labour MP Tracy Brabin wearing a dress which bared her left shoulder, then receiving a Twitter tongue-lashing – but her self-effacing response to the trolls.

"Hello," Brabin writes in a tweet shared by the BBC. "Sorry I don't have time to reply to all of you commenting on this but I can confirm I'm not… a slag / hungover / a tart / about to breastfeed / a slapper / drunk / just been banged over a wheelie bin. Who knew people could get so emotional over a shoulder?"

She goes on to say, "They were playing Top Trumps on how rude they could be." It's a perfect summary of how many choose to use Twitter: trying to one-up the abusive post above them, without considering that there's a human being on the other end. Fair play to Brabin for taking a stand while maintaining her sense of humour.

Friday 7 February

It's fun to stay at the YMCA. It's never fun to join the school PTA. This was the advice given to me by a selection of friends upon my eldest graduating from nursery, and I followed it ardently for all of six weeks. Then I attended my first PTA evening in support of a mummy mate, blurted ideas before my brain could stop me, and within a year had ascended to the role of vice chair. Cheers, brain. No, we cannot share another Oreo right now.

As you'll recall from the Prologue, I've since volunteered myself into the chair role, figuring that time away from social media would need to be occupied by something practical in addition to scribbling gibberish in this book. Today is my first event, a school disco, and in the most predictably alpha-geek of developments, I have assigned myself the role of disc jockey.

ATB-Dub. Benno Brookes. Fatboy Unslim. Daft Lunk.

Being the dweeb of dweebs this isn't the first time I've manned the decks (AKA a free DJ programme on my laptop), but it's my debut at doing so using the AUX socket on a dust-shrouded sound system which looks more ancient than the school itself. Sensibly, I went in two days ago to check everything works. Inevitably, on the night, nothing does. For 25 minutes I fiddle with wires, and output settings, and show Herculean mental strength by not dropping F-bombs in the middle of a church school, surrounded by increasingly restless children – each yearning for pop, pizza, and Panic At The Disco. Your PTA chair already has that last one well covered, kids.

Finally something plugs into something else and the Mesozoic speakers burst into life midway through Gangnam Style, and I've never been so relieved to hear a hyperactive manboy spouting Korean chat-up lines. The rest of the night is a belter: forget every cliche you've heard about PTAs. Mums and dads muck in to sell cake, and Coke, and candy in 50p bags, and small people roar and ride shotgun and shake it off, and the curfew time of 7pm flies by with the hall still more than half-full. We are harbingers of rebellion! For 10 minutes. At which point parents and teachers gather to clear up and reset and have one last boogie to Bad Guy, and the treasurer counts some pennies, and announces that we've raised £286. A titanic sum for a tiny village school.

Amid this clean-up, the head teacher reveals to me that the secret to eating a Terry's Chocolate Orange is to have it with a glass of red wine. There's some culinary advice you'd never have got from Twitter.

The disco would have occurred without my social media departure, probably with a different chair, certainly with a more competent DJ. But it's another experience which has justified my walking away. Because it's concrete proof that PTAs aren't the cult-like monstrosities they're made out to be, and I'm now looking forward to committing some proper time this year to building on events such as this without the distraction of internet inanity. Just as soon as I've persuaded the committee to invest in a pair of deafeningly loud Wi-Fi speakers.

Tuesday 11 February

As Britain recovers from Storm Ciara, my insides are making a poor attempt at combating some aggressive sniffles. After despatching the girls to their places of education, I slump back to bed and unearth a blog from one Rohit Kumar Neralla.

While this may be the first book on giving up social media for a year, I can't claim to be the first person to write about it. Neralla went through a similar process from February 2018 to 2019, then shared a comprehensive post about his experience. "Who the hell are these people?" he writes about scrolling through Facebook in early 2018. "Why am I sharing my life with hundreds of half-forgotten friends if I don't remember them?" I flash back to the nervous wait for my biopsy experiencing the same sensation.

"I felt an existential unease right after deactivating Facebook," he continues. "'I will be forgotten,' I feared. 'Forgotten and friendless'." Ditto.

One of Neralla's observations is that many of us suffer from 'novel information addiction' – seeking nonsensical info to stave off boredom or discomfort. That's why we waste lunchtimes or evenings scrolling inanely and endlessly, soaking up news stories and memes and pictures of friends pouting into camera phones. It's an addiction. Much like cigarettes and alcohol, just without an accompanying Oasis anthem.

Neralla says he overcame the drive for novel information by journalling – a process which I'm also finding useful. From there, he reconnected with his hobbies. "I discovered the joy of mindfulness, reading, singing and writing. Try disconnecting for 30 days without telling any of your friends and see what that feels like. You may also get some insights on what you are truly interested in."

Most intriguingly, he found that staying away from social media eliminated 'appearance bias' from his life. "Appearance bias in social media means we immediately believe the image or post we see is true and honest. This is one of the more deleterious side-effects of social media." That then makes us jealous of our friends, to the point of potentially disliking them. "Since envy is a part of our human nature, we cannot help but think that others have it better than us."

His closing bombshell tallies with my limited experience so far. Step away from social media and no one will notice. "This is not because you are unimportant but because most people are too self-absorbed to care about what you are doing. They only care about how they are being perceived. Save yourself from this misery before it's too late. There is no joy in keeping up with the Joneses. In fact, it should liberate you that people don't really care about you as much as you think they do."

Friday 14 February

Being a big old soppy bollocks, I've been dreading Valentine's Day. Single for the first time in 20 years, it's loomed over my calendar like a towering cumulonimbus. That changes with a crack-of-sparrows text from January Girl – our first exchange since going no-contact.

"Being a big old soppy bollocks, I bet you've been dreading Valentine's Day."

"Errrr… yes."

"Just so you know, Valentine's Day is crap and makes most people feel like cack."

"Errr… yes."

"Seriously, Ben, I can imagine it's a difficult day for you. But ultimately it's just commercial bullshit. Lots of self-love (but not that kind) for you today, please. Do something nice for yourself. You deserve it."

My mood is transformed. In fact, it's a relief to be avoiding social media, ducking loved-up posts from friends and family, and not having to create fictional ones of my own. Mrs E and I spent recent Valentine's Days tagging one another in gushing updates on all that was right with our world, when aside from the kids little was right with our world. It's the greatest relief for us both not to have to do that.

As for January Girl's request that I do something nice, that transpires by way of another surprise text, from Steve. He and Bethan are also Valentine's Day cynics, and thus he suggests a film night. It's true bromance. He rocks up at 8pm with a rucksack of beer to watch *Fighting with My Family*, the highly amusing tale of British wrestler Saraya 'Paige' Bevis. It brings immense cheer to a day I'd dreaded, and particularly spirit-lifting are cameos from Stephen Merchant and Dwayne Johnson. From rock bottom, to Rock solid.

Saturday 15 February

46 days into this project, I receive the first enquiry as to my whereabouts, from a Palace-supporting pal called Naveed: "Hey mate. Thought of you this morning as haven't seen you on social media for a while. Hope all is okay."

I thank him by text and follow it up over email with the first chapter of this book.

"Bloody hell! I did enjoy that, and I'm glad I checked in," he replies. "You know, next time you're at the doctor's and want to tell someone something, I'm here. Always. Despite you being wrong on Wayne Hennessey." This is a football reference to which we shall return later.

There's likely some truth in Rohit Neralla's analysis regarding people being "too absorbed" to notice a specific mate disappearing from Facebook, but clearly it's unfair to tar every past acquaintance with that brush. Being absorbed in their lives – aren't we all? – doesn't mean they lack compassion.

I've enjoyed stepping away from my circle of influence, but know Nav's message is genuine, and that I also need to uphold my end of the bargain. I can't expect people to be there for me if I'm not there for them. I need to make a conscious effort this year to check in with nearest and dearest. The evening is spent firing off text messages to Andy S in Abu Dhabi, and my three younger brothers, and various other friends just to see how they're doing. I end up chatting to pals over beers until 1am, just like in my London days. Without the prospect of falling into a sozzled stupor and leaving an £89 monthly travelcard on a night bus back seat, mere hours after purchasing it. [Two decades later, I'm *almost* over that one.]

Sunday 16 February

Caroline Flack, whose up and downs have often showcased social media at its worst, has died by suicide, aged 40.

Flack spent half her life in the public eye, presenting shows such as *Gladiators* and *The X Factor*. From a professional standpoint she's best known for fronting *Love Island*, yet her love life generated as many column inches as her career. A brief relationship with One Direction's Harry Styles, 14 years her junior, generated endless clicks and social media abuse, and she was about to stand trial for the alleged assault of current beau Lewis Burton.

Sections of the press had already implicated Flack as being guilty. Newspapers published photos of apparently bloodstained bedsheets, accusing Flack of attacking Burton with a lamp. Domestic violence is a serious offence, and the evidence against the presenter looked compelling, at face value. But that's what court cases and establishment of facts are for. Convictions come via judge or jury, not social media.

In theory.

In practice, tabloids repeatedly implied that Flack's case was clear cut, and thousands of Twitter and Instagram users took that as a cue to pile in. She stepped down from her *Love Island* role, yet searching for her name continued to deliver wave after wave of criticism and memes. Cancel culture damned her before she'd had a chance to have her say. In response, she put out a simple, powerful 10-word Instagram message last December: "In a world where you can be anything, be kind."

I've no wish to downplay a charge of common assault, or portray Flack as faultless. But she at least merited the opportunity to defend herself. As would anyone. Think of the biggest error you've made in the last 24 months. Imagine it being amplified to an audience of millions, with minimal consideration for your perspective, or whether you regretted it, or whether it changed you. Supposed 'experts' whipping up the general public to chastise you for it. Abuse wherever you look, day after day. What do you do? Where do you turn? Humans are prone to mistakes, even famous ones. Formats such as Twitter make it easy to forget or ignore that. 280 characters offer next-to-no nuance.

I don't need to check social media to know that all those click-chasing journos who've spent months haranguing Flack will be lamenting her death, and sharing the number for the Samaritans, and promoting mental health awareness. That's a good start, but it counts for little if tomorrow they return to openly bullying, say, Meghan Markle. Until those habits change, until we stop trying to mask our own flaws by magnifying those of others, there will always be a chance of desensitised social media abuse leading to very real human tragedy. Here's hoping Flack's sad passing sparks genuine change.

Wednesday 19 February

The midway point of my first school half-term without social media. A bowling playdate with Lady S's friend Shark Boy yesterday raised smiles, but sibling squabbles and lack of routine make half-terms a minute-my-minute challenge, and I'm struggling.

Not only because of the childcare aspect: My mind repeatedly drifts to the Caroline Flack story which feels like it should have been preventable. Also of concern are widely reported predictions that the virus which started in China, Covid-19, has a strong chance of developing into a pandemic, threatening life worldwide in a manner not seen since the Spanish Flu of 1918.

Uncertain, deeply worrying times.

Thursday 20 February

Today I cannot peel myself from the bedsheets. I text Mrs E – one room away! – to ask if she can manage the girls' morning routine. (Which, during half-term, amounts to watching as much *Peppa Pig* as possible while steadfastly refusing to get dressed.) For the next half an hour it feels as if my shoulders are pinned down by an invisible force. When I do eventually manage to unclamp from my mattress, I have to use the bathroom towel rail to stay upright. An entire five-minute shower is spent shoulder to wall, like my legs have no connection to the rest of my body. I am stricken. Shattered. Finished.

I'm unprepared for this. If yesterday was a foreshock, this is my mental-health earthquake. That's the real horror of depression: the manner in which it blindsides you with minimal warning or logic. All my running, and a gluten-free diet, mean I'm as healthy physically as I've been in my entire adult life. Last night I went to bed nervous about the concerns listed yesterday, but generally calm. Today there's nothing left in the tank. Every inch of my mind and body feels utterly drained.

One benefit of avoiding social media at times such as these is being oblivious to the modern world's most odious term: 'man up'.

It conveys a choice, that somehow serious depression can be overcome by channelling a cinema-trailer voice inside your head which wills you on to be fixed. Newsflash: I've tried 'manning up' many times. I've no doubt the distressing number of men who die by suicide every year – 5,185 in the UK in 2018, making it the deadliest killer of men under 45 – have tried it many times. It doesn't work, and its casual promulgation by journalists and celebrities and influencers who should know better undoes the endless hard work of mental-health charities.

On days like today there is no 'man' left to 'up'.

Mrs E kindly arranges to work from home. I slowly piece all my fragments back together, on autopilot, knowing I have to go on for my kids. But, good god, it's hard. So many anguished suicide stories involve friends saying, "we knew he was low, but we never expected this." But that's the key thing: often there is no premonition. Nothing within me announced at 11pm last night that I'd feel apocalyptic seven hours later. Yet here I am, a sorry shambles, wondering what the point of anything really is.

It'd be an exaggeration to proclaim myself suicidal. My kids have always been sufficient to pull me away from the darkest thoughts. But I relate to the catastrophic pondering that can overwhelm men my age, sometimes inexplicably, and desperately want to do more to change it. We can, and should, all do more to change it.

Somehow I get through the day. But every second feels like a minute, and every minute feels like an hour, and every hour feels like a century. I go to bed with no idea of whether it'll repeat tomorrow, or I'll wake up without a care in the world.

'Man up'?

Get fucked.

Friday 21 February

It's tough to wake up without a care in the world when you get zero sleep.

I spend the first half of the night staring at the ceiling, helpless. Shortly after 3am, emotional and exhausted, I let the tears flow and sob for… actually, I've no idea how long. It feels like an eternity but is probably 30 minutes. I have a long drive ahead of me today, for a belated 40th birthday surprise from my mum, and the more I tell myself I need to sleep, the more my brain yells back 'no chuffin' chance, mate'.

At 4am I'm up and eating a breakfast which in my pathetic state feels like the height of self-destruction: four slices of gluten-packed toast and a can of Coke. Ah, Twitter hive mind, if only you could see me now. Sequels to legendary musicals could surely be penned around such insurgent acts. *One more hour, one more slice, one slice more.*

By 6am I've achieved a modicum of peace, by emulating last Saturday night: messaging close friends and family to enquire about how they're doing, and sharing a potted two-sentence summary of my struggles. Andy S in Abu Dhabi, already awake given the four-hour time difference, immediately replies offering sympathy and encouragement. A fabulous ex-colleague, Gemma, also up thanks to the waking habits of two young boys, responds with her news and we go on to swap parenting stories which mainly involve the words "half-term" and a dictionary's worth of swears.

The experience eases my hysteria, and by late morning I'm finally able to eke out two hours' kip before jumping in the car and motoring south-east.

Monday 24 February

Mum's 40th surprise for me is a stay at an adults-only hotel on Hayling Island, a small square of land just off the coast of Portsmouth. One bridge in, one bridge out. Within three hours of arrival I'm watching a bunch of octogenarians dance to S Club 7's Reach at half the song's pace, and grabbing for my phone to write a cynical tweet, only to clock that I can't. Old-people-watching habits die hard, as the saying goes.

An epiphany follows. I've spent this book lambasting the cruelty of selected Twitter users, without being self-conscious enough to recognise that I'm part of the problem. Shaming for humour's sake – mocking the generation above for dancing to a pop song despite the protestations of their knees and hips – is a shitty human trait, even if there's no individual target. It's in such situations that Caroline Flack's motto of 'be kind' should apply. So I resolve to adopt a positive outlook for the rest of the weekend – and book, if possible.

It's a curious three days. I chat to a waiter, Steven – Scottish, mid-thirties, a mini cyclone of plate-whisking and tea-pouring – about the clientele and he tells me the average age of guests is 75, and that after five years in the job he still loves their company, as everyone wants to chat, everyone is there for some 'young again' enjoyment. That comes in the form of a Peter Kay tribute act called Lee Lard, and cover bands dedicated to ABBA, The Jackson Five, Queen, and ELO. Lard obliterates my cynicism for 90 minutes, unafraid of dropping near-the-mark jokes about advancing age which the audience laps up. The covers acts are less consistent, but for a pop junkie like me it's still difficult to resist toe-tapping along to Waterloo and Another One Bites the Dust.

Once more, being away from social media frees up time. I spend three enjoyable days reconnecting with the old dear, plough deeper into my current read, *The Body* by Bill Bryson, and again run further than ever before. My 15km Sunday morning furrow covers practically all of Hayling Island, and consumes an hour and 38 minutes. It's important thinking time after the depressive relapse of midweek.

The long weekend acts as a much-needed post-half-term reset, with two moments lingering. On the Sunday afternoon we take in the Elton John-inspired film *Rocketman*. A vaguely accurate biopic of the piano-pop king's youth and wonder years, it sticks with me not for the A-grade tunes or B-plus performances – Richard 'Robb Stark' Madden is deliciously hateable as John's vulgar lover and manager – but one line towards its close. "Real love is hard to come by, so you find a way to cope without it." Something I must do in the months ahead, if this project is going to be about more than heartbreak and depression.

The second memorable moment is an entirely positive one. The ELO covers band launches into When I Was A Boy, and a lady in a wheelchair at the end of our row happily echoes every line. One verse in, the gentleman next to her – clearly her husband – pulls her up out of the chair, bears her weight, and rests her head on his shoulder. From here, she softly sings every remaining word into his ear. The gentle shuffling of his shoulders suggest the man is sobbing. Mother and I are too.

It's an unforgettable sight, the very essence of romance. Proof that real love is hard to come by… but whether you're 18, 25, 40, or the sum total of all those numbers, it isn't an unattainable dream.

Tuesday 25 February

My eldest daughter's seventh birthday, and the first we've celebrated while in the Facebook wilderness. Or it would be, save for the realisation that I forgot my monthly check on the 15th. I do it today instead and find a video my mum shared at the weekend of me dad-dancing to Bruno Mars' Treasure. Still need to work on those Inbetweeners tendencies.

A refreshingly mobile-free birthday meal follows, where my focus is fully on the kids, and Mrs E and I converse about future plans for childcare and houses – rather than stare at our phones and use Facebook checks as an excuse to avoid conversing. As had been the case at every family meal in recent memory.

Saturday 29 February

Two months of the project complete. Amid the fallout from February's biggest, saddest news story, Caroline Flack's death appears to have triggered desire for genuine change, with a petition for stronger tabloid press regulation doing astronomical numbers.

Petitions on gov.uk which rack up 10,000 signatures are assured of a government response, while those which amass 100,000 signatures are considered for parliamentary debate. Titled 'Caroline's Law', this one has surpassed 750,000 – the only catch being that it was started on campaign website 38 Degrees, meaning those in power could ignore it entirely. Still, it's all too easy for hashtags and social media mantras to fade away following initial, well-intentioned sharing. 'Be kind' patently hasn't.

My own mental health remains a helter-skelter, but I finish the month in reasonable spirits, helped by the weekend away with mum and text exchanges with old friends. Time off social media continues to provide physical benefits. My wanton sleepless night of fizzy pop and warm bread aside I'm eating better, and clocked three hours more running than in January – dropping my weight below 15 stone. It's a boost after three difficult weeks.

Beware the Ides of March? I will, but it's a relief to have February in the can.

End of month stats: February 2020

Weight: 14st 12lb
Twitter followers: 5,012 (-10)
Facebook friends: 836 (-3)
Instagram followers: 226 (+1)
Average sleep: 6h 26min
Books read: 3 – Jean-Paul Flintoff: How to Change the World, *Andrew Grumbridge & Vincent Raison:* Today South London, Tomorrow South London, *Bill Bryson:* The Body
Distance run: 85.5km
Time running: 8h 23min
Best 5K time: 23min 57s
Best 10K time: 57min 7s

MARCH

Sunday 1 March

My first attempts at 'distance' running occurred aged 17. By this point we lived on a sprawling Carshalton council estate, where every second day throughout the summer I would undergo a comprehensive warm-up, then do 'laps'. One lap took about six minutes. Often that one lap would be sufficient to send me back to the flat, wheezing the rest of the day away. Laughably, I blamed my asthma, usually while inhaling a bag of Haribo to replace the energy lost in 360 seconds of speed-walking.

That union of poor fitness and laughable excuses meant I never pushed myself. A dismal diet didn't help. Teenage me would regularly espouse the notion of 'everything in moderation'. One-a-day? Yes please! One bag of crisps, one chocolate bar, one bottle of Coke, one XL portion of ketchup-drenched chips. Little wonder I couldn't keep my legs moving as every corpuscle did its utmost to fend off diabetes.

23 years on, diet transformed and body no longer mirroring the Stay Puft ghost, my outlook has switched completely. Initially, 'running' meant gently jogging around the local village, as an escape from two barbarous toddlers. 5km took nearly 40 minutes, but it was 40 minutes of thinking time. This became especially useful as I began to understand my mental health woes, and address the challenges of CBT.

As my fitness and times improved, Steve recommended an app called Strava. This was especially surprising given his eschewing of social media, but he insisted it would foster a sense of competitiveness, and that it was "bullshit free". I signed up and discovered that he was correct.

It's impossible to fake stuff on Strava. You run or ride or swim, and it tracks your time and route, then shares it to your profile, and your friends' news feeds. Achieve a Personal Record (PR) and a gold medal shows up against that activity. Over time you can easily monitor your own improvement, and the progress of mates and family. Competing against your own previous times is strong motivation, but so is the app's authenticity. On Facebook or Insta you can mask a bad day by posting a smiley photo of your kids. On Strava, there's no such fiction, only fact.

Now, aged 40-and-a-bit, I love running. It's still my respite from parenting, but much more too. It's time to indulge in loud music, to get lost in my own thoughts, to process and overcome past failings, to assess hypothetical future ambitions. Entire paragraphs of this book have been constructed in my head while pounding local pavements. It's competitive yet strangely relaxing: a time of unapologetic self-preservation, where I'm free not only of Twitter and Facebook and Insta, but also email and text messages and any other contact.

Today, with a sense of clarity that went missing throughout February, my legs feel as if they could run forever. I turn My Chemical Romance's darkly operatic *The Black Parade* album up to maximum volume, and keep my calves and feet moving until I have to stop myself from keeling over. Synapses firing, evening sun accompanying a calm breeze, it's one of the highlights of this snakes-and-ladders year, only possible due to the time freed up from quitting social media.

When I do stop Strava clocks me at 17.7km, not far off half-marathon distance. I've been on the move for an hour and 48 minutes, a period 17-year-old me would have considered unfathomable. For a few seconds, before nonchalantly returning to his Coke and chips.

Thursday 5 March

World Book Day delivers pangs of guilt for being off Facebook. It's a key event for school and nursery parents, and giving one another a digital thumbs up over home-made *Harry Potter*/*Super Mario*/entire-cast-of-*Frozen* outfits is a positive tradition I can take no part in. We've not bothered to make stuff, instead buying in matching Matilda dresses.

To distract from social media temptations, I revisit Rohit Neralla's concept of novel information addiction. Not by logging into Twitter, but via two recent copies of *Mendip Times*. It's a monthly magazine charting local happenings across Frome, Glastonbury, Shepton Mallet, Street, and Wells, which I figure will both engage the brain and raise a smile via some quintessential Britishness. It doesn't disappoint.

Take the story of local artist Lydia Needle, and her 'Fifty Bees: The Interconnectedness Of All Things' display in Frome. It features 50 bees sculpted from wool, embroidery thread, and "vintage Kamibari gold", then housed in simple containers such as old tins and matchboxes. Each bee is then paired with a companion piece created by an artist or writer. Needle is up to 200 bee sculptures, with her overall target 275, one for every type of British bee.

Similarly kooky is a guide to making the perfect borsch, a Ukrainian dish which seems to have no local connection other than the writer, Adrian Boots, read about it in a recent copy of *National Geographic*. "Historically hogweed was collected in the spring, chopped up and covered with water and left to ferment, creating a form of sauerkraut," Boots explains. "This was then used to make a sour soup. Not a disgusting sour, more of a savoury sour… this spring, why not try fermenting some wild hogweed and having a go?" Sadly I'm all out of wild hogweed. There will be no Benjamin Borsch.

Most novel is a tech-expert column warning against the potential perils of decade-old computers. "Windows 7 users will no longer receive security patches that keep their machines safe," it reads. "Running an unpatched machine means flaws in the code will never be fixed. As exploits become known and widespread, your chances of being successfully attacked grow very rapidly." There is some truth in there, but the apocalyptic tone does feel a touch *Little Britain*.

Computer says… run! And hide! In the attic! Now!

Friday 6 March

A second enquiry regarding my social media absence arrives, from another Crystal Palace comrade, Anna W. As with Naveed's, I respond by sending her the introductory chapter of the book.

"Wow! What you're doing is fantastic," she replies. "I've considered it before but then never done anything because I'm too scared to. You have my full admiration. That [biopsy] scare must have been awful. I can't imagine what it must have felt like. I'm a message or phone call away though – I appreciate many will say that when reading that chapter, but I genuinely am."

We arrange to meet for a real-life drink the next day.

Saturday 7 March

Off to my first Crystal Palace fixture of this year. My normal matchday routine involves catching a mid-morning train from Bath to Paddington and spending the entire 90-minute journey scrolling though Twitter, digesting team news and discussing the afternoon's fixture with fellow Palace fans. This process repeats himself on the ride home, with social media being used to discuss key points of the match and argue vehemently with fellow Palace fans.

That's not an exaggeration. Win, draw, or lose there is always a vociferous Twitter minority who spend their Saturday nights taking potshots at manager Roy Hodgson or goalkeeper Wayne Hennessey, and I've spent far too many half-drunk rail rides engaging with the naysayers. Last season I was covering our away game at Manchester United for a national magazine. Palace fought bravely to a 0-0 draw. Yet once my copy was filed I spent the evening not hitting the trendy bars of Ancoats, but using hotel room internet to defend Hennessey's performance – a clean sheet at the biggest arena in British football not enough for the Twitics. It's a relief to have cut those distractions from my life.

With Twitter out-of-bounds I change my routine and drive, parking up at my mum's place in South London. This affords time to properly catch up with family and friends, both before and after the game. Such mini reunions often prove superior to anything that occurs on the Selhurst Park turf. I share a pint with Anna W in the build-up to kick-off, then meet Dave and Claire, a couple I've known for more than two decades, following the final whistle. It's all more leisurely and fury-free than my old routine.

The match experience is different, too. That Twitter blue tick means I've long considered it my journalistic duty to provide pithy live updates on stuff the stay-at-home fan might miss: curious off-the-ball occurrences, witty chants, sarcastic one-liners yelled from the stands. This is a recurring headache, given that 25,000 people inevitably drown out the 4G signal, and Palace's attempts at Wi-Fi are powered by a cup and piece of string. Today it's a relief to put my phone away, switch off my brain and simply enjoy the football at face value – especially as Palace overcome Watford 1-0.

I spend the evening in Tooting Market, getting hammered with a friend called Lou. It is endlessly preferable to being holed up in a Mancunian hotel, being hammered about Welsh goalkeepers.

Tuesday 10 March

Uh oh, uh uh oh, uh uh uh oh, uh oh oh, uh oh oh, uh uh uh uh uh uh oh, uh oh oh. Not only the bridge to a five-star Beyoncé track, but also my reaction to a *Guardian* news headline: "Glastonbury and Hay festival organisers press on despite coronavirus fears."

Being off social media has enabled some avoidance of Covid-19 developments, but the fast-dawning reality is that it's embedded in the UK now. One death is too many. To date, there have been five. It's clearly going to get worse before it gets better, however optimistic the Eavis family may be. As such, while it matters little in the grand scheme of things, I need to carefully consider this project's future. Can you complete a book inspired by Glastonbury if Glastonbury literally doesn't happen?

Thursday 12 March

Positive Glasto news as, at 7pm, Emily Eavis reveals the first line-up poster. Travel buddy Lauren sends me a screenshot of the line-up and Eavis' accompanying Instagram message: "After much consideration given the current circumstances, and with the best of intentions, here is the first list of musical acts for Glastonbury 2020… No one has a crystal ball to see exactly where we will all be 15 weeks from now, but we are keeping our fingers firmly crossed that it will be here at Worthy Farm for the greatest show on Earth!"

Our WhatsApp group is immediately alight with chat which illustrates our range of music tastes… and birth dates.

"Lightning Seeds! Manic Street Preachers! La Roux! Pet Shop Boys! Bet it doesn't happen!" I write.

"Sooo good! Elbow, Lianne La Havas, Laura Marling, Robyn OMG," replies Lauren's best friend Sarah – a fellow journalist but, like Lauren, eight years my junior. "Sam Fender! The Staves!" she continues. I don't dare admit I've never heard of Lianne La Havas or The Staves.

"Looking forward to Skunk Anansie and Taylor Swift," adds Andy H, who will also be celebrating his 40th at the festival.

"It's one of the worst Glasto headliners line-ups I've ever seen," Lauren writes. "But there are other people I will go see, so…"

"Crowded House!" I write, alongside a string of sarcastic laughter emojis. Before recalling that both Don't Dream It's Over and Fall At Your Feet are bangers, if indeed it's possible to class easy-listening acoustic ballads as bangers.

"Actually, I do quite like Crowded House," I add, guiltily.

"Er… who's Crowded House?" replies Lauren. Wait, what?

"Literally have no idea who they are, lol," adds Sarah. Wait, WHAT?

"Oh god Andy, WE ARE SO BLOODY OLD," is all I can muster in response. The group goes silent for the rest of the evening, so I shut down WhatsApp, pop on my slippers, tear open a bag of Pontefract cakes, and blast out Weather With You on the gramophone. Live your best life, and all that.

Saturday 14 March

An aim of this project was to reconnect with friends in real life rather than on social media, so I'm currently in Salisbury, staying with one of my closest mates. Colum is originally from Ballycastle in Northern Ireland, and we met at university 20 years ago. Upon his first introduction to my mum she demonstrated a baffling inability to grasp his name, utterly insistent that it was something other than the definitive word on his birth certificate.

"Are you sure it's not Colin?"

"No, Mrs Wilson, definitely Colum."

"Ciaran?"

"No, that is Irish, but every letter is completely different other than 'C'… 'Col-um'…"

"Ohhh, with a 'U'? And an 'M'? So it's Callum?"

"No, [as politely as he could muster] C, O, L, U, M."

"Gollum?"

At which point we both gave up, and began plotting a seemingly interminable quest for a magical gold ring.

Along a similar theme, in a marginally speedier time frame, I rattle off an enjoyable 16km run through the quaint villages of Wilton and Quidhampton on an overcast yet dry Wiltshire morning. Upon my return, Colum raises the idea of a late-afternoon Stonehenge visit. With clouds looming eerily yet prettily, and crowds absent due to coronavirus concerns, it's a masterstroke of a call. Somehow, I've gone 40 years without visiting this most famous British landmark, and today we have it almost exclusively to ourselves.

The stone circle has been fenced off since March 1978, but even at a short distance there's nothing so humbling as the aura of a monument erected around 5,000 years ago – 125 times my own age. A forceful reminder that we're on this rock for a bewilderingly infinitesimal amount of time, and should make the bleeding most of it. This notion taps into my daft, soppy romantic side: in the suddenly felt absence of January Girl, Colum is my only option for a snog by the stones. He responds to my amorous cheek-peck with a fist to the ribs. Fair's fair.

Our manly embracing over, an amiable American family approaches to ask if we'll take their photo. They're from Missouri, and we swap tales of watching their hometown Kansas City Chiefs win the Super Bowl from very different vantage points. They're supposed to be in Kiev right now, and have only ended up here after a flight diversion necessitated by a sudden travel ban to Ukraine. Quite the destination change.

I snap a few images of my own but find myself compelled to just take in the stones and scenery, rather than consider the best angles for Insta, or puns to annotate a Facebook gallery. This wouldn't have been the case three months ago. It's immensely liberating.

In the evening we head into Salisbury proper, for a humongous curry, and to visit the Bishops Mill pub – which became infamous following the poisoning of former Russian double agent Sergei Skripal and his daughter Yulia. The Skripals spent 75 minutes here in the early afternoon of 4 March 2018, before being found unconscious on a park bench. It was closed, decontaminated, and completely refurbished over a 13-month period.

The pub has been decked out like an upmarket JD Wetherspoon. I ignore the internal voice hounding me to order a White Russian, as we sink a succession of BrewDog IPAs while tapping our feet to tunes of an unapologetically poppy nature: S Club 7, Little Mix, Spice Girls. Alas, nothing by Tatu. The clientele is mostly twenty-somethings, but twinkly disco lights don't entice a single one to dance, even to the near-faultless refrain of Miley Cyrus' We Can't Stop. I try to drag Colum up in time for the middle eight, and he looks at me as if I've just poiso… actually, best not to finish that joke.

Salisbury may have been declared Novichok-free, but that doesn't mean I escape its historic embrace without some sickness of my own making. Exhaustion from this morning's run, enhanced by spiced meats and Soviet-strength hops, overcomes me shortly after leaving the pub – and I finish the night vomiting into the River Avon from one of England's oldest bridges. Quest failed. Instead of Legolas, I am merely legless.

Sunday 15 March

While watching a review of the morning papers with Colum I make a mental note to pick up the *Sunday Telegraph* on the way home.

The reason for doing so is its lead sports headline, and the accompanying story does not disappoint. With professional football suspended, the back page is given over to the Oxfordshire Senior League clash between Garsington FC and Summertown Stars. Headline: "Match Of The Day". Final score: 1-0. Match fees: £5 a head.

Which is to say, each player paid a fiver to play, rather than receiving any remuneration for their efforts.

The report treats the two clubs as if they were Tottenham and Arsenal, with Garsington's Joe Ryan (star man) and Brad Dalton (scorer of the winner) enjoying a day of recognition every pub-team player in the land dreams of. It's a smile raiser amid a miserable time, with some well-placed dry wit. "Summertown had brought quite a contingent, swelling the attendance to 31," writes correspondent Jim White.

Once home I carry out my monthly @ replies check. It is uneventful, other than another batch of missed birthdays. As with my social calendar, I've long been reliant on Facebook to keep track of when friends were born. I'm flushed with guilt to learn that three of my favourite people had birthdays in the last week, and I shunned them all.

So, Sarah Head, Rob Sutherland, and Sean Foster, let me set that right in everlasting print. Many happy – if somewhat belated – returns.

Tuesday 17 March

No word on Glastonbury as yet, but one event central to this project will no longer occur. Six days ago, the coronavirus outbreak was labelled a pandemic. As a direct consequence, Euro 2020, which was due to take place across 12 separate host cities such as Munich, Rome, and Dublin, has been postponed by a year.

Locally all remains calm, although my attempts to book an online shop are farcical despite government pleas not to panic buy. Tesco: no slots available. Sainsbury: no slots available. Asda: can't even load the home page. Finally, Ocado brings joy. For six seconds. I get onto the website and am told that I've successfully joined the queue. "You are position 10569 of 10641. Your wait time will be more than two hours."

Pasta in a saucepan for the entire household until further notice it is, then.

Wednesday 18 March

Glastonbury cancelled. Fuck fuck fuck fuck fuck fuck fuck. Fuck.

Thursday 19 March

Able to view yesterday's announcement with more perspective today. The country is shutting down, with schools and nurseries closing and the government pressing home the need for anyone at risk to self-isolate for 12 weeks. Deaths in Italy alone have passed 3,400. For now music festivals and other forms of entertainment must wait.

I message mum, reaffirming the situation's seriousness, with London case numbers escalating rapidly. Then I give my head a wobble and finally grasp the bigger picture.

I've been asthmatic since contracting pneumonia aged nine, during the 1989 ambulance strike. I remember being stretchered into an army truck and rushed to hospital, at which point a male nurse attempted to implant an intravenous drip in my left hand. After a couple of minutes spent waggling a needle around unsuccessfully, he attempted to attach it to my right hand. Another extended, painful failure. So I spent the night on a bed with an oxygen mask over my face, desperately frightened, my mum's face ashen with fear at my bedside.

Hundreds of thousands of people are living that same nightmare across the world. But they're alone: the threat of the virus means friends and family aren't allowed into hospital with them. A great many will not survive it. It's appalling to comprehend. So yes, losing Glasto is a personal blow, but I have to get a grip on reality here. It's a brilliant party in a field. It is not life and death.

The small piece of good festival news is that the Eavises are generously carrying existing tickets over for 2021. After a heavy, thought-provoking day I use that as motivation to hammer a 22:10 PB on a sunset run.

Friday 20 March

I am a wreck at school drop-off. The thought process behind this project was to drop social media contact; now the government advice is to have minimal real-life contact for 12 weeks. It's tough bidding farewell to fellow parents and staff, and to abandon all PTA plans until who-knows-when.

Following yesterday's perspective-shifting reality check, I make a snap decision while sat in the car outside school. Last Sunday was the Bath Half Marathon. My January paranoia was misplaced: I feel ready to take on the full distance of 21.09km, and regret not having signed up. Instead I'll have my first ever crack at stumbling one on my own. Tomorrow. Why wait?

I'm fairly confident that my legs are capable of lasting two hours, but have no idea about fuel. My usual pre-run 'carb load' is two bananas and two Jaffa Cakes. In normal circumstances I'd crowdsource foody tips from friends via Facebook, but that's not allowed, so it's over to the experts instead.

Firstly, what should I eat the night before? "Dinner should be relatively small, but carb-heavy," writes Dimity McDowell of *Runner's World*. "Eat on the early side so you have lots of time to digest."

"You want to wake up race day hungry – not full from the night before," adds Monique Ryan, author of *Sports Nutrition For Endurance Athletes*. Goddit. Chicken breast and jacket potato added to the pre-run shopping list.

What about breakfast? Porridge is the top choice, according to *Runner's World*'s Alice Palmer. "The unofficial king of the race day breakfast, oats are healthy, filling and 70 per cent carbohydrate – perfect for running," she writes. "Stir through honey, maple syrup or fruit compote for a dose of fast-acting sugar, or add raisins or dried fruit – blueberries and cranberries are delicious. Adding sliced banana before heating makes for a sweet, healthy and heartier pre-run breakfast."

Porridge and banana. I can do that. What about during the run itself?

"Your muscles can store about 2000 calories worth of glucose, which fuels your brain and muscles. Any run longer than 60 minutes needs fuel," explains Windsor Half Marathon expert Nicola Joyce. "[Go for] purpose-made running gels or shots, carbohydrate drinks, or soft/easy to eat bars. Jelly sweets, pretzels, banana, oranges, or dried fruit – if you are OK with the fibre content. These will have the carbohydrates you need and be easy to digest."

I head to the local Co-op to stock up. It's heaving with virus-evading panic buyers, but all the essentials are collected: slab of chicken, gigantic spud, bag of oats, mound of bananas, trolley's worth of Lucozade Sport and Haribo. Plus tonic water and a bottle of Limehouse Pink Gin. The latter pairing is an incentive to finish the run, but should also keep me temporarily sane once the euphoria has worn off and I'm left with one long summer, two untameable children, and no place to go.

You know what? I might even have a glass now.

Saturday 21 March

Up at 7.05am. Porridge and bananas are demolished by 7.20am. I play Peppa Pig with the kids for an hour, which is how I assume Eliud Kipchoge relaxes before a championship dash, then hit the local roads.

The early few kilometres ease by. I set a pace of 5:56 minutes per km, which has become my standard for longer runs, and breeze through the first third. Here my perspective changes. My recent tactic when out jogging has been to go for as long as I can last, with no specific distance target. So I am constantly counting upwards in terms of ground covered, and therefore buoyed by it. On those occasions, when I've needed to stop, I've done so.

Here, stopping is no option, and I'm effectively counting downwards: I need to run 21.09km. So when I pass 10km, instead of celebrating a reasonable distance negotiated, my reaction is, 'Ahhh shit. Still more than halfway to go.'

Even with the Lucozade Sport and Haribo providing sugary goodness, my calves and thighs begin to wilt at 14km. I live at the top of a valley, and the homebound sector involves lumbering up a 43-degree gradient. Every step feels leaden. The temptation to jack it all in accompanies every breath. But I persist through 2km of hell, and once back on level terrain pick up my pace. The 21st, and final, of the lot, is quickest at 5:46.

It's done. In two hours five minutes precisely, I've completed my first half-marathon.

I'm elated, but the sensation is different to past sporting triumphs. I've captained teams to five-a-side medals and even scored twice on the Crystal Palace turf – as any Facebook friend or Twitter follower will tell you, because I crow about these achievements all the cocking time. They're my 'look at me' fallbacks, deployed in order to coax shallow backslaps at times of maximum insecurity.

I feel no desire to broadcast today's big W, other than on Strava where the numbers speak for themselves. It's something I could not have done without the time, and head space, afforded by axing social media, and this project's first sign of true self-betterment. I hope there will be more to come. But for now, I have gin to drink. Exquisite, therapeutic, very pink gin.

Monday 23 March

When embarking upon a year without social media I anticipated a year of change. I did not expect, on its 83rd day, to be homeschooling my children. Homeschooling my children without any aid from social media.

This is the new normal. I'll have the kids from 7am until 1pm, then work in the afternoons. Mrs E will do the same in reverse. Meaning their education, for however many weeks, falls on me.

We've set up a school WhatsApp group to exchange ideas for educational tasks and fun activities – my issue being that most of the links are to Facebook.

D'oh. But a handful of useful ones are unearthed. At 9am each day YouTube fitness favourite Joe Wicks will be hosting a PE session. That will ground our day and be our official start time. Half an hour to loosen up and get their legs moving, then a mix of traditional necessities. 9.30am: spelling. 10am: reading. 10.30am: maths. 11am: seventh cup of tea. 11.30am: gentle cry.

A slight problem with this timetable is my children's surprising over-keenness. I'm dragged out of bed by the eldest at 6.15am, and they're both yapping around like stray dogs 45 minutes later. Lady S has spread eight weeks' worth of books and printouts across the living room, while Little Blue insists on turning out Play-Doh to mimic her favourite nursery activity.

Kettle on. Might need to bring forward that gentle cry.

We co-exist through to 9am and the next three hours are a pleasant surprise. Little Blue throws herself into Wicks' PE session – which at one point has 840,000 viewers – with uncharacteristic abandon, and Lady S applies herself to work with diligence and thought. It turns into a special daddy-daughter occasion, collaborating on the simple things such as '-ough' words and times tables.

One of her projects is to research Florence Nightingale, then pen a pretend letter to the iconic nurse's sister. It's a learning exercise for me as much as Lady S. I discover both Florence and sibling Parthenope were born in Italy and named for their places of birth. That Nightingale's legend was such that, to avoid media scrutiny, she often travelled under the pseudonym Miss Smith. That she had a pet owl called Athena.

It's all rather humbling. We've worked together many times on homework, but there's always been a get-out clause in my head: if it's not done properly, a teacher will fix it. Now there's no such luxury. This is an essential part of her development which is my responsibility alone.

To end the morning we discuss coronavirus, and what it means for the wider world. Lady S, already fastidious in her hand-washing after guidance at school, is a worrier like me and hangs on every word – particularly the concern of a hospital beds shortage. We chat about it again at dinner so that she can relay what she has learned of both Florence Nightingale and Covid-19 to Mrs E.

"Mummy, when I grow up I want to be someone who runs a hotel, where people can go to when they're not very well," Lady S announces.

Not wishing to be left out, Little Blue chimes in immediately afterwards.

"Mummy, when I grow up I want to be…"

[There's a pause as she reflects on her own day, and Lady S's new-found social conscience.]

"…Elsa from *Frozen*."

Thursday 26 March

"Daddy, can we have our own YouTube channel"?

Oh lord.

I grew up watching and adoring *ThunderCats, Transformers,* and *Care Bears*. Wait! I mean *Teenage Mutant Ninja Turtles*. Let's never mention the *Care Bears* thing again. But I never wanted to be Lion-O or Optimus Prime or Donatello. Merely to build an evil action-figure alliance of Mumm-Ra, Megatron, and Shredder which for long joyous afternoons would appear insurmountable, only for those good guys to save the universe seconds before dinner time.

In contrast, Lady S and Little Blue *do* wish to be their idols. Their idols being talking doll versions of Anna and Elsa from *Frozen*, whose YouTube escapades include (and I'm quoting Lady S here) "painting wooden stuff" and "having a birthday party". And the characters from *Grace's World*, where Australian teenager Grace Mulgrew provides voices for the doll-based adventures of Barbie's daughters Annabelle and Isabelle. Best episodes, again as chosen by Lady S: "when they go to park" and "when Chelsea has a sleepover".

Grace's World has 2.2 million subscribers. *Come Play With Me*, host to the adventures of Anna and Elsa, has 7.3 million.

As a result, I am repeatedly asked to set Lady S and Little Blue up with a YouTube channel. My stock answer – to this, and 98% of all questions posed by my children – is "no".

But we're home for the summer. A summer that could last months, as two days ago prime minister Boris Johnson placed the UK under lockdown. The homeschooling is ticking over, but we're going to need other things to do. That they're already watching two films per day to maintain my sanity is the type of confession which would cause parenting manuals to spontaneously combust. So before I can stop myself, before I know what I'm committing to, a different word spills forth from my silly, silly mouth.

"Yes."

Oh no.

Lady S is indescribably pleased, rehearsing her "subscribe to our channel!" pleas into an invisible camera in the corner of the living room. Little Blue's stock reaction to the answer "no" is throwing a tantrum so spectacular that within 45 seconds she can't remember which activity she was being denied in the first place. Give her a "yes" to any request and she offers a brief smile, then moves on to something entirely different, eagerly awaiting the next opportunity to throw a 45-second tantrum. As is the case now. Oh, to be four.

I know what you're thinking: YouTube is social media. This is totally cheating on the rules. My response to which is, "but no, your honour." Much like watching Joe Wicks' PE sessions, our intent is to use it as a broadcast-only medium, not for public interaction. The only people I can share it with are friends and family, via WhatsApp. Plus it's in the girls' name, not mine.

As we're now best friends, I hope you can agree that's all fine? Phew!

Lady S and I discuss ideas, and come up with a plan. Recently Mrs E has spent most evenings rehearsing for a theatre play; one of my favourite tasks with the girls has been mimicking mummy's performances by learning Taylor Swift songs on the guitar, and recording them on video. So we'll extrapolate that idea, and YouTube-ify it with other family favourite tunes. *The Greatest Showman*. Little

Mix. The Original 1985 *Care Bears* theme. No, wait, the girls nix the last one. Swines.

I log into a personal YouTube channel set up years ago but since rendered a barren wasteland, and rename it in the girls' honour. We tune the guitar, then spend two smiley hours recording and re-recording three songs: *The Greatest Showman* theme, Swift's The Man, and another in-car favourite: Chvrches' impeccable torch song Graffiti.

On numerous occasions it goes awry. The girls repeatedly disappear out of shot. I mess up lyrics or chords. Our recording tool of choice – my iPhone – falls off the 'stand' I've haphazardly created for it [a pile of DVDs] three quarters of the way through Graffiti. We complete The Man, upload it, watch it back – and swiftly have to delete the entire video, on discovery that Little Blue flashed her downstairs bits during the final chorus.

Overall it's a hilarious bonding experience, and by day's end all three videos are on the channel for friends and family. I reflect that it's nice not to have the temptation of sharing it on Twitter or Facebook. My career involves maximising internet traffic in everything I do. As a freelancer you never pitch something simply because it sounds fun; it's imperative that any proposed piece can attract the eyes of its target audience. So committing to something in the same field without any pressure on figures is immediately gratifying. The girls and I can simply enjoy this for what it is, rather than striving for perfection.

Not that Lady S shares this sentiment when we watch the videos back before bedtime.

"Do we have a million subscribers yet, dad?"

Just a little way to go, darling.

Friday 27 March

Shave my head for the first time in 22 years, aware that the only other option now barbers are closed for three months is to grow it into a bedraggled mop with 3ft sideburns, as popularised by 1970s Panini albums.

I've never done this in the social media era for fear of two psoriasis patches on the back of my head being 'outed' on Facebook, but it feels like a physical symbol of this project, and is therefore here to stay. No more covering up my flaws online in order to portray a character that isn't me.

Tuesday 31 March

Among my aims when starting this book was determining ways in which quitting social media can improve the minutiae of daily life. Eating more healthily. Getting fitter. Sleeping better. Re-establishing close friendships. Going five days at Glasto without being stapled to Insta.

90 days on, the landscape of both this project, and the wider world, has been remoulded unimaginably. I've just re-read the Prologue. If I'd predicted that within three months my family and I, like so many the world over, would be in quarantine, hiding from a hideous pandemic which has so far claimed 38,000 lives, these pages would have been classified as sci-fi. But this is very real, and very scary.

Yet I'm not going to change anything written previous to March. Even the part about being so offended by friends ducking a birthday party, which seems so precious and cringeworthy in the light of current events. It was honest. It captures not only my pre-coronavirus mentality, but also that of everyone in the UK: going about our business watching football, attending playdates, planning for festivals, getting drunk. Close human contact with zero thought as to how easily we could swap deadly germs, just by going about our daily life. This virus will ease to some extent in a year or two. But what of the after effects? Will those norms ever truly return?

What of this project, too? After wavering, it feels right to keep going. There will be no calendar year quite like this one. The girls and I are going to be indoors, save for the occasional run, until summer. Where this was conceived as a diary about social media isolation, it's now one about human isolation too. With my mental health history that's a concern. Again, it's convinced me to push on. Keep being honest. Write about the hopeful moments and the horrible ones.

That hope begins with a Glastonbury replacement. I've been thinking on it for the past 13 days, since the announcement of the event's cancellation.

The book will continue.

The festival will go ahead.

Just in a different location, with a streamlined set of artists, and a couple of hundred thousand fewer people in attendance…

End of month stats: March 2020

Weight: 14st 11lb
Twitter followers: 5,004 (-8)
Facebook friends: 836 (NC)
Instagram followers: 227 (+1)
Average sleep: 6h 31min
Books read: 3 – Shaun Bythell: The Diary of a Bookseller, *Jill Armitage:* London Underground Ghost Stories, *Danny Wallace:* Friends Like These
Distance run: 131.3km
Time running: 12h 6min
Best 5K time: 22min 10s
Best 10K time: 53min 0s
Best half marathon time: 2h 5min 0s

APRIL

Wednesday 1 April

If I can't attend the world's most fabled music festival – the very event that kickstarted this entire book – then it will have to come to me.

Goodnight, Glastonbury.

Hello, Glastonbenny.

This isn't an April Fool. Instead of sleeping in a tent in a field for five days, I'll sleep in a tent in the garden for five days. Instead of watching Taylor Swift or the Pet Shop Boys perform live in the flesh, I'll watch them perform 'live' on YouTube or Netflix. I'll still have to pack for almost a week camping in Somerset, still have to cower in a sleeping bag hoping to avoid Biblical flooding should the heavens open. All without a word to social media.

I'm excited. The pandemic has triggered anxiety and uncertainty – not just in me, in everyone I know. News reports talk of exit strategies and vaccines but both positives seem a way off. My family, like so many others, can only take things day by day. But this is something to plan for in the not-too-distant future. The prize, of sorts, for enduring 12 weeks of isolation. If you can call five nights sleeping on dried mud, while nursing increasingly hellacious hangovers, a prize.

It'll need substantial planning, too. My last festival was T In The Park, near Edinburgh, in 1999. I went up on a coach with my university mate Alby. As he was eight years my senior I let him big-brother me: organising travel, putting up the tent, sparking conversations with strangers. I've mentioned *The Inbetweeners* a couple of times in this book. At T In The Park, I was Will. In truth I still am a little bit Will. I've never even erected (simmer down, Jay) a tent on my own.

For Glasto, I was relying on Lauren for the same manbaby-nursing role. She does two festivals per year and happily suggested playing tour guide and resident expert during 'Farewell EU' night, given that Andy H, Sarah, and I are all Glastonbury virgins. That option is gone. I can tap into her advice over the phone, but in practical terms Glastonbenny will have to be a solo thing.

Actually, that's not quite accurate. It'll have to be predominantly a solo thing, with the added bonus of getting Lady S and Little Blue involved. It'll be a few years before we're comfortable with them attending a real festival, and even then the chances of both Mrs E and I being there are slim. This is a chance to give both daughters a taste of Glasto, and one of my challenges will be creative ways to include them. Skye from Paw Patrol headlining the Pyramid Stage is suddenly an all-too-real consideration.

Saturday 4 April

Keir Starmer is named the new leader of the Labour Party, seeing off the challenges of Emily Thornberry and Rebecca Long-Bailey. It's a startling reminder that I've been oblivious to politics since abandoning social media.

The news brings clarity on how much time, energy, and heart I lost in the build-up to the general election, debating policies on the local Facebook forum. Throughout November and early December I spent most evenings on there. At least two hours a day, every day, for six weeks. Three-and-a-half days of my life lost to disputes with 12 villagers on the internet. Or, for all I know, three villagers under four aliases.

I don't regret debating those with opposite perspectives in the election build-up. There has to be a place for rational discussion where politics are concerned, no matter how partisan individuals become over issues such as Brexit, and whether you're debating with one person or one thousand. But it's clear I got the balance wrong.

Everyone has a right to respectfully fight their corner on a global or national scale, but it's important to self-preserve at the same time. Throughout November and December, incandescent from those late nights arguing politics, I was Lord Grumpytits with both daughters over the most trivial of things. In fighting for my kids' future I was spoiling their present, by burning myself out day-to-day over matters which I couldn't change single-handedly. It massively impacted our Christmas, and is something I look back upon regretfully.

In all likelihood I'll still be an opinionated, insufferable bore when the 2024 election rolls around. But hopefully for a small, self-contained chunk of each day, rather than allowing it to consume my, and my family's, existence.

Sunday 5 April

5.35pm. The Hard Rock Hotel, Chicago. I am 28 floors up, sitting on a window ledge spanning the entire width of my room, small can of Heineken in hand, staring out at the city's spectacularly eclectic architecture. A collection of spires and shapes in myriad sizes and colours. Spherical buildings that start off as car parks then metamorphose into residential properties a third of the way up. The oversized, flipped Lego cubes of the Sears Tower. It's a view that makes zero sense, and is all the more mesmerising for it. A low sun peeps through the scattergun skyline, filling my room with a welcoming orange hue.

A complimentary CD has been left on my bed upon arrival. *Us and Them*, by Shinedown. I grab a second beer, and set the disc playing on the in-room stereo for a third time. Heavy, dirty rock, not usually my sort of thing, but one track hooks me in – the catchy, almost poppy I Dare You, with its mellow, dwindling verse and drum-heavy bridge and exultant just-try-not-to-sing-along chorus.

Every single time I hear this song in the coming years it will immediately, and happily, transport me back to that window ledge.

To my first ever night in America.

To my first ever WrestleMania.

Indeed, I'm listening to it right now in 2020, in a small village in Blighty. Because it's WrestleMania weekend, but I am not in Chicago. Or indeed Tampa, where this year's event was due to take place. Due to the pandemic, no crowd is permitted at WrestleMania.

2006 was a very different time. Twitter didn't exist. My only social media presence was a Myspace account where having to select a 'top eight' friends for display on your homepage was a recipe for in-office passive aggressiveness. Who ever figured it would be anything else?

At this point of the mid-noughties I was months into a new job as reviews editor of *Official PlayStation Magazine*. I'd been obsessed with wrestling since the summer of 1991, when a family friend recorded SummerSlam off Sky Sports thinking I might enjoy it. He was right. I watched Bret 'Hitman' Hart and Curt 'Mr Perfect' Hennig knock the pretend stuffing out of one another, and immediately decided that real-life cartoon characters brawling were a step on from anthropomorphic felines and talking robots. Being tasked with going to see the launch of a new wrestling game was therefore seismic news. With one tiny problem: when accepting the job my only condition was that I'd never have to board a plane.

My editor Tim knew this.

It's why he took me to a private room in February 2006, four weeks ahead of the trip, to pick my brains.

"Some amazing news, Babus," said Tim. [Babus is my work nickname. It's Latin for 'manbaby'.]

"Go on," I replied.

"THQ are announcing WWE Smackdown Vs Raw 2007 just before WrestleMania. And you're on the media list for it," said Tim.

"[many expletives.]"

"There's one catch."

"Okay…"

"It's in Chicago. By just before WrestleMania, I mean the day before WrestleMania."

"So I'll get to go to WrestleMania?"

"If you want to. But it means having to fly. How do you feel about that?"

"I can't do it. I can't go. I'm sorry."

"Think on it for 48 hours," said Tim. "Then if you decide not to go we'll ask a freelancer."

I did think on it for every single second of those 48 hours. It consumed me. I knew I couldn't turn down my first professional assignment in a different continent. On a personal level, I also knew that I'd permanently regret skipping WrestleMania, and the opportunity to see the USA for the first time. Super-sized food portions. Sports bars with 17 separate screens showing everything from baseball to basketball to synchronised tractor pulling. Beautiful Lake Michigan. Spherical buildings that start off as car parks then metamorphose into residential properties a third of the way up.

I had to go. But I couldn't fly. Could I?

One fellow journalist had been invited: a colleague on a different magazine called Fred. An hour before having to give Tim my decision, I sat down next to him to pick his brains, offering a five-minute soliloquy on my plight.

He didn't need five minutes to respond.

"Look at it this way, Babus," said Fred. "If our plane makes it over there, we'll have a great time watching WrestleMania in Chicago. And if it doesn't, let's just say we won't know about it anyway."

Weirdly, it did the trick. I returned to my desk green in the face but told Tim, before I could change my mind, that I was in. The flight was fine. America was – is! – phenomenal. To the point that in the ensuing decade I did four more WrestleMania events. Three for work, one in Miami for pleasure. I'm a very, very lucky manboy.

In Detroit, in 2007, a year on from Chicago, I was posting updates on a new sharing site called Facebook.

By San Jose in 2015 I was live-tweeting every movement, including interviewing arguably the most famous wrestler ever, Hulk Hogan, and fielding questions from fans on Twitter. They were all exceptional experiences, and I'd never try to paint them as anything but. Yet reflecting on them today, after three months away from social media, I now realise that my enjoyment of them all was defined by Facebook and Twitter reactions to what I was doing – rather than my own.

After interviewing Hogan we posed together for a photo at my request, then chatted for another three minutes off the record. Jimmy Hart, Hogan's long-time representative, joined us. It was a dream scenario for any fan who grew up watching '80s or '90s WWF wrestling: 180 seconds to chat any subject with its biggest star, and mouthiest manager. Yet to this day, I have zero clue what we spoke about. Because instead of focussing on the conversation at hand, I spent that entire three minutes zoned out, pondering how many Likes the photo would get on Facebook and Twitter. 100? 150? 200? "Thank you Mr Wilson. Hulk, this way please…"

It's hard to parse that entire scene as I reflect now. What should have been an incomparable private moment, sacrificed at the altar of boast posts. The nadir of a decade playing the same 'look-how-great-my-life-is' game I've bemoaned elsewhere. As a result Chicago, 14 years ago, remains my favourite WrestleMania. Not merely because it was my first. But because it's the only one I enjoyed as myself, rather than a character I wanted the rest of the world to see. 28 floors up, listening to Shinedown, staring out at Marina City, drinking tiny Heinekens, with no one to tell, no pressure to overstate the experience.

Tuesday 7 April

Awake to the news that prime minister Boris Johnson spent the night in intensive care with worsening coronavirus symptoms. Our politics will never align, but it's a terrifying situation and I can only will him through. I daren't imagine how this news is going down on social media, and am relieved to be out of it.

In a cheerier development, Strava has announced an 'NHS Active' campaign. Users donate a fiver to the NHS and then do a minimum of 10 minutes' activity every day for 12 days. My intention is to run 5km each day, and the first scamper round the village passes without incident. By bedtime the event's JustGiving page has totted up more than £120,000 in donations.

Wednesday 8 April

A genuine relief to read that Boris Johnson is stable after a second night in hospital.

Thursday 9 April

The girls' YouTube channel continues to trundle along in radiant anonymity. Our most popular video, featuring outtakes of the girls messing up song intros, is our highest-watched clip with 85 views. I'm still loving the opportunity to do something vaguely media-related with no microscope. Lady S and Little Blue continue to enjoy dancing and singing for friends and family – and a mystical, mythical audience.

With the third week of quarantine approaching its close, we discuss what Lady S misses most from school. One of her responses is singing in assembly. So we record her favourite school song, Count On Me by Bruno Mars, together then pop it on the channel and send the link to her head teacher. Two hours later we receive a reply:

"Thank you! You've reduced the whole staff to tears! Happy ones! Take care and happy Easter."

Lady S is made up. Whisper it, but I am a little bit too.

Saturday 11 April

Easter Weekend used to mean four days of videogaming, Facebooking, and tweeting for me, with Mrs E freed from work and enjoying uninterrupted mother-daughters time. This year it's all change. We're splitting parental duties, as I use the time I would have spent uploading *FIFA 20* Ultimate Team acquisitions on house-move prep.

My plan is to declutter every room with the aid of Marie Kondo. Countless friends have recommended the tidying guru's KonMari method, where you gather up your belongings by a single category type – clothes, or shoes, or Avengers Funko Pops, not that I'd ever consider being parted from Infinity Gauntlet Hulk – and then sort through them one-by-one, disposing of any that don't deliver 'tokimeku'.

In literal English that word translates as 'flutter, throb, palpitate', but in practice it means you ditch anything that does not immediately 'spark joy'.

Tackling my T-shirt drawer is today's sole target. The workload instantly quadruples on recalling that my T-shirt drawer extends to two whopping boxes in the back of a wardrobe. By the time everything has been emptied on the bed it resembles a dormant volcano of cotton and polyester. Technically I'm already doing KonMari wrong, as I should be going though all clothing at once rather than just shirts, but even assessing this lot will take hours. And I have *FIFA* to play… sorry, children to look after. I wonder whether Mrs E could do with a break right this second.

I call down.

"Nope, we've just put the girls' tent up in the garden. Fine for a couple of hours at least."

Bollocks.

Into the pile. I start with reds: the Mission Burrito shirt I 'earned' for finishing a greedy-guts food challenge. Joy! The Cross Hatch tee with the misshapen collar that I waited too long to take back, but refused to throw away because it cost £15.

No joy! Into the chazza shop box! After 10 minutes, the rouges are done, and the keeps are folded compactly back in their drawer, and the box for our local branch of Mercy In Action has already amassed a pleasing pile.

The pile on the bed looms as large as ever.

There's a scene in *Ghost* where Oda Mae (Whoopi Goldberg) is forced to hand over a cheque to charity by the apparition of Sam (Patrick Swayze), but she can't let go of it after learning that it's worth four million dollars. At the risk of sounding tight – ostensibly because I am – that's the toughest challenge here. Knowing that a shirt cost 30 quid, and getting rid of it for nada, breaks my skinflint brain. Joy or no joy, I go full Oda Mae on a dozen occasions. But eventually, one by one, items that I no longer wear, many of which are basically rags with sleeves, drop into the box.

It's two hours before the process approaches its climax. En route I learn that I own precisely one pink T-shirt – sporting the logo of wrestler Bret Hart – and far too many grey ones, which is probably a sign that I like things safe and drab and dull. After a tense start, I relax into it as the volcano regresses to a small hill and then a satisfying plateau, and find the process of letting go easier once a few hard decisions have been made. The idea is you thank each item for its service before declaring it redundant, and my canary yellow Lion-O rag-with-sleeves gets an especially fond farewell. No tears, but I may have given it a peck on the collar.

Clearing the bed really does bring on a sense of catharsis and serenity. Unlike this time last year, I've unquestionably earned at least one game of *FIFA*. I lug the box downstairs, dump it by the back door, and walk – literally – straight into my youngest.

"Daddy, we're bored of the tent now," Little Blue announces.

"Just in time!" comes Mrs E's voice from the garden. "They're all yours."

Double bollocks.

Sunday 12 April

Up to six runs in as many days for the NHS Active challenge. I'm beginning to feel it in my knees – I have next-to-zero cartilage in the left one as the result of footballing injuries – but the hamstrings and calves feel okay, and I'm determined to see it through. Halfway there, with no need to bow my head and channel Bon Jovi.

In more consequential news, Boris Johnson has been discharged from hospital, confessing that things "could have gone either way" and praising two nurses who stood at his bedside for 48 hours – Jenny McGee from New Zealand and Luis Pitarma from Portugal. It's a relief to hear that he's recovering, and being so specific in his praise for those working on the frontline. I can only hope such sentiments are echoed across Facebook, Twitter, and Insta.

Wednesday 15 April

A traumatic Facebook notification arises amid my monthly check. It concerns a new post from a friend named Paul, who was a pillar of support throughout my CBT course. He has lost his father to coronavirus.

I message Paul with my sincerest condolences, explaining that I'm off social media but he can call or text at any time. Covid-19 has been widely labelled as an old person's disease, almost as society's way of disconnecting itself from the risks of catching it. And the majority of UK deaths so far have been persons aged 60 or older. But each of those – 10,000 and steadily rising – is still a mother or father or uncle or grandmother, taken before their time, leaving behind family enduring what Paul is having to endure.

Paul soon replies with a two-minute WhatsApp voice message. It's dignified and staggeringly free of self-pity. He can attend the funeral but not even hug his own mother or son because of social distancing. He has every right to be a wreck. Yet he is composed and philosophical: "I've lost my best wingman, but when you go through defining moments in your life it either breaks you or makes you stronger. And I'm strong, mate."

It's a life lesson from someone who has been through much worse than offensive social media posts and a cancer scare. And a wake-up call after my early year wobbles. I message back with love and best wishes, and we arrange to catch up over the phone next week.

Friday 17 April

One day to go of the Strava NHS challenge. Physically it's become taxing, if only for the wear and tear on my knees and shins. Mentally, however, I feel determined to run big. 5K today, 10K tomorrow, done.

I've always found motivation to be an intensely personal thing. I have relatives who swear by pull-quote memes, and share them liberally on Facebook. With utmost respect, I can't say I miss that aspect of social media.

Instead I lean on past experiences to drive myself on. At Dulwich Prep I was fully aware of being the lone council estate kid among the well-to-do. It embarrassed me at the time, but is an invisible tattoo I wear proudly now. Much of that relates to the actions of an English teacher, who we shall call Mrs R, when I was nine. Upon enquiring in class as to which newspaper we read at home, hands shot up for *The Times*, then *The Telegraph*, then *The Guardian*, then *The Independent*, and finally the *Daily Mail*. By this point I was the only child not to have committed to a publication.

"What newspaper does your family read, Benjamin Wilson?" asked Mrs R.

"The *Daily Mirror*, miss," I replied.

She laughed! Actually laughed. Out loud. As did the rest of the class, without any suggestion from its figurehead that doing so was perhaps unkind.

"Mr Wilson, don't you want to be a journalist when you grow up? Children who read the *Daily Mirror* do not grow up to be journalists."

I was humiliated. But 31 years on that 'advice', and the Nelson-Muntz-style mirth which followed, still bounces around my brain every single time I write anything for anyone. At the very top of the manuscript to this book is a note to myself: 'Prove her wrong, Ben.' It's an attitude which has stood me in good stead. I ended up writing for the *Daily Mirror*, and three of the five broadsheets deemed acceptable household reads to a judgemental primary school teacher back in 1989.

Thank you, Mrs R, for lighting a fire that burns to this day.

My conversation with Paul has sparked a similar attitude towards the Strava challenge. My legs are flagging, but I feel as motivated as I have done all year. Every penny raised for the NHS is going to matter to some family somewhere amid this crisis. Who knows how many lives that will save? I want to complete this knowing I gave it my all. Not for Facebook or Twitter backslaps, as would have been the case a year ago. For Paul, and his dad, and every family and NHS worker affected by Covid-19.

Saturday 18 April

True to my word, I push myself for every footstep and smash out the fastest distance run of my life: 10km in 49 minutes and 14 seconds. For all the reasons mentioned yesterday. It's a PB I'll never break, spurred on by the NHS and Barrington Burrell. By the weekend's close Strava's campaign has raised £440,000. I'm proud to have played in infinitesimal part.

Sunday 19 April

My youngest brother, Harry, spends the day haranguing the rest of the family to participate in a quiz evening over Skype. One by one we give in to his charms and by 8pm, six of us are gathered for his big reveal. Which is… *Pointless*.

Pointless is like an inverse *Family Fortunes*. You're asked a series of questions and have to give correct answers that are different to 100 members of the general public. Take countries ending in the letter 'E'. While Chile gets you 44 points, Sierra Leone scores one, and Côte d'Ivoire a glorious zero. Making it a pointless answer. The lowest score at the end of the quiz wins.

Harry has dredged up the official *Pointless* book in order to ask questions, and devised a card-based scoreboard to mirror that of the actual show. Each time we give an answer, he lowers a rosette representing that family member downwards from 100 to the appropriate figure, with a descending sound effect to match the broadcast version. If it was carried out by a pissed-up Dalek.

It's hilarious throughout. As fun an evening as we've had as a family not just while in lockdown, but for a good couple of years. Competitive too, especially as the alcohol consumption racks up and the questions get tougher. Bridges over the Thames. Top 40 hits by the Sugababes. Characters from the film *Gladiator*. A couple of risky failures by eldest little brother Marc gift me the win – Harry's even made a tiny paper trophy for the occasion – but that's not the most memorable part of the evening. There are two, actually.

The first is a simple naming mix-up featuring two very different household favourites from our youth. It comes when middle bro Dean is asked to name a *Neighbours* character from 1988.

A long pause ensues. You can sense the cogs whirring.

Toadfish Rebecchi? Slightly too modern.

Charlene Mitchell? Too obvious, everyone loves Kylie.

Then, pressured by time…

"Howard Donald."

If only Madge could have known at the time that her bespectacled husband would one day swap coffee shop ownership and scout group leadership for a spot in all-conquering UK pop group Take That.

"It's *Harold Bishop*, Deano!" the family responds, as one, in stitches.

The second is especially amusing because our darling mother has spent the last 40 years telling us that geography was her favourite subject at school.

"Name a city in Ireland," says Harry.

Mum nominates Dublin. I say Cork. Marc chooses Galway. Sister-in-law Bea picks Belfast. Dean opts for Kilkenny.

"All decent answers," says Harry, "but there's only one pointless one. And it's… Lisburn."

Four glasses of white wine down, and buoyed by an evening's worth of laughter, mum is apoplectic.

"Whaaaaaaat?" she exclaims in the broad Devonian twang which only emerges when back in the South West for a few days and/or in her cups. "That's not in Ireland! It's the capital of Spain!"

Thursday 23 April

"I don't believe anything in life is random, Ben. Everything happens for a reason. The good and the bad."

I'm catching up with Paul for the first time since the death of his father. This is his third colossal loss since we became close friends, after lining up at centre-back together in a Clapham Common kickabout, in the mid-2000s. His wife Joyce died of cancer in 2014. His best friend Phil was taken by a heart attack, aged just 49, last year. Now his dad is gone too.

Paul has every reason to feel aggrieved as he approaches the most poignant of 50th birthdays. For days I've been worried about how to uphold normal conversation in the wake of yet another tragedy, thrust upon one of the most selfless people I know. Yet what unfolds is 80 minutes of positivity. Paul is as upbeat as I've ever heard him.

"I'm gutted mate, but I don't see this as the end of the journey," he tells me. "It's the principles of being a Christian. For my dad this is the process of going from a caterpillar to a butterfly. I live in hope that I will see him again one day."

I've never been especially religious, and one of Paul's loveliest traits is that he doesn't preach. He has his beliefs yet is respectful of all others. His mental health has held firm by developing what he calls "a relationship with Jesus", but when he enquires about my challenges with depression – questions I feel embarrassed to answer, given what he's going through – there's no one-size-fits-all solution, no suggestion that prayer is my answer. Plus he's still a bloke's bloke. Goes to the football. Loves a filthy joke. Drinks like a teenage Nemo.

He's found human loss brings out the very best in people on social media.

"When I posted on Facebook about my dad passing the response was heart-warming," he says. "I knew he was a great man. But to have 160 well-wishers, wow. It was nice to see how much my dad was loved. Meant the world. And I responded personally to every one of those 160 people."

"I have to use Facebook to keep up with family around the world," he continues. Paul's roots stretch back to Jamaica – his dad emigrated from there to London in 1962. "While people embellish things on there, you never see the whole story of their lives. The key is looking past that, and reaching out when you know a friend needs it. Like when you posted about your mental health last year. I could sense you were going through similar troubles to me, even before you announced it publicly."

Paul's positivity is infectious. I can see how his belief in something bigger than skin and bone steers him through difficult periods. "Focus on the things in life you can control, Ben, and let go of those you can't," he says. Hope is his anchor. I come away from the conversation determined for it to be mine. In a literal, rather than spiritual, sense. Health and happiness for my children.

Amicable paths ahead for myself and Mrs E. A meaningful relationship with someone new. Achievable, tangible ambitions.

He's changed my attitude to this project, too. I've realised that when I started, there was a silent, subconscious agenda. I wanted to prove that social media was bad. That was my USP: take a year off Facebook and Twitter and Instagram, achieve self-improvement, provide a watertight template for anyone who fancies doing the same.

Yet social media isn't simply 'bad'. Spaces such as Facebook have nuances. Paul's suffered three terrible losses yet been able to celebrate those lives with friends and family across the globe, finding sparks of joy in the saddest times. We live in a diverse, interconnected world. When Steve and I discussed the ease of getting our family news away from social media, we were doing so as two white English dudes whose essential contacts live within a two-hour radius. For the millions like Paul, with family spread across different time zones, Facebook is a more preferable means of staying in touch than 3am phone calls to distant cousins.

That's something to be celebrated. So too is Paul's courage, and his father's memory.

Tuesday 28 April

Another project milestone as I complete my tenth book of the year: travel presenter Simon Reeve's memoir *Step By Step*. As discussed in January, I struggled to get through one book per month before ditching social media. Indeed, a YouGov poll reckons only 31% of Brits make it into double figures for an entire calendar year.

"You can always read more, if you decide to read everywhere."

Three years ago long-time friend and colleague Joel Snape penned the above words on his website, Live Hard. He was adamant that we can all read more if we so wish, and listed some beautifully written, attainable goals. Have the

Kindle app on your phone. Ditch the devices at bedtime and keep a book next to you instead. Aim for 20 pages a day. Read everywhere.

"Seriously: make reading your default time-killing activity, and you'll be amazed."

I loved the piece, but fired Joel a tweet to tell him that such ambitions were impossible with kids clambering on my arms/legs/soul at all hours. I now realise that was a lazy excuse. He was right. Even as parents, we still get snatched moments of solitude – a cuppa while the kids watch *Frozen* for the gazillionth time, five minutes on the khazi – where it's possible to rattle off 10 pages. It's only habit which dictates that these times are instead used to glance at Twitter or upload to Insta. On those occasions I'm now churning through words, rather than defaulting to Facebook.

In the process I'm filling the old grey matter with Rohit Neralla's novel information, via the most old-school entertainment medium going. The best chapters in Reeve's book cover countries that aren't official countries, a bunch of which he visited for the series *Places That Don't Exist*.

Take Transnistria, a stretch of land between Ukraine and Moldova. The UN considers it part of the latter, but the state itself – a presidential democracy – heavily disputes this claim. Reeve visits then-Moldavian president Vladimir Voronin and shares an incredible story: tensions are so high that Voronin has not seen his own mother in two years, because she lives in Transnistria.

A more upbeat tale concerns Somaliland. This former British colonial outpost is a de facto state of 3.5 million people that has its own parliament, flag, currency and maintains a border with Somalia, even though it's internationally considered part of the latter.

Somalia is infamous as one of the world's most dangerous nations. Yet when *Guardian* journalist Joshua Keating visited Somaliland's capital Hargeisa in 2018 he found it defied expectations: "Hargeisa is one of the safest large cities in Africa, and, aside from the pollution and the traffic, there's not too much to be concerned about when you're walking around." Reeve echoes this view, with tales of war-torn Hargeisa being rebuilt with little outside help, and ancient rock paintings dating back thousands of years, and – how ace is this? – meeting a nurse delivering a baby who also happens to be the state's Foreign Minister.

No matter your political alignment, it's tough to envision Dominic Raab in that role.

Thursday 30 April

The six of you who are a. statisticians and b. paying attention to the monthly tracker will note that for all my gleefulness about competing a tenth book, it's the only one this month. That's compared to three apiece for January, February, and March. Confession time: I'm drifting back into old habits.

Whereas from January through March I was reading books at all those times Joel suggested, I'm back to grabbing my phone the instant I get a moment's down time. Not to hit social media, but the BBC or *The Guardian*, seeking out the latest coronavirus updates. Many of which are justifiably apocalyptic – which only drives me towards reading more. I'm addicted to bad news.

In all likelihood you are too. A study by University of Michigan scientist Stuart Soroka strongly supports the notion that we're all "neurologically or physiologically predisposed" towards negative information. It's based on a lab experiment where participants viewed a variety of real-life TV news stories while Soroka and his partner Stephen McAdams tracked their heart rate and skin conductance, i.e. sweat levels.

"Negative network news content, in comparison with positive news content, tends to increase both arousal and attentiveness," explains Soroka. "In contrast, positive news content has an imperceptible impact on the physiological measures we focus on."

"Indeed, physiologically speaking, a positive news story is not very different from the grey screen we show participants between news stories."

So when I reach for my phone before getting up in the morning, or dashing to the loo, it's likely a subconscious effect of being human. We're all looking for bad news. No wonder clickbait headlines shared on social media are constantly negative. Sadness sells.

It's a downbeat discovery to end the month, but otherwise I've managed to follow Paul's lead and pick out the positives. I've loved the personalised catch-ups and quizzes with friends and family, and found joy in the silly YouTube channel made with the girls. The KonMari continues to prove purgative, with a load of tat listed on eBay, and three bumper charity boxes loaded into the boot of the car, awaiting the end of lockdown.

All that daily jogging has paid dividends too. In addition to being for a good cause, my weight has dropped by almost half a stone. You're the run for me, fatty.

End of month stats: April 2020

Weight: 14st 7lb
Twitter followers: 5,004 (NC)
Facebook friends: 835 (-1)
Instagram followers: 231 (+4)
Average sleep: 6h 10min
Books read: 1 – Simon Reeve: Step By Step: The Life in My Journeys
Distance run: 116.3km
Time running: 9h 55min
Best 5K time: 23min 19s
Best 10K time: 49min 14s
Best half marathon time: N/A

MAY

Friday 1 May

With Glastonbenny etched into the calendar, my mind turns to the other summer event for which I own tickets: football's Euro 2020 finals. The tournament has been rescheduled for 11 June to 11 July 2021, which is a sensible decision – but falls outside the scope of my year without social media. Yet I'm determined it still needs to play a part.

So I'll play the entire tournament out on my own.

On the Streatham council estate where I grew up, four tall sets of flats encircled a compact patch of grass. Two pairs of trees at each end were just the right distance apart to form goalposts, and many a summer afternoon was spent haring up and down with friends of all ages, treating a friendly kickabout like the European Cup final. However, I was… different… to those friends. They'd come out to play football in the afternoons, then splinter off into games of knock down ginger and 40-40 and patball and runouts.

I just wanted to play football. All the time. So I did.

In the summer holidays I would go out at 8am, with most of the estate still asleep, and re-enact the best games and goals from recent memory. I vividly remember Coventry beating Tottenham 3-2 in the 1987 FA Cup final and choosing to relive the deciding moment as losing captain Gary Mabbutt: kneeing the ball into my own goal to gift Coventry the unlikeliest of wins, then lying forlorn on the Streatham mud, pretending it was Wembley, as though a crowd of 96,000 were watching from the surrounding flats.

I was an odd kid.

Not much has changed, and so for a few seconds, I consider taking the same approach to playing out Euro 2020. I could stick a mini goal at each end of the garden and, for each fixture, attempt five shots per team. Trouble is, there's no effective way of mimicking a country's identity. Other than placing a blindfold around my head to replicate an English penalty taker.

Instead, I'll just do it on PlayStation 4.

The videogame *Pro Evolution Soccer 2020* has recently announced a batch of extra content, with official Euro 2020 branding. All the teams, all the kits, the correct tournament ball, a digitised version of Wembley.

Sorted. Across one super-geeky July weekend I'll play every fixture myself. I will still be in attendance for the final; it'll just take place in a sleepy village near Bath, rather than North London. Maybe I'll make a local delicacy, such as Sally Lunn buns. Or borsch. There will be a winner, a runner-up, a top scorer. But with no social media presence, it'll be our secret. Exclusive to this book. As you read this, your nation might be the reigning European Champions, without you ever having realised. Exciting, right?

Just promise me one thing. If our digital final is decided by an own goal, thereby casting your country as runners-up, don't recreate it in a public space overlooked by at least 80 residential properties. It seems fun in the moment, but the expressions of concern it draws from neighbours hanging washing on their balconies will leave you scarred for life.

Monday 4 May

A theme of the opening chapter of this book was impoliteness. Brexit splitting the country in two (give or take 4%), a general election with results delivered on Friday 13th, playground squabbles about diving footballers. By giving up my social media access I knew I'd be shielded from such binary topics for 366 days.

In real life, all those tensions still existed. I knew there was every chance of bumping into those I'd had political debates with in Tesco, and primed myself for the fallout. Passive-aggressive looks. Loud tutting. Pinching the last loaf of bread and holding it aloft like the Coupe du Monde. All possibilities were prepared for.

Yet the spread of coronavirus has transformed those attitudes. My morning runs pass dozens of houses with hand-coloured rainbows in the windows, as symbols of hope in a troubling time. Mostly drawn by children, but their positivity has translated to adults too. 99% of people I sidestep while socially distancing wave hello. That's 98% more than were doing so in February.

I regularly see villagers chatting to passers-by from a safe distance, and have again been struck by the politeness of others on supermarket trips. I don't believe it's just a local thing, either. Friends and family in Leamington and London share similar stories, of neighbours posting notes through doors inviting shopping requests, of volunteering to help the NHS, or other assorted acts of kindness. Coronavirus has torn the country apart from a socialisation perspective, yet fostered a sense of nationwide togetherness at the same time.

The best example has been on Thursday evenings, with the nation encouraged to 'clap for carers' at 8pm. This involves standing on your doorstep and applauding for one minute in tribute to NHS workers, care home staff, and all those others who've risked their lives during the pandemic. In my village – full of people I'd sneered at for taking political potshots – that's meant the beeping of car horns, clanging of saucepans, release of fireworks, and other assorted celebratory noise.

Week after week after week. And it's been brilliant. Completely brilliant.

Whether that attitude has translated to social media is beyond my sphere of knowledge. Perhaps people are being polite in public, then unleashing inner fears and frustrations online. Which would be a real shame. If the majority of us can find ways to be kinder in real life in response to a pandemic, we can certainly soften our online personas when it comes to discussions of politics or sports or celebrity mis-steps. Though as a Crystal Palace fan you may need to remind me of this at 4.52pm every Saturday.

Wednesday 6 May

Back on track with the reading. The first book completed this month is *How to Grow Old* by the comedian John Bishop. This was a Christmas present from the ex-in-laws (what do you call in-laws after a marriage ends? Let's roll with that for now), delivered with unknowing prescience on their part. There's an entire passage entitled 'Anti-Social Media'.

In it, Bishop explains that he has a Facebook account to keep in touch with friends which he rarely looks at, and Instagram and Twitter accounts used primarily for work – the use of which has been reduced as a result of random negativity. Celebrity doesn't eradicate the need to keep up with the Joneses, either. While Bishop is far more famous than Steve or I could ever hope to be, his attitude to online grandstanding mirrors ours.

"Even famous people who I know do not have perfect lives can post things that make it look like everything is perfect," he writes, "or certainly at that moment in time they appear to be winning at life. This makes me feel that, by contrast, I am not, which is bonkers. I'm 52, fairly successful, financially secure, confident and healthy with decent self-esteem, and I still see social media posts that make me feel that I'm a bit shit."

The revelation is simultaneously reassuring and deflating. If a bloke that packs out arenas across the country and feels in control of his anxiety and depression can be felled so easily by Twitter, Facebook and Instagram, what hope the rest of us?

Sunday 10 May

Boris Johnson is due to address the public on upcoming lockdown steps tonight, and I wake full of anxiety. Six months ago, instinct would have propelled me towards my Facebook echo chamber for some instant fix gallows humour. Today, a voice in my head compels me to bung some gear on and run.

And run.

And run some more.

My second half-marathon. Just like that.

I end up clocking a sub two-hour time. This is an advanced achievement for someone of my escalating years and doughy build, particularly with zero preparation. For my first half-marathon in March I mapped everything out meticulously. Today it's just a case of going as far as my legs will carry me. 21km, on a whim.

It's restorative and uplifting and categorically would not have occurred anywhere near this soon with the distractions of social media.

The unclear Covid-19 advice is a real comedown. It's officially changed from 'Stay Home' to 'Stay Alert' – like we're all Ross from Friends, brushing up on our Unagi, in readiness to defend ourselves from a dozy mugger. Mrs E reports widespread disgust on Facebook, but I request to be kept in the dark as to further social media reactions. Paul has taught me that little good can come from ruminating on matters I've no control over.

Monday 11 May

If you'd asked me in December to summarise the worst element of Twitter in two words, I'd have replied "Piers Morgan".

The ex-*Mirror* editor and professional wind-up merchant built his brand on picking fights with celebrities over controversial and/or trivial topics, then setting his seven million followers on anyone who dared disagree. Vegan sausage rolls, body-positive models, millennial snowflakes, any and every blue-tick that dares challenge him: no issue is off limits when it comes to aggressive caterwauling in the name of self-promotion. Pick any recent culture war and Morgan has usually been found at its heart, whipping up his passionate support in order to fan the flames.

Imagine my shock, then, on opening Apple News to see him interviewed by the *Sunday Times* under the guise of being Britain's go-to guy amid a global catastrophe. "In the upside-down world of the coronavirus crisis, Morgan has emerged as something approaching a national hero in his efforts to speak truth to obfuscating power," writes Decca Aitkenhead. Huh?

I learn that he's pledged to pay for every NHS worker's parking ticket accrued while in service. Okay, that's a strong gesture. Fair play.

I learn that Morgan has U-turned on former close friend Donald Trump, publicly calling out his handling of the current crisis. Crikey.

The most remarkable development of all is Morgan showcasing humility, and confessing to trolling for the sake of doing so. "Did I really, really feel in my heart of hearts that the great hill I was to die on was the Greggs vegan sausage roll? No," he says. "But was there anything else to get my teeth into at the time? No, not particularly. I like arguing with people, I like controversy, I like being at the centre of a firestorm. But there's also, for me, now a sense of self-awareness."

"Let's put all the stupidity and the nonsense and the silliness and the point-scoring and the culture wars behind us," continues Morgan. "All that stuff has to be changed, we have to put all our concerted energy into being different people coming out of this. Better people… if [the coronavirus crisis] doesn't make everybody recalibrate in some way, there's something intrinsically wrong with you."

He's right, and Morgan's new-found drive for positive change merits commendation – assuming he's committed to it long-term. Seven million followers amounts to a powerful hive mind. One that can be a tool for widespread outcry and abuse, but also a force for good at a harrowing time. If Twitter's most prominent fire-starter can clean up his act, anyone can.

Wednesday 13 May

An extended evening run accompanied by Steve provides my first company with an adult human other than Mrs E in seven weeks. It's super, though I'm not sure which he finds more exhausting: the physical act of jogging, or an hour of me singeing his lugholes with two months' worth of forthright opinions which in a different time would all have been broadcast on Facebook and Twitter.

We arrange to do it all again at the same time next week. I suspect Steve may bring earplugs.

Thursday 14 May

Coming up to three months after Caroline Flack's death, more than one million people have signed a trio of petitions asking the government to tighten up laws on press harassment. One, the Caroline's Law petition mentioned in February, wishes to make it a criminal offence "not dissimilar to corporate manslaughter", and has 862,000 signatures. Another started by campaigner Joshua Brandwood, and calling for an inquiry into British tabloid behaviour, has 270,000. It's good news, in theory – but despite surpassing required threshold numbers, the UK government has shown no interest in furthering the debate.

Brandwood's petition has been rejected by Jacob Rees-Mogg, Leader of the House of Commons, because it was set up on change.org rather than the official government website. He describes the response as "dismissive and completely invalid", telling Sky News he had "no choice other than to set the petition up elsewhere as the parliament e-petitions website was down at the time".

Holly Maltby of 38 Degrees, which set up the Caroline's Law petition, echoes Brandwood's view: "The fact that the Leader of the House of Commons is using small print and loopholes to avoid debating what the government should do to end bullying and harassment in parts of our press is doing the public a disservice. 860,000 people hope he reconsiders." It feels like those hopes will be in vain.

Friday 15 May

Nothing to report from the monthly Facebook and Instagram @ replies check, but Twitter does throw up a couple of intriguing developments.

The first is a post from a Palace-supporting friend, Rob, from 3 May. It simply wonders aloud, 'Did @BenjiWilson give up Twitter?'.

Naveed's is one of four kind replies, explaining that I've taken a break to work on a secret project. I drop Rob an email containing the first chapter of this book by way of explanation.

The second comes from back on 20 April, and is from Glasto buddy Lauren, circulating a challenge to share six books you love. She knows full well that I'm unable to reply on Twitter, so I will do so on these pages instead. Once I've slept on my choices.

Saturday 16 May

I've chosen not to tell Lauren that I've accepted her challenge, with the answers only to be revealed in (at least) eight months' time. Six books I love, then, and why…

Ronald Reng: *A Life Too Short.* A thorough, essential read for anyone interested in sport, or mental health, or both. Author Reng was a close friend of Robert Enke, the German international goalkeeper who died by suicide at the age of 32. This biography of Enke brought to prominence the concept that fame and money don't ward off depression; that even in the public eye, a smile can hide a million insecurities. As such, this resonates now as much as when it picked up *William Hill Sports Book Of The Year* honours in 2011.

Jim Dwyer & Kevin Flynn: *102 Minutes.* This masterpiece documents the fall of the twin towers based on eyewitness reports and comprehensive research. It's inevitably a tough read, but there are uplifting tales too – of the firemen who made the ultimate sacrifice, of the two secretaries who guided an elderly Italian man down 89 flights of stairs, of the Polish window washer who used the edge of his squeegee to gradually break down a wall after he and five others were trapped in a lift shaft. Memorable, moving, essential.

George RR Martin: *A Storm of Swords.* Despite my self-confessed geekery, I didn't do fantasy reading until watching the first series of *Game of Thrones* and forcing myself into the books because I was too impatient to wait for season two. I then became that worst kind of *Thrones* fan, boring everyone by telling them that the books were better (true) and looking smug for knowing spoilers. Which is no longer the case, as Martin releases one book roughly every millennium, and the TV show finished in 2019.

Dave Gorman: *America Unchained.* A road trip with an inventive twist, as the British author/comedian/ex-flatmate-of-Danny-Wallace attempts to cross America in a 1970 Ford Torino, while restricted to mom-and-pop gas stations and independent hotels. Laugh-out-loud funny but heart-warming too, featuring numerous tales of amiable general store workers and local business owners enjoying the simple life.

Matt Haig: *How to Stop Time.* My most recent read, but still worthy of a spot here. 41-year-old Tim Hazard is an 'albatross' who ages 10 times slower than a normal human, and so has been alive for nearly five centuries. Themes of ageing, parenthood, romance, and social media are masterfully interwoven with clever peeks into the past. Encounters with William Shakespeare, Captain Cook, and Lillian Gish fit the story rather than feeling contrived, and it also features a breathtakingly worded kissing scene.

Bill Bryson: *Notes from a Big Country.* Bryson tackles returning to his home nation of the US after two decades living in England, and all the quirks and idiosyncrasies thrown up by the move – such as an 18-seater jet disappearing off radar close to his local airport and vanishing without trace, despite the efforts of 11 helicopters and 200 volunteers on the ground. Fret not, there are many cheerier tales too. My favourite book of all time. Must pack it for Lauren to borrow at Glasto 2021.

Sunday 17 May

Football is back! In Germany, where the Bundesliga has resumed inside empty stadiums, with balls being disinfected when not in play, and players asked to socially distance as best as possible – such as when celebrating goals.

I tune into Dortmund's 4-0 hammering of Schalke. It's surreal, ghostly viewing, though hearing elite pros' instructions echo around as if this were

Hackney Marshes rather than the 81,000-capacity Westfalenstadion provides some novelty.

I listen out for the German equivalent of "just fucking twat it, Dave!" but it is sadly not forthcoming.

This limited action has piqued my interest in the Premier League's return, but I still have no inclination to debate sport on Twitter.

Oh, and because I know you're now wondering… "Zerschmettere es einfach, Dave!"

Monday 18 May

A return mail from Rob.

"Wonderful stuff," he writes on the book, kindly. "Intriguing and amusing. Sorry about Glastonbury. But, mate… Taylor Swift?!"

Guessing he's not had the privilege of hearing Death By A Thousand Cuts on vinyl. I let it fly.

"I think your project will resonate with loads of people," he continues. "I quit the Crystal Palace forum six years ago, and thought I'd never do without it – but I've never once even browsed it since."

"On the subject of friends, and not knowing who to contact with your cancer scare – I've been doing an experiment over the past few years," says Rob. "When I decided to pack up work nearly six years ago many people vowed to 'keep in touch'. We exchanged emails periodically to keep up to date with each other's news. But it suddenly occurred to me that I only ever heard from people if they wanted something, or as a direct response to me getting in touch. So I decided to only continue these correspondences if THEY wrote to me first, to see how I was doing. I don't expect you have to guess how many of those relationships continue to this day…"

In his next email Rob confirms the answer is none. It's a bleak prospect, but the reassuring messages from Naveed and Anna W during mid-monthly checks, and support from the likes of Gemma and Andy S amid my February meltdown, give me faint hope that this project won't end in the same manner. So long as I reciprocate when and where possible.

Tuesday 19 May

"Hello Lauren! I have some unconventional news for you."

"Hey! Unconventional news?! How intriguing…"

"Glasto is still happening! Er, in my back garden."

"Okay. Are you trying to tell me you're throwing a socially distanced Glasto party?"

"Well, I don't know if anyone can attend in person. That depends on the government guidelines at the time. But instead of Glastonbury, I am doing Glastonbenny. Packing bags for five nights, camping out for five nights, watching the same bands on YouTube or BBC iPlayer…"

"Oh Christ!"

"… Making it as close to the real Glasto experience as possible. Just with working loos."

"Hey, if you don't have to queue for half an hour to pee with the smell of urine almost overpowering you the whole time, then you haven't been to Glastonbury."

"Fair enough. Maybe I'll get Little Blue to wild wee around the garden throughout the five days, to make the experience authentic."

"Ha! So, let me guess: You need something from me to help with this experience?"

"Um… Yes. As my festival guru, I was hoping you could come up with four essential things one has to do at the real Glastonbury, that could also apply in a back-garden version. Hard drugs, and making out with an octogenarian hippie, probably aren't feasible. But anything else is in play: a drink, type of food, essential band, game, experience (yoga?) – I'm open to ideas. I'd like a flavour of Glastonbury even though I'll be 21 miles down the road in a cramped garden."

There is a pause. A lengthy pause.

"Work is a bit mental at the mo. Let me get back to you…"

Wednesday 20 May

I have a sudden recollection that my close friend Matt, a comrade on multiple Stateside wresting trips, celebrates his birthday in May. With no access to Facebook – the foundation of my social calendar, don't forget – I cannot recall on which day.

So I drop him a line to ask.

Perhaps forgivably – as he knows of this project – I've missed it.

Less forgivably, I'm reminded that it was his 40th.

So a project motivated in part by friends silently missing my 40th, has led to me silently missing a great mate's 40th. I'm not sure whether this fits with the Alanis Morissette definition of ironic, but it quite rightly leaves me floundering in guilt.

I send Matt a grovelling apology, which he accepts, because he is one of the loveliest men I know, and we arrange to share a belated celebratory beer or six once lockdown is over.

Hopefully this book has provided various reasons for you, dear reader, to consider a break from social media if you ever feel that it all gets too much. Before you commit to doing so, please heed my lesson and make handwritten lists of the following pertinent information.

Phone numbers, in case you lose your mobile.

Email addresses, in case you lose your mobile and tablet.

Friends' birthdays, and friends' children's birthdays, so that you don't end up looking a right old Benjamin three weeks into your supposedly relaxing social-media hiatus.

Favourite alcohol brands for all your nearest and dearest, in readiness for the occasions when you misplace the above lists, or find that they've been defaced by a seven-year-old with a new pack of colouring pens, and thus have retrospective grovelling to do.

Matt's birthday BrewDog order will land on his doorstep before the weekend.

Saturday 23 May

A new story emerges of a female celebrity dying by suicide in the wake of social media abuse. Japanese wrestler Hana Kimura, a cast member of Netflix reality show *Terrace House*, took her own life after revealing that she no longer felt capable of handling online bullying. Kimura was 22.

I can't access Twitter to see her final post, but it's been translated from her native language by a range of news sites:

"Nearly 100 frank opinions every day. I couldn't deny they hurt me. 'Die', 'you are disgusting', 'you should disappear'. I believed these things about myself more than they did. Thank you, Mother, for the gift of life. My whole life I wanted to be loved. Thank you to everyone who supported me. I love you all. I'm sorry for being weak. I don't want to be a human anymore. It was a life I wanted to be loved. Thank you everyone, I love you. Bye."

Her final Instagram post, again translated widely, is even more sobering: "Goodbye. I love you, have fun and live a long time. I'm sorry."

Wrestling journalist David Meltzer explains the background to this dreadful event. "In an incident on *Terrace House* filmed in early January, a male housemate named Kai washed his clothes while her [wrestling] outfit that she wore at the Tokyo Dome was in the washer and then threw it in the dryer and ruined the outfit. She lost her temper and knocked his hat off his head."

"Since that incident aired, she had been getting hate messages from people all over the world and it sent her into depression," continues Meltzer. "It was getting worse in recent weeks."

It's easy to connect dots and point fingers at the social media sites themselves when horrible incidents such as this occur. But individuals have to take some blame too. Just because social media offers the opportunity to be a dick with anonymity doesn't mean you have to.

Would keyboard warriors have inundated Kimura with abuse if they'd seen her outside a show, or in a bar, or on the subway? Would they have continued their tirade – over the flipping of a hat! – or asked for a photo or an autograph? It's easy to commit an act of cowardice, and ignore that someone is a real human being, when sat staring at a screen. But it's also easy to take a few seconds before posting on social media, or sending an email, to remind yourself that there's a person at the other end. If the next time you had a barney with a mate 100 randos appeared to call you every name imaginable you'd feel abysmal.

During my CBT I discovered a quote which reads: "The true measure of a man is how he treats someone who can do him absolutely no good." As discussed in April I don't often go for pull quotes as life advice, but this one stuck, even though the internet has cast doubt on its widespread attribution to Samuel Johnson. Cynics may laugh this off as holier-than-thou liberal sanctimony, but it's something I subsequently tried to apply to all my online actions. My aim was to address a person – friend, family, stranger – as if they were in the same room as me, rather than behind a computer screen. Sometimes I got shouted down, especially during the general election, but often it turned initial abrasiveness into respectful discussion.

My sense is that genuine tragedies linked to social media would be significantly reduced if the majority were able to adopt a similarly considerate stance. Maybe I'm just a big woke wally – but something has to change. Hana Kimura represents another young life senselessly lost, with cyber bullying cited as a critical factor.

Sunday 24 May

A day I've been nervous about for a while: Mrs E and my first wedding anniversary apart – yet still under the same roof, thanks to lockdown.

We're still listed as married on Facebook, so for all I know my account is flooded with reminders of the occasion. It's for the best that I can't see them, or celebratory messages from friends who may not know we've split.

There's no sombreness though. We met 20 years ago and married in 2008. At 21 and 19 you have near-endless time to share one another's interests, plan and enjoy nights out, and sashay off on romantic holidays. At 40 and 38 with two kids, jobs, grown-up responsibilities, and school/nursery taxi driver commitments, that time to bond has eroded naturally. As a dating notion, 'opposites attract' worked at the turn of our twenties. It ended us as we approached our forties.

Mutually acknowledging that, and still wanting the best for our children, has enabled us to remain friends. Thankfully, the wedding-anniversary-that-isn't turns out fine. We take the girls on a sunny family stroll, KonMari some old cuddlies and cushions, enjoy an afternoon film – Vanessa Hudgens' teen musical comedy *Bandslam* – and rustle up the least romantic dinner possible: microwaveable burgers and chips.

It's the least fractious anniversary either us can remember since having kids. More tellingly, it's the one the girls have enjoyed most. For years following Little Blue's birth we slapped sticking plasters over gaping wounds in our marriage, "for the kids." Today is final confirmation that the best thing "for the kids" is for us to be apart.

Tuesday 26 May

It's 10 minutes to midnight and, with Glastonbenny less than a month away, I'm wide awake in bed thinking about a man named Andy. I've not heard of him for many many months. But I need him. Urgently. Now.

Andy L – not to be confused with Andy S in Abu Dhabi, or Glasto buddy Andy H – was one of the design whizzes on *Official PlayStation Magazine*, and an element of social media I miss is catching up on his latest projects.

So I've come up with a project which enables me to reconnect with him and make the festival-in-my-garden feel more official.

It's five to midnight now. I won't sleep unless I text him.

"My Iron Leung! Long time no hear. Sorry to text at this hour. Hope all is well. Do you have any availability over the next fortnight? If so, what would the cost be to design a poster for an entirely fictional music festival?"

Text sent. Rumours that I drift off imagining Andy drawing me like one of his French girls are unfounded. Or are they?

Wednesday 27 May

Wake to a reply from Andy L, sent 20 minutes after my message. When I was sparko. In the absence of Twitter banter, my own insomnia is mocking me.

Anyway, it's good-ish news.

"Hey buddy! Yeah, been a while! I'm not too bad thanks. Bored of lockdown. Hope you're doing well. I'm still working but I have time. Not going anywhere, lol. What's the poster for? If it's work related, I charge [a very fair rate] an hour. If it's a personal thing, we can do a deal."

"Cheers man," I reply. "It's kind of both. I'm writing a book about giving up social media for a year. It was inspired by the idea of doing Glasto without Facebook, Twitter, and Instagram. But Glasto isn't happening. So I'm doing it my garden instead, and calling it Glastonbenny. And I got the sudden urge to ask whether you'd be up for designing a poster for the 'event'."

"I did wonder if you'd given up social media. How are you finding it? Earlier this year I tweeted you something about our old five-a-side league, and never heard back."

This must have raised alarm bells. I never resist the opportunity to bleat about five-a-side feats on Twitter. Usually amounting to, 'did not score my customary own goal this week. Success!'

"Sorry dude. I've not told many people. It's been a positive change for the most part. Running more, catching up with long-lost friends, using my phone less. Can't believe it's been nearly six months!"

It does mean I've missed Andy's most exciting news of 2020: "Dude… I got the *Friends* Lego set during lockdown, but couldn't tell you!"

"Oh mannnnnn, amazing," I reply. "I got one for Christmas and have been saving it for the new house. Have also seen a special acrylic display case for it that costs 50 quid. Might treat myself as a moving present. Best not mention that in the book though. Way too nerdy."

Oops.

"The book sounds interesting!" says Andy. "I'm up for doing something for you."

"Thanks so much. I'll send over some ideas shortly. But please let me pay you something."

"Okay. I'll see what the workload entails and let you know about payment. Or just buy me the *Fast & Furious* Lego Technic set."

I know Andy is half-joking. I also know he loves Vin Diesel and jet-propelled cars even more than I love the vainglorious broadcasting of five-a-side triumphs. The Lego set is ordered, and the poster is go.

Friday 29 May

Lauren messages with her four essential Glasto tasks which can definitely maybe still be done at home.

"The first is the trickiest," she writes. "On the first night everyone walks up the big hill to watch the festival start as night comes in. It's essential – but I don't know how you'd replicate that at your place?"

Okay. A fairly light challenge to start with. An extended stroll up a steep-ish gradient.

"So you suggested yoga in your original message," continues Lauren. "Yes, try it! They normally have classes at the Healing Field. You also need to have your own Ultimate Power party – the thing I keep inviting you to Bristol for. They have their own slot at Glasto and it's epic. Bonnie Tyler, Meat Loaf, The Final Countdown: all your favourite power ballads."

"Yes! Those two sound ace."

"For the last one, have a look at this…"

A hyperlink follows. It's from NME and begins with the words, 'make a cucumber trumpet.' Cripes. "In the Greenpeace area… you are invited to attend the Vegetable Instrument Workshop, where you can fashion carrots, cucumbers, peppers and pumpkins into flutes, trumpets and pan-pipes all of which, we confidently predict, will sound like shit."

Right-o. Midway through day two, Lady S and I are attempting to make a watermelon drumkit. Then blaming Lauren when it all goes – quite literally – pear-shaped.

Sunday 31 May

Snowed under by homeschooling most mornings, and busy with work, reading, and Glastonbenny planning in the afternoons, social media has at last become an afterthought in my daily routine. Yet over the past six days, one Facebook video has been unavoidable. With good reason: the clip has played a pivotal role in highlighting racial inequality in the starkest manner imaginable.

On 25 May, an African American man, George Floyd, was arrested in Minneapolis for allegedly using a counterfeit $20 bill in a grocery store. Floyd was handcuffed face down in the street before a police officer, Derek Chauvin, knelt on his neck for eight minutes and 46 seconds. Floyd died, with the official autopsy report attributing the cause as 'cardiopulmonary arrest caused by subdual and restraint'. Two days ago Chauvin was charged with third-degree murder and second-degree manslaughter.

The game changer here is that a passer-by, Darnella Frazier, filmed the entire incident and uploaded it to Facebook. I haven't needed to be on social media to view the 10 minute, eight second video. It's quite rightly gone viral, been shared by numerous news sources, and triggered action across the globe. What will surely go down as the most impactful social media post of recent times hasn't come from Piers Morgan, or Donald Trump, or a sportsperson or movie star or some other kind of influencer, but a 17-year-old high school senior who happened to be strolling down a Minnesota street with her cousin on a Monday afternoon.

The reason this is so powerful is you cannot argue with it. There can be no fact-twisting. When someone posts an opinion piece or incendiary Twitter thread the debate often obfuscates the original point. As such, even well-meaning hashtags get diluted and lost in the mire. I suspect, sadly, that the ethos of Be Kind may go that way long before my social media return. But this video? It is unedited, unfiltered, unspinnable. It is an appalling and inhumane watch, wherever you stand on the political spectrum. And it is single-handedly driving change.

Since its dissemination, protests have taken place not just throughout America, but in London, Liverpool, Milan, Rome, Berlin, Copenhagen, Abuja, and Monrovia – indeed, the full list of cities is too numerous to include here. Seven years after its inception Black Lives Matter, a decentralised political movement seeking criminal justice reform, is dominating the news. Police reforms, including the banning of chokeholds – as soon as tomorrow, in San Diego – are being mooted across the USA. In New York, officers joined protestors in taking a knee to support the campaign. The NBA (National Basketball Association) has pledged to address inequality. Many other significant organisations are following suit.

In some areas the strength of feeling has spilled over. There've been fires in DC, LA, New York, and Nashville, looting in numerous locations, and continuing civil unrest which has necessitated curfews in more than 30 American cities. My standard take on such events is that violence solves nothing, but who am I to even merit a take? A decade of tweeting has conditioned me to feel as though I have to say *something* about *everything*. This year I've realised I don't. I'm a white dude living in middle-of-nowhere, UK. I can't begin to imagine experiencing this sort of systemic prejudice.

While the use of violence in situations such as this is a divisive issue, the need to curb racism in our societies should not be. I'm moved by the balanced words of Calvetta Williams, founder of Mothers Against Violence, and organiser of a peaceful protest in Des Moines, Iowa. While she was determined that her event should remain calm (and it did), she also understands why current events have motivated some to take physical action.

"I'm a black mother with two black sons, and I'm tired of using hashtags with the names of people murdered by police officers," Williams tells *USA Today*. "We can't just sit on the sidelines anymore."

"I think [the violence] enhances the message," says Williams. "How many times do we have to say our lives matter?"

"A building can be put back up. George Floyd, he can't be put back home."

End of month stats: May 2020

Weight: 14st 6lb
Twitter followers: 4,969 (-35)
Facebook friends: 835 (NC)
Instagram followers: 234 (+3)
Average sleep: 5h 37min
Books read: 3 – John Bishop: How to Grow Old, Matt Haig: How to Stop Time, Ed Hawkins: Bookie Gambler Fixer Spy
Distance run: 155.8km
Time running: 14h 54min
Best 5K time: 24min 10s
Best 10K time: 53min 39s
Best half marathon time: 1h 58min 29s

JUNE

Monday 1 June

My history of camping comprises the grand total of two memories.

The most 'recent' occurred some 21 years ago. T In The Park 1999 was one of the best weekends of my life: four days in Scotland watching the Manic Street Preachers and Blur and Fun Lovin' Criminals, bonding with my flatmate Alby, and talking bobbins to strangers while banjaxed on Tennent's Lager. Hardcore. I remember everything about the days and nothing about the nights.

For the other memory we must rewind a further decade. To 1989, and a one-o'clock-club sojourn from Streatham to a remote corner of Norfolk. After nagging until every adult acquiesced, nine-year-old me was named coach DJ, which meant playing both sides of Jason Donovan's *Ten Good Reasons* cassette on a loop for the entire three-hour journey. I suspect a handful of now-grandparents living in South London still experience unsettling flashbacks upon the opening riff of Too Many Broken Hearts.

I would remember this trip as fondly as T In The Park, save for one calamitous incident. You know about my latest love life failure, so we may as well cover the first. I'd been madly in love (or so I thought at nine years old) with Sara, a girl from our council estate, for a while, and one morning we ended up alone in my family's tent. From nowhere, I developed the confidence to ask for a kiss. To my complete shock, she agreed and a hurried liplock followed.

My first kiss! I was on a high for the rest of the day. Until…

That afternoon a few families went for a walk in woodland near the campsite. We chanced upon a rope swing, attached to a tree over a shallow pool of water.

Everyone present knew me to be the softest kid in all of SW12, but supercharged by the Sara kiss I swaggered over, sat on the makeshift seat, kicked both feet against the tree for momentum, swung out over the water…

… and felt the seat give out under me, before plunging hard into the drink.

Everything hurt. My elbows. Knees. Backside. Pride. Tears emerged. Two older kids jumped down to help; as they pulled me to the bank I noticed the full range of expressions staring down at me, from concerned parents to sniggering teenagers to Sara's younger sister, Claire, laughing and pointing with unquantifiable glee.

I caught Sara's eyes. She gave a nervous smile, but everything else about her expression said what she really thought:

"I can't believe that four hours ago I kissed this doofus."

And she never did again.

I have no idea what Sara is up to these days. But I can confirm that there will be no rope swings permitted at Glastonbenny.

Wednesday 3 June

Tent-buying day!

This is an exercise I'd be more confident about with social media access. Our most recent car purchase was made after asking my Facebook hive mind for an affordable, reliable family vehicle recommendation. It's served us superbly for six years. If Facebook pals can pick a kid-ferrier for us, I have absolute faith in their ability to choose me a Glasto tent.

Instead, text messages to friends and customer reviews have to suffice. Two separate mates recommend I scout decathlon.co.uk, where I'm drawn to the Quechua 4-Man Arpenaz. Partly because it sounds like a jug of cocktail on offer at JD Wetherspoon. Chiefly because it boasts ample space for Andy H and I to share at next year's Glasto, including a bespoke living room area.

"I've had this tent for nearly five years now and it has been used for numerous trips," writes the mysteriously named 'P' in the customer reviews. "We've had weather ranging from glorious sun to cold, torrential prolonged rain and strong winds in the North Wales mountains. The tent has not let us down."

Awesome. Steve's done a handful of Glastonbury Festivals, so I message him with a link, seeking approval.

"Is this too big for Glasto, mate? Will I look like a twat?"

"Yes and yes!"

Oh.

Back to the search. For a moment I consider sticking two fingers up at Steve and taking a punt on the Air Seconds 8.4, an inflatable tent with room for eight people. Except, a. it's 700 quid and b. customer Jay was not impressed:

"We took our six kids on a camping holiday after buying this tent. We drove nearly 400 miles, got to the camping park, went to put the tent up and found the tent poles were missing. All of them. We had to find a hotel for the night then drove the nearly 400 miles home. Kids were all upset, and our holiday completely ruined. I will be returning it for a full refund. Absolutely disgraceful."

It does sound disgraceful until you read Decathlon's official response, from staff rep Joe. "The Air Seconds 8.4XL FB is an air tent and therefore requires only a pump to set up and thus no poles – apart from the two small porch poles which are not structurally integral to the tent." Ah man. Poor Jay.

Such talk pulls me out my depth so I resort to the trustiest of old friends, a pal who has seldom let me down over four decades' worth of buying stuff: the Argos catalogue. Even the book of dreams draws a blank. Amazon's range is more promising, but I decline to purchase when I learn that the 'Amazon choice' for a 3-man camper is the 'Amazon Basics Tent'. Cheeky.

Back to the Quechua range. If a 4-Man Arpenaz is going to make me look a tool, surely there's a three-person version which Andy and I can get away with?

Computer says yes. Actually there are seven different versions, but the one I'm drawn to, the Quechua 3-Man Pop-Up Tent 2 Seconds 3.0 Blue (catchy) is backed by some persuasive words from a chap named Geoff.

"Probably the best pop-up tent I've come across. Very quick and easy. Keeps the rain out and a sensible size too. We now have 30 of these and they are great."

30! It's so good Geoff has purchased 30! And I only need one. Compelling.

I pop back to Amazon to cross-reference reviews of this model and get the confirmation bias I need from a man (or woman) who calls himself (or herself) 'Amazon Customer'. Subtle.

"The most exciting tent I've ever owned," writes AC. "Pops up in two seconds after you unclip everything. Haven't used it in rain/wet ground yet, but it was great on my weekend trip in Tahoe."

It's basically never rainy or damp in England. And I've always fancied a weekend trip to Tahoe. It's a sign!

AC does drop one nugget of info which could prove problematic: "I'm 5ft 2 and can sit up with at least 8 inches from my head to the ceiling."

Errrrr...

I'm 6ft 2. Andy is 6ft 4. I wonder how tall Geoff is? Why don't these sites include reviewers' heights along with their punchy screen names?

Sod it. Geoff has bought 30. AC says it's the best he's ever owned. Ever. Who needs social media? I'm in an impulsive mood, keen to get Glastonbenny motoring. Quechua 3-Man Pop-Up Tent 2 Seconds 3.0 Blue ordered. Might need to give it a shorter nickname though. Tenty McTentface?

Saturday 6 June

Deliver an essay to my original Glasto crew – Andy H, Lauren, and Sarah – via WhatsApp.

"Hello beautiful people.

This is going to sound a bit unconventional but I'm still going to Glastonbury. In my back garden. And calling it Glastonbenny. (Lauren already knows this.)

Sadly we can't be there together, but I'd still love you guys to be involved – by choosing which bands I go to 'see'.

Using YouTube, or Netflix, or iPlayer I'll be 'watching' live concerts by six artists from the confirmed line-up each day. The three headliners (Kendrick Lamar, Paul McCartney, Taylor Swift) have to be in their correct time slots, and I'll choose two acts each day myself.

Crowded House are on the list. No arguing.

If you're up for it, I'd love for you guys to choose the remaining nine – so three per person. Does this sound like a fun thing? Even if this doesn't sound like a fun thing, and it leads to Sarah writing me off as a fruit loop and never speaking to me again… do you think you could help me out please?

Thank you! And, er, sorry…"

Thursday 11 June

Sarah is the first to deliver her band choices for my pretend festival. "You definitely need to include Elbow, I saw them live once and they're amazing. Lianne La Havas too: amazing stage presence. Pop mixed with old school blues and some folk. And Laura Marling. A poet who just happens to have an incredible voice. She's very introverted, which means it's strange when you see her play."

Andy H is more to the point: "Editors, Groove Armada, and Skunk Anansie. Three very obvious ones. Metronomy is a good shout too. I'd have seen all of those bands." Ooh, a cheeky bonus fourth choice.

Lauren is last to play her hand.

"I assume someone has already said Tay Tay?"

Ah rebellious Lauren, always attempting to break rules.

"Yep. All three headliners are on the list automatically."

"Okay. Dizzee Rascal, then. Robyn. And… Manic Street Preachers."

Love the Manics choice – they were the highlight of T In The Park all those years ago. I now have six days to locate live sets, and get the finalised artist list to Andy L for the poster.

Saturday 13 June

One issue with planning a festival in my back garden is food and drink. At Glasto, I'd have to pack supplies into a rucksack but otherwise make do with what's available on site, at some expense. My local news outlet, Somerset Live, says that, "over the five days you should expect to spend around £80 on food. Satisfying your appetite doesn't come too cheap on site, with a pastry or hotdog at lunchtime costing around £6 each."

The old devil called booze, which I plan to imbibe hourly from sunrise onwards, is also steep – £4.50 per pint on average. "If you have two bar drinks a day that will cost you £45 over the five days," summarises Somerset Live, whose journos are welcome at my place anytime to homeschool Lady S on the 10 times table.

All of which means that taking 12 steps into the house to rustle up a ham sandwich and grab a Foster's from the fridge feels like cheating.

Rather than do that, I've devised a cunning – if inordinately expensive – plan.

Lady S and Little Blue love utilising their play kitchen, and pretending to be stallholders using fake money hoarded from board games.

For Glastonbenny, they'll be the real stallholders, using real money hoarded in my wallet, which I will never see again.

Other than items I can cram into a rucksack alongside clothes and essentials, I'll need to purchase all food and drink from them. Lady S and I will venture to the supermarket together in order for her to select stock, and Mrs E has gamely agreed to help her prepare cooked items.

The money spent won't be for show. Lady S and Little Blue will split 40% of it between them once the event is over – a good chance to earn some bonus pocket money while Daddy lounges in the garden. The other 60% will go to Glastonbury's 'Worthy Causes' partners Oxfam, Greenpeace, and WaterAid.

In an immediate, and profligate, display of my commitment I toast this plan by jumping onto the Glastonbury event website and purchasing this year's official 'Hope Shines Brightest In The Dark' T-shirt, all proceeds from which go to those causes.

Triumphantly, I buy it in L rather than XL. Five-and-a-half months going without social media, and the running time created by doing so, has caused me to drop a T-shirt size.

Monday 15 June

Nothing to report from my monthly @ replies check, save for a friend, Nicola, tagging me in a Facebook 'league football grounds visited' challenge. I used to be obsessed with this type of content and make a great fuss of trumpeting the stadia I'd racked up following Palace around the country. Today I smile at Nicola's number, but have no desire to figure out or broadcast my own.

Wednesday 17 June

Via Netflix, YouTube, and iPlayer the entire line-up for Glastonbenny is ready to go, though not without late drama. I've decided to include all of Andy H's recommendations, taking the overall tally of artists to 19. That leaves an uneven number for each day. So I bump it up by two and send the finalised list to Andy L for the poster. As the song goes: it's my garden party and I'll fiddle with the guestlist at the last minute if I want to.

Just don't tell Lana Del Rey, who's the lone must-see act I can't find room for.

Thursday 19 June

There's a mid-afternoon knock at the door. It's too late to be the postman. It's too early to be an Amazon delivery. Am I finally under arrest for crimes against popular music?

Mercifully not. It's a man in front of a van with 'Glastonbury' on the side in large letters.

"I've got a yard of ale for you," he announces in a West Country burr. Eh?

He really does. He disappears into the van and re-emerges with a long rectangular box, which is then carefully placed in my doorway. Small windows carved into its facade reveal beers with names such as Mystery Tor and Lady Of The Lake. "Have a great festival," he chimes, before clambering into the van then driving away. This is odd. Brilliant but odd.

Nice-yet-random Westie guy has left an envelope on top of the box, with a note inside.

"Happy Father's Day to a great dad. Here's a little something to make your Glasto experience more authentic. I hope the sun shines and the bands are good. Sending huge hugs, Mum. xxx"

Amazing! Flaky knowledge of Portuguese capitals or not, she's a keeper.

"Thank youuuuuuuuuuuuu," I text.

"No problem!" she replies. "What a fab company – a family business, they were really helpful. They went out of their way to deliver them. I told them about your project, and that you were doing Glastonbury in your garden. They loved the idea so much they insisted on going out of their way to hand-deliver them."

I am awestruck and a bit humbled. Glasto to our house is 21 miles, and a 90-minute round trip. I should jump on Twitter and thank them publicly, but can't. Hopefully mentioning their handle, @GlastonburyAles, in a book about social media goes a little way to making up for that.

Saturday 20 June

Starting tonight, English top-flight football is being broadcast live on terrestrial TV for the first time in 28 years as a feelgood gesture. Sod's law given my social media silence, it's a Crystal Palace game up first, against Bournemouth – and we scream into an unassailable 2-0 lead within 23 minutes.

It's the first time in months that I feel tempted to re-enter Twitter's footballing fray, but a merry distraction curtails the urge. With no supporters allowed in the ground, the BBC has constructed an on-screen montage of fans reacting to the action at home. One of whom, tucked away in the top-right hand corner, is… Paul! After his tough recent experiences I'm made up for him, and redirect my social-media temptations his way.

"Looking good on the Beeb, mate!" I message. I get two hearts – one red, one blue, AKA Palace colours – and a thumbs-up emoji in reply.

Sunday 21 June

After 40 years, six months, and two days mustering the courage, it's time to brave putting up a tent on my own for the first time ever. On Father's Day, because if you don't have social media to mock your failed attempts at completing a two-decades-overdue rite of passage, two squawking children are the next best thing.

Happily, and unusually, the girls don't get to revel in my fatherly shortcomings. '2 Seconds' is a misnomer, but it really is up in under two minutes. We spend the afternoon inside playing board games while Mrs E takes a much-deserved break.

The fun begins when it's time to disassemble our home-for-a-day. Folding the tent away involves flattening it to the ground so it takes on the appearance of four stacked hula hoops, then folding it into a figure of eight, then folding it again. Even with the guidance of explanatory YouTube videos my initial efforts are dismal, and Mrs E fares no better, despite her having a degree in astrophysics. We leave it outside collecting rain for two hours.

Eventually I return and taken the traditional male approach: using brute force and hoping for the best. Poles bend but don't break and with some faffing it's eventually slotted into its carry case, ready to be unfurled again on Wednesday. I can't argue with the 'Pop Up' element of its name. For accuracy's sake, however, Decathlon might want to add 'Wrestle Down' as a subtitle.

Monday 22 June

I sadly won't be spending this week with Lauren and Andy H, but nonetheless a message from the former kicks it off with gusto.

"Hey mate, Andy and I just remembered you're off social media at the moment so probably haven't seen the news…"

There follows a photo of Lauren's left hand, sporting an engagement ring.

Amazing!! I'm chuffed for them both.

Steve's point from January is again emphasised. Even without social media, the salient news has its way of finding you.

Tuesday 23 June

The Glastonbenny food menu is finalised, by way of a supermarket order at the weekend and dash to the local Co-op with Lady S. It's her first trip out since last week's lifting of lockdown, and she has much fun grabbing costly gluten-free items to sell on at even more exorbitant fees.

We spend a tranquil afternoon typing it all up together, which is enhanced by an email delivery from Andy L. He's designed seven different posters and they are all incredible. I can't choose a favourite, and the temptation to spoil the whole thing with a grand Twitter reveal is tough to quash. I manage to do so by spamming Andy with thank you messages, and sending the poster to a few select pals, including my original Glasto WhatsApp crew, and Steve. [Once this book is out it'll also be visible on my Instagram, @benjiwilson79.]

I need my main man's help on a day one activity. I've been thinking on how to tackle Lauren's first Glasto task, strolling up the big hill and watching the sun go down. Helpfully, Steve lives at the apex of a steep hill – with arresting views of fields, farmland, and two twee villages. Squint and it could be Worthy Farm, just with 79 less stages and zero portaloos.

The promise of two cans of Foster's warmed by a day in my backpack is sufficient for him to invite me over tomorrow, although his place is only 15 minutes' walk. To make the task feel more 'real' I'll do an hour's stroll round the village before heading to his. By which time the beers in my sagging pockets should be volcanic, and therefore festival appropriate.

Wednesday 24 June

With a morning's homeschooling behind me I decant to the garden. Glastonbenny is go. Lady S insists on helping put up the tent, which in practice means trampling dirt all over my mattress as soon as it's inflated, and putting her fingers perilously close to each peg as I wallop it earthwards. Unlike my bedding she escapes without a scratch. It's the hottest day of the year so far, and within minutes the tent's innards are warmer than Venus, so once unpacked it's left vacant for the rest of the day.

The ramble round the village is an emotional hour. Left to my own thoughts on a mellow summer's eve, the truth hits home: I should be on Worthy Farm right now, settling in with Lauren and Andy H and Sarah and 199,996 other music-lovers. It was the entire point of that angst-filled morning in October, the inspiration for this project, the celebration of 40 years on this rock.

Yet I can't feel forlorn. I'm fortunate to be able to do this, and involve my children, in the first place. Many families have spent the last three months cooped up in flats like those I grew up in, or having to cope with grief in the same way as Paul. Homeschooling has been relentless, but in the grand scheme we can count ourselves very lucky. I've tried to gently impress this on the girls where possible. And I'm determined to let that sense of perspective fend off any 'wish-I-were-there' blues.

My mood lifts once settled in Steve's backyard. The cans of Foster's are authentically toasty – so Steve refuses his, preferring to grab one from the fridge. "Just like buying a cold one from a proper bar at Glasto," he protests. "Enjoy yours, though." And I do. The weather has held and the sunset begs to be photographed for Instagram. I grab a selfie, but settle for sharing it with two friends on WhatsApp. First test passed.

The Quechua fares similarly well on its debut night in the wild. It's cosy enough to form a homely base, yet sufficiently roomy to stash all my needs for five days, catch Zs and sit up in. Those fears about headroom come to nothing. My first night camping in 21 years goes okay, kip wise. Two bouts of heavy rain puncture my slumbers, but otherwise I get a restful night – safe in the knowledge that for once I won't be startled awake by the flapping, flailing hands of a wandering child.

Thursday 25 June

Startled awake just after 8am by the flapping, flailing hands of two wandering children. Lady S and Little Blue are trying to get into the tent to take my breakfast order, using the zip technique common to impatient toddlers: yank it 'til it snaps, along with Daddy's temper. In a panic about four nights of cold air (and spiders) raiding an unfastened front porch I open up, then send them off with half my life savings in exchange for the world's smallest bagel and a microscopic portion of jam.

Our first guests arrive soon after: Little Blue's godmother Sam and her son Shark Boy. Mrs E has kindly helped construct a garden-based take on

Glastonbury's famous Kidzfield, with baking tasks, paddling pool, and football goal. The latter attraction sees more balls thud into new tent than old net, so I politely request that baking takes priority.

While the kids make ice-cream bread I'm humbled by a revelation from Sam. She was one of the few friends sent Andy L's Glastonbenny poster two days ago, and has reconfigured it into a lanyard using an official Glastonbury neck strap picked up on a past visit. Again very Instagram worthy, but more special because I can't share it.

Sam and Shark Boy have lives to lead away from fake music festivals and so mid-afternoon sees them depart, and Lady S and I turn to tackling Lauren's vegetable instruments task. It's both amusing and a chance to nab some free food. Scooping out a watermelon to turn into a drum means I'm able to ferry away the odd mouthful under the auspices of "checking its acoustic properties". Lady S is seven, but not stupid, and rolls her eyes.

Hilariously, the drum works! Lady S and Little Blue take turns bashing it with a carrot, and the results are surprisingly sonorous. However, things unravel as I attempt to transform their makeshift drumstick into a flute, and end up with a troublingly phallic orange stump boasting zero musical capabilities. You carrot be serious.

Our pepper shaker fares only marginally better. The instructions are to cut off a lid, hollow out the innards, then tip in a cup of rice and replace the lid. Trouble is, I've hacked out pepper's placental region, meaning there's nothing to hold the lid in place once restored. Our pepper shakes, then collapses in on itself. Then shakes, then collapses in on itself again. A passable impression of me on a university night out, but rubbish as plant-based instruments go.

The carrot and pepper are repurposed in our cucumber trumpet. This time we drill out the central cucumber core by hand, then fashion a carrot mouthpiece and slide it snugly into one end of the cucumber. Over the other end goes the decapitated pepper, creating the trumpet's bell, and amplifying the sound from the cucumber tube.

Miracle of miracles, it works!

"Daddy!" announces Lady S. "It sounds just like a farting chicken!"

Good enough.

The evening brings a switch to the Lauren task I'm looking forward to as much as any element of Glastonbenny. Ultimate Power is a club night she and Andy H frequent regularly, offering exactly what it says on the tin: hour after hour of power ballads, mostly from the '80s. In a task as epoch-defining as any time capsule, journalist Clare Zerny attended one such event and wrote down by hand every song played, then posted it on the internet. It's that tracklisting, in order, which I shall work my way through tonight.

Here I Go Again by Whitesnake to start, then Don't Stop Believin' by Journey, then Bonnie Tyler's Total Eclipse of the Heart. What an intro! Nik Kershaw's Wouldn't It Be Good takes the tracklist into double digits and I'm already on beer two. The girls have provided an honesty tin for post-bedtime purchases, and the move from lager to cans of gin and tonic sees it fill at an alarming rate. But the music's too epic to care about my funds ebbing away. We Are The Champions, If I Could Turn Back Time, Take My Breath Away, just one more final can…

Roxette. It Must Have Been Love. Brilliant!

T'Pau. China In Your Hand. Better!

The Bangles. Eternal Flame. Best!

I have the strongest sense of déjà vu as Susanna Hoffs croons about her fiery fella's stethoscopic abilities. It's 1989, I'm nine, cycling round the Streatham council estate with trees for goalposts, listening to the Top 40 through headphones (yes, on a bike – someone call health and safety), happy as anything as the ladies from LA hold onto the UK number one spot for a fourth consecutive week.

32 years later, this song still washes away all my problems for four minutes and two seconds.

Once Zerny's set is played out I add my own personal flourishes, with songs whose balladry is certain, but power dubious. Tomorrow I will find videos on my phone of I Swear by All-4-One and Baby I Love Your Way by Big Mountain being mimed in near-total darkness, silhouette of a pink gin can being swayed side-to-side. Glastonbury? Glastonbenny? Wherever I am, it feels stupendous as the night's fourth repeat play of Eternal Flame echoes through my headphones beneath a starlit sky.

Friday 26 June

11.45 Lightning Seeds (Dalkeith 2018)
1.15 Haim (Lisbon 2018)
2.30 Laura Marling (Bristol 2016)
4.15 Metronomy (Glastonbury 2017)
6.00 Editors (Glastonbury 2013)
8.15 Pet Shop Boys (Glastonbury 2010)
10.15 Kendrick Lamar (Reading 2018)

After two sweltering days, waking to the gentle patter of rain on the tent roof is a relief – even if it's 4.45am and I'm hungover. I assume that means I'm doing Glasto right. The girls soon emerge seeking my breakfast order, and I cough up £6 for three teaspoons of porridge and the smallest croissant known to restaurant-kind. Suspect that means they're doing Glasto right too.

I've decided this will be a dry day after two nights of unchecked liver-dousing. A favourite band, the Lightning Seeds, are up first; three songs in I'm handing Lady S £4.50 for a can of Hawkes Dead & Berried Mixed Berry Cider. Ah, such resolve. A beaming midday sun has chased away the drizzle, and Lady S and I spend 45 minutes happily dancing around the garden to Change, Lucky You, and The Life of Riley. Released in 1992, the latter track gained fame as *Match of the Day*'s Goal of the Month music; the Riley of the title is lead singer Ian

Broudie's son. Today he's on lead guitar, belting out a song written about him while in the womb. Cool.

Less cool is my right shinbone, badly bruised when I over-exuberantly waltz into Mrs E's chiminea during Sugar Coated Iceberg. In the 50-year history of Glasto, that's surely a first.

I take it easier for Haim, a sister act who take no shit. In 2018 the all-sibling group fired an agent after discovering they'd been paid 10 times less than a male performer who'd appeared one act above them on a festival bill. The likeable bolshiness isn't an act: the Californian trio launch straight into a head-turning three-person drum solo, then maintain this zeal for 57 nod-along, super-sweary minutes. Even sat on my backside it's energising.

Laura Marling pens incisive, folky psalms made to be enjoyed in June heat. Sure enough a blazing sun has come out to play – but I was born south of the Watford Gap, and so enjoy them in June shade. Her sardonic lullabies have me close to drifting off, making the up-and-at-'em synths of Metronomy a welcome change of pace. This the first of today's sets originally filmed at Glastonbury, and the sea of flags and beaming faces bring a little piece of the real thing to my silly garden party. Especially rousing are the Depeche Mode bleep-bloops of Lately and marching-band beat of Love Letters.

I've had 10 years of Twitter friends espousing Editors' excellence, but they've never been my thing. Where others hear melancholy, I sense only misery. Frontman Tom Smith does have a commanding voice, which Lady S and I use as background noise to a catch-up over dinner (tomato soup) and a non-alcoholic drink (she's already had her fortnightly shot of absinthe). During Papillon she disappears into the house before emerging with complimentary popcorn for last track Honesty, so I'm still counting Editors' set as a success.

Pet Shop Boys' 2010 Other Stage slot is legendary. Mum's Glastonbury ales are fished out from my rucksack, and 90 minutes of timeless pop ensues. Is it possible to have one favourite PSB song? You're adamant it's Go West, then Neil Tennant bursts into Always On My Mind. That's your undisputed number one…

until Chris Lowe taps out the opening bars of Suburbia. So the process continues, through What Have I Done to Deserve This?, and Domino Dancing, and It's A Sin.

It's a minefield of dazzling uncertainties, but at least you're inebriated, happy, and making mental notes to ape Tennant by wearing a red cube over your head at next year's festival. Okay, that one is just me.

Kendrick Lamar's Friday night Pyramid Stage slot was on course to define Glasto. The Black Lives Matter movement continues to pick up support, with police reforms confirmed across America – such as the banning of chokeholds in Denver, Chicago, and Phoenix. Premier League footballers have been using their fame for good too, kneeling at the start of each match. In such an environment Lamar's performance would have symbolised hope and peace: the fundamentals of Glastonbury going back to its 1970 inception. Watching him play Reading on YouTube in my garden can't recreate that. Even mentioning standout songs – such as Swimming Pools, whose chant-along chorus is subverted by lyrics about alcoholism and addiction – feels like lip service.

I enjoy it all, but it's a performance that needed to happen in real life, in the now. As is best evidenced when Lamar stands tall in front of a supermassive video screen image of the Stars and Stripes before launching into XXX – in which his friend's son is killed as a direct result of systemic racism, and the rapper struggles to explain the loss to the grieving father. The song's final line cuts off mid-sentence, representative of so many black lives cut short. In a parallel timeline the sudden silence, followed by a supportive, elongated roar for justice, would have been the singular most powerful moment of Glastonbury 2020.

Saturday 27 June

11.45 Camila Cabello (New York 2019)
1.15 Crowded House (Glastonbury 2008)
2.30 Robyn (Barcelona 2019)
4.15 Groove Armada (Glastonbury 2010)
5.30 Skunk Anansie (Vieilles Charrues 2019)
8.15 Manic Street Preachers (Isle of Wight 2018)
10.15 Paul McCartney (Glastonbury 2004)

A true *Game of Thrones* night in the garden: dark, full of terrors, distressingly absent of Ygritte towards its end. At points I contend with incessant rain, wild wind, a creaking fence, and the biggest false widow I've ever seen glaring at me in bright torchlight when I go to check that the fence isn't coming down.

The drizzle continues all morning, making Camila Cabello the first cast-iron beneficiary of Glastonbury being postponed. The sassy Havana and positively scorching Senorita – 2019's best pop song, no returns – are delivered without fault, but these are not tunes tailor made for West Country rainfall.

Blustery conditions are of less concern to Crowded House, purveyors of three meteorological hits: Weather With You, Four Seasons In One Day, and Distant Sun. All get an airing today, and I like to think the Crowdies would have won Sarah and Lauren over. If not for the music, then lead singer Neil Finn's humour. Between the band and the crowd are a wall of blue-shirted security staff, who Finn can't resist teasing to face the stage: "168, you're a legend! Look what glory awaits you!" [Cue a raucous cheer when 168 glances back at the band.] This all peaks at the climax of the band's best song, Don't Dream It's Over, as Finn adapts the outro refrain on the fly: "We know who they are / Specialised security / Well, we won't let them win."

Senorita may not have worked on this washed-out afternoon, but Robyn's equally supreme Dancing On My Own does. She stands back to let the crowd chant the first chorus and the response is universal, as you suspect it would've been among Pyramid Stage viewers.

That's one highlight of a virtuoso performance. Love Is Free's spaceship disco lasers are the closest I'll get to Glastonbenny psychedelia, closer Call Your Girlfriend is up there with the best of Scandi pop supremos a-ha, and the Swede's unconventional dance moves, cut loose each time there's more than a second's gap between verse and chorus, make each moment unmissable. Again, you suspect a muddy, mildly delirious Glasto crowd would have responded in kind.

Metronomy's snappy electronics arrived at just the right time for a late-afternoon Friday pep up. In the same slot today Groove Armada have the opposite effect. A claustrophobic morning has ground me down, and I spend much of the set pacing the garden, trying to walk off the grumps – and the drizzle. Handily, end-of-set stalwarts Paper Romance and Easy are just the right tempo to match my manic perambulations. It's not quite sand dunes and salty air, but they've chased off the clouds.

Dinner time, and Lady S's long-awaited opportunity to charge me £8 for a gluten-free katsu curry, brings about the first hitch of Glastonbenny. Remarkably, it's not me tearing down the tent in protest at pricing policies. Skunk Anansie's Skin is the unknowing cause: as Lady S hands me said curry on a paper plate, the effortlessly cool singer offers a one-line summary of I Can Dream: "This song is all about fucking." My eldest isn't remotely fooled by my tale of the hip bald lady's love of pond-based bread throwing.

If you're over the age of 30 you know more Skunk Anansie songs than you realise. Half an hour before the set I couldn't name a single one, but You'll Follow Me Down, Twisted (Everyday Hurts) and Weak all trigger 'oh yeah, this one!' reactions, and flashbacks to simpler times. All are surpassed by a track I haven't heard before, 2019's What You Do for Love, with its wailing guitars, throaty vocals and rapid-fire percussion. Spotify it now. Hang on! After you've finished this page, I mean. [Thanks.]

I was foolish to question Robyn's dance moves earlier. By 8.16pm I'm pulling unorthodox shapes of my own as Manic Street Preachers launch into the insurmountable Motorcycle Emptiness. Opening with their best song has grave repercussions for my pint of Glastonbury Cold Gold: a quarter of it ends up sloshed around our picnic table as I flail about, miming every word. Hit after hit follows: You Stole the Sun from My Heart, Everything Must Go, A Design for Life. They're the commensurate sun-setting, fifth-drink-of-the-day band, and I'm as chilled now as I was grumpy four hours ago.

Not just me, either. A passing fly is so into Tsunami that it decides to drown itself in the froth of my beer, the poor winged numpty.

Paul McCartney solo project. Four words which fill me with as much dread as 'sugar free Dr Pepper' or 'Lady S's fractions homework'. I understand the need for Glasto's 50th anniversary to bring the festival full circle, but my three co-attendees had all agreed that we'd avoid Macca's set within seconds of his being announced. Yet the Glastonbenny rules – which dope made those? – leave no choice.

I'm wrapped up in my sleeping bag as opener Jet fails to take off, and on the verge of kip as Hey Jude is strung out for eight... minutes? Hours? Years? Live recordings of this song exist in their own space-time vacuum, sufficient to accommodate an entire series of *Doctor Who*.

Anyway, Yesterday and Let It Be wake me sufficiently to crack open a late-night beer, and Follow Me is a surprise mobiles-to-the skies (or tent roof) moment. Macca has just about turned it round, to that point that I'm ready for him to close out the show with a self-effacing We All Stand Together frog chorus. Which, sadly, never comes. Bom, bom, bom, bollocks.

Sunday 28 June

11.45 Thundercat (Glastonbury 2017)
1.15 Lianne La Havas (Glastonbury 2013)
2.30 La Roux (Glastonbury 2015)
3.45 Diana Ross (Las Vegas 2018)
5.45 Elbow (Glastonbury 2017)
8.00 Dizzee Rascal (Glastonbury 2010)
9.30 Taylor Swift (Arlington 2016)

Begin the final day of Glastonbenny with the last of Lauren's challenges. Recent running highs have convinced me that 23 minutes of beginner *Yoga with Adriene* – 7.8 million YouTube subscribers can't be wrong, surely? – will be easy going.

I've never been more wrong about anything, and I predicted a 2017 Labour election win.

My calves and hamstrings hold up fine, but I've not considered the toll of four nights sleeping on hard ground. Halfway through the session Adriene introduces a standing dog and my shoulders scream in agony. I swear I actually hear them plead "WD40, WD40!" Returning upright merely shifts the pain to my sternum and shoulder blades, and for the next hour there is no comfortable position available. 'Loosening up' with some neck rolls feels more like being caressed by a branding iron. If we do yoga at Glasto 2021 I'll need a year's worth of beer money for post-session massage therapy.

Thundercat is on the move, Thundercat is loose. On an iPad screen in my tent, because outside it's bucketing down with Mumm-Ra ferocity. Camila Cabello wasn't the sole beneficiary of Glastonbury's postponement after all; by this point we'd all have been trudging through quagmires and quicksand. Thundercat's quirky jazz-funk, and Lianne La Havas's soothing melodies, contrast splendidly with the inclement weather, providing the serenity missing from this morning's yoga session. A break from the monsoon would be welcome though – there's a festival VIP due.

The guest is a mummy friend, Amelia, together with her daughter, Mini-Meils. The Kidzfield is reopened, now with added sandpit, so that within 15 minutes of their arrival our own authentic Glasto mud bath has formed. Lady S, Little Blue, and Mini-Meils' princess dresses are soon caked, in keeping with the festival vibe – under 12s go free to Glasto. For us adults, ciders and quality La Roux tunes flow: if you're in the market for a modern dance-rock band with '80s sensibilities, there's none finer. Bulletproof is their famous track, but Uptight Downtown, Kiss & Not Tell and Sexotheque are all subtler and more sophisticated. They're so great I want to replay the set in full.

That would, however, deny us Diana Ross in the traditional Sunday afternoon legends slot. I ask Lady S if she and the girls would like to dance to one of the great soul singers of any lifetime; her response is, "what's Diana Ross?" Blasphemy. No stugged-in-mud Supremes today, then. Instead, with the drizzle finally clear, Baby Love, Stop! In The Name of Love, and You Can't Hurry Love are an optimal accompaniment to my and Amelia's catch-up.

With teatime looming our first visitors depart midway through Elbow – a band I will never, ever 'get'. Sorry, Sarah. In the interests of kindness I should point out that frontman Guy Garvey seems a true gent.

Dizzee Rascal's onstage arrival heralds new guests: Lindo and Hazel, almost six months after our impromptu drinking session which triggered a mental health spiral. I'm much more confident about handling a similar slump tomorrow, and smiles for miles accompany the rest of the evening. Dizzee is in equally lofty spirits, leading a devoted Glastonbury crowd (and three contented Glastonbenny revellers) in energetic renditions of Jus' a Rascal, Dirtee Disco, Dance Wiv Me, and Bonkers.

How can a middle-aged dude flip off Elbow, then proclaim Taylor Swift the best pop act on the planet? It helps that she is. Delve beyond the preconceptions and headlines and there's no one better at recycling four chords into catchy earworm harmonies. Plus I've always disliked music snobbery. It's a subjective medium. Don't conform. Like what sounds good to your ear.

Two hours of Swift sounds immaculate to myself, Hazel, and Lindo, and I'm grateful to my neighbours for ignoring our loud music and even louder chatter. Mercifully, tall fences mean they're spared our dancing. This set was recorded in 2016, meaning Swift's outstanding recent album *Lover* – whose sway-along title track and feminist anthem The Man would've lit up real Glasto – are absent, but there are still storming tunes galore. Blank Space and Shake It Off deliver the hit factor, but the night-drive undertones of Getaway Car and breathy Dress work just as well on this summer's eve.

Pick of the lot is a track never released as a single. Penned about her break-up with Jake Gyllenhaal, Swift's slow-building heartbreaker All Too Well is the finest five minutes of music she's ever recorded, and sounds more raw and real than ever stripped down to just her and an acoustic guitar. Had I and tonight's comrades listened to this the day after our early year night out I'd have been a complete wreck. Okay, even without listening to it I was a complete wreck. Yet here it feels triumphant. A paean to five months of letting go. Of my ex-wife, of January Girl, of the fear that I'd be forever alone.

I'm still single, but dealing with it. For all my mentions of love in this book, the middle of a pandemic is not the time to go searching, and I've made my peace with that. Paul's April pep talk is also in my mind daily, and has given me a stronger handle on my mental health than at any point in those early weeks. And friends have come though, not only in the sense of attending Glastonbenny, but also being at the other end of a WhatsApp message or phone call when needed. I dearly hope they'd say the same in return.

Swift's set closes out with This Is Why We Can't Have Nice Things, and the three of us share one last drink to bring Glastonbenny to a close. It's not on a field in Pilton, as originally planned – but nonetheless 24 to 28 June has provided the personal pinnacle of this rollercoaster year.

Monday 29 June

Did I say I was redirecting 2021 beer money towards post-yoga massage? Let me upgrade that to private shoulder surgery. My right side feels as if it's been trampled in the night by four centuries' worth of wandering druids.

It makes packing up a wince-heavy experience, but even that – and more rain! – can't dampen my mood. Glastonbenny has been fun yet uncharacteristically intimate: a project that took three months to plan, and five days to enjoy, but fewer than 10 people know about. I've kept a video diary in order to eventually promote the book, but otherwise it's been something for me and a handful of close friends and family. It still won't match the real thing, but it's quite right that the real thing was cancelled.

My festival has one substantial advantage to the one in Pilton. The return journey takes four weary footsteps, rather than four traffic-clogged hours. The evening 'back home' is spent enjoying all my favourite alpha-male indulgences: a warm bath, pink gin that I'm not required to pay for twice, and my own bed. It's the dream finish to an unforgettable five days. I am completely relaxed, and for once sleep like a milk-bellied newborn.

Until I'm startled awake 15 minutes after midnight, by the flapping, flailing hands of a wandering child.

End of month stats: June 2020

Weight: 14st 4lb
Twitter followers: 4,945 (-24)
Facebook friends: 834 (-1)
Instagram followers: 233 (-1)
Average sleep: 5h 53min
Books read: 3 – *Pete May:* There's A Hippo In My Cistern, *Marcus Berkmann:* Rain Men, *Miriam Moss:* Girl on a Plane
Distance run: 56km
Time running: 5h 19min
Best 5K time: 25min 29s
Best 10K time: 56min 29s
Best half marathon time: N/A

JULY

Wednesday 1 July

I've not posted on Twitter, or Facebook, or Instagram, for six months.

Being able to write that sentence on 1 July 2012 would have prevented half a decade of mental health anguish.

These were my *Official PlayStation Magazine* [*OPM*] editor days, the pressure of which already had me taking nightly antidepressants to help me sleep, and ward off neurological symptoms. Even so I was unprepared for a costly Twitter mistake.

Trade show E3 is the focal point of the gaming calendar, and takes place in Los Angeles each June. In this particular year our magazine deadline fell in the middle of the show, meaning it was imperative we had as much coverage as possible set up beforehand. This is a fairly standard procedure across all forms of journalism, where you see a film or listen to an album ahead of release, but an embargo prevents you revealing any details until a specific time.

Earlier in the year I'd visited the London HQ of Sony, makers of the PlayStation console, for a look at their upcoming line-up in readiness to pen news stories and previews when the games were unveiled. Most of these had long been rumoured, but the very last one was a complete surprise – so secret that I was asked not to even tell my own team about it until the night of the E3 conference. I'd been a journalist for 11 years, I was used to embargoes, this was no issue at all.

The Sony event, with the reveal of the secret game as its climax, was due on the Monday night. I flew into LA on Saturday. By Sunday evening, rumours were flying around Twitter of a new game called *Beyond: Two Souls,* developed by French studio Quantic Dream and featuring a pair of Hollywood-calibre actors. On Monday afternoon, a reputable UK gaming website announced that its sources had confirmed the game.

Inexplicably, I took this to mean that it was safe for me to add my two dollars' worth.

"I saw Beyond back in February," I tweeted. "It looks incredible. A massive step up from [predecessor] Heavy Rain. Two HUGE A-listers in the lead roles. Will steal E3."

Tweet sent, I stepped into the shower to freshen up for the press conference.

My phone had gone haywire when I picked it up again 15 minutes later.

On my Twitter client, RTs and @ reply numbers just kept escalating. Journalists welcome attention – but most also have a strong radar for the good and bad kind. I knew the rate of shares was not a good thing.

My day-to-day Sony contact was first to call. "Ben, man… what have you done?" I could tell he was trying to maintain a veneer of professionalism, but was disconsolate at the same time. Justifiably so. "The tweet is everywhere… I don't know how I can explain this."

I deleted the tweet, but too late. A popular news site had by this point made it the focal point of a front page story titled 'OPM outs Quantic Dream's Beyond, Ellen Page mentioned in leaked shot'.

The leaked shot came from elsewhere, but the first two paragraphs focussed on my tweet alone. (The two actors I'd alluded to were Page and Willem Dafoe.) PS3 was the biggest console in the world at the time. Its proprietor was a company worth billions. Some jumped-up nobody had just blown Sony's key summer reveal in 140 thoughtless, self-indulgent characters.

Tim, still my superior as the brand's editor-in-chief, was next to call. "Just seen all the Beyond stuff. Are you sure this is okay? I trust you Benji, but it's everywhere…"

I gulped and spluttered an answer. I have no idea what it was.

The next 10, 15, 20 minutes were the lowest I had ever ever felt. [And would remain so until the Twitter threats aimed at my daughter.] I sent a nine-word text to my publisher, James: "I'm sorry, and would like to offer my resignation." Then I curled up on my hotel room bed and willed the world to go away.

In those moments I had no desire to face another human being again. My colleagues, friends, family, wife, mum, anyone. There were no tears. No anger. Just a void. Complete, total emptiness. I've had dark times since. In February I wrote about feeling pinned to my bed by a colossal weight. This was a thousand times worse. Indeed, I didn't think it could get worse until *that* Eden Hazard incident five years later.

If all of this sounds hysterical, that's a good thing. It reinforces my point that what's trivial to one person can seem world-ending to another.

At some point I dared to pick up my phone again. There was one text. "You okay, Babus?" A kind ex-colleague, Rachel, had been watching events unfold on Twitter and sensed what my reaction would be, spurring her to check in. As her former editor I should have responded with a show of resolve and imperviousness and bravado.

"Nope."

"Take a breath. Have a cuppa. It will blow over."

Somehow I dragged myself off the bed and brewed the kettle. Rach's calmness and positivity heaved me out of my Twitter funk, at least temporarily. I'm indebted to her to this day for it. And to James, for his casual reply to my resignation offer: "Don't be daft. Get yourself to the press conference, and enjoy it."

I tried to. I got through the remainder of E3 on adrenaline and alcohol – which for all my flippant jokes in this book, is not a long-term solution to a depressive episode. As I discovered upon my return to England. I developed eye floaters which severely impacted my vision for months. I ate and ate and ate until a friend nicknamed me John Goodman. At least once a week Mrs E would find me slumped in the kitchen insistent that I couldn't face work that day, and pull me to my feet and put me back together. Our futures lie apart, but I will always be grateful for that.

Eight years on, I still cringe about that tweet. I screwed up. I knew it then, as I know it now. I'd been stupefyingly unprofessional, and will never forget the horror of looking at my phone and instantly knowing I'd made a mistake, in the public eye, which could not be retracted. The escalating Twitter numbers, that news headline I had zero control over. I paid a heavy toll for it with years of anxiety and depression.

That doesn't deserve sympathy, but I hope it triggers consideration as regards online bullying. Everyone cocks up occasionally. At home, in the workplace, in text or WhatsApp messages to friends, and on social media. I'm trying to teach my daughters that errors of judgement are a fundamental element of being human, whatever your age. Make a mistake, own it, grow and change as a result. So while some people in the public eye deliberately bait controversy and ill-feeling, plenty of others know when they've done wrong, without thousands of strangers piling in. My mantra to the girls is, 'place yourself in someone's shoes before judging their issues.' I believe it's a strong MO to apply to conduct on social media, too.

Thursday 2 July

A laid-back day turns dreadful with a phone call from my mum. Her brother-in-law, my marvellous Uncle Dave, has died.

Dave, my Aunt Lynne, and cousins Scott and Kim were a fixture on our summer holidays to mum's home city of Exeter. Dave was football obsessed and we would 'watch' fixtures together on Teletext, in the days before Sky broadcast multiple live matches each weekend. From as young as I can remember, spoofing Trigger from *Only Fools and Horses*, he nicknamed me "George" as he knew I would protest that it wasn't my actual name. In 40 years I never once heard him call me Ben.

I feel like I'm letting my family down by not signing in to Facebook to pay tribute, so shall share a fond final memory here instead.

I last saw Uncle Dave half a decade ago. Lynne had warned me that his brain had been impaired by dementia, and there was a high chance not only that he'd tell the same stories over and over, but also that he'd have no idea who I was. I walked into the family living room in which I'd enjoyed so many childhood moments playing Super Cup Football with Scott, and listening to Brother Beyond with Kim, and there he was: Uncle Dave. Thinner than I'd ever seen him, but in the same old dapper clothing, with the same big grey moustache, and same big blue eyes.

Uncle Dave looked over at me. Paused for a second or two. Then smiled from ear to ear.

"'Ello, George."

Saturday 4 July

Still catching up with real-world events, following Glastonbenny and a sombre end to the week.

My festival may have been a mere masquerade, but it's convinced me that I could do the real thing without social media. Even with just my children and overactive brain for company, I was too busy to trawl the internet, let alone jump into apps. It's taken a week to discover that Labour's Rebecca Long-Bailey has been sacked by Keir Starmer for sharing an anti-Semitic tweet. During last year's election I'd have known that inside two minutes and spent the rest of the day digesting the fallout across Twitter and Facebook.

There were practical lessons to heed. To skimp on baggage space I packed three pairs of shorts and zero trousers, and chose to forgo a coat in favour of a lightweight waterproof running top. Meaning my legs went five soggy days and nights without any protection from the cold, and my clothes clung to my torso within minutes of leaving the tent in a downpour. Given the conditions across

Saturday and Sunday it's no exaggeration to say that I'd have been risking hypothermia at real Glasto.

Tenty McTentface turned out superbly, however. No wonder Geoff bought 30. It's been such a success that the girls won't let me take it down, and we've spent the last nine days having hourly arguments about over-aggressive zipping.

Sunday 5 July

A sad postscript in the tale of Hana Kimura, the Japanese wrestler who died by suicide in May. News magazine *Shukan Bunshun* features an interview with Hana's mother Kyoko, in which she claims producers of reality show *Terrace House* manufactured the incident which triggered widespread social media backlash.

"The incident that led to her being attacked through social media was largely set up," reports Dave Meltzer. "Kyoko said Hana told her that they wanted her to slap Kobayashi in the face, but she didn't want to do that and instead slapped the hat off the top of his head. She said she thought slapping him would be wrong and wouldn't come off as professional or help the women's pro wrestling business, which was her goal [of] the show – for exposure to the mainstream."

According to *Shukan Bunshun*, Kimura also texted a friend that, "My ring uniform just got destroyed and the staff wanted me to act mad in front of the camera."

It's yet more evidence of the dangers in playing judge and jury on social media without applying nuance, or context, or knowing the full set of facts.

Monday 6 July

My first Monday back on the freelance clock following Glastonbenny presents the toughest professional aspect of the challenge thus far.

I mentioned in the month's opening entry that journalists court attention, ideally of the positive kind. To that end, I spent much of May and June on a titanic work project: a comprehensive history of the rivalry between two football videogames, *FIFA* and *Pro Evolution Soccer*, for UK newspaper *The Guardian*.

It involved interviews with developers past and present, PR representatives, ESPN commentator Derek Rae, Sky Sports presenter Michelle Owen, and a considerable amount of research. Now it's live on *The Guardian*'s website, and doing impressive numbers – 88 shares, 292 comments – but I've no way of promoting it personally, or interacting with readers on Twitter.

It feels against the spirit of the project to scratch my itch by offering personal replies to those comments, so I refrain. And must confess that doing so is a dent to the ego. I see now why John Bishop feels the need to keep his accounts active despite slurs from randoms. Adopting a broadcast-only stance shields you from abuse, but it also prevents you from interacting with those keen to discuss your work objectively, or even (god forbid) deliver praise.

Tuesday 7 July

Message from Lauren. "Ben! It's Andy's 40th tomorrow! Afternoon drinks in Bristol?" Oh god, I'd almost forgotten yet another key birthday. I'd be there even if the rules didn't decree that I have to.

Wednesday 8 July

Back in Bristol's picturesque, clandestine Famous Royal Navy Volunteer to celebrate Mr H's Andy-versary. The experience is night and day compared to 31 January, and not only in the sense that we start drinking at 3pm and are bidding farewell by 5pm.

Covid-19 concerns mean we all have to register with an app upon entry, paper menus and table service replace queueing at the bar, social distancing means there are no hearty embraces to usher in Mr H's fifth decade, and the atmosphere throughout is of groups keeping to themselves while speaking in hushed tones. It feels apposite to such a quaint venue, even if the unspoken truth is that we're all too nervous about microscopic droplets to loosen up.

Still, it's great to see much-missed friends and we toast Lauren and Andy's recent engagement, his big birthday, six months off social media for me, and the prospect of Glasto in 2021. On Worthy Farm rather than in my garden.

After two pints I require a couple of hours to sober up before driving home, and spend it under a setting sun on the dewy grass of nearby Queen Square. I finish Harry Thompson's engaging around-the-world cricket diary *Penguins Stopped Play*, then take a little time to silently reflect on my own personal contrast between today and 'Farewell EU' night, and shake my head at its preposterousness.

Ask me to steer my small family through an unprecedented pandemic while homeschooling, and cohabiting with my ex, and I can hold things together – albeit with a heavy heart over the wider damage Covid-19 has wreaked. Ask me to get over a special lady? Can't do it until I've had more meltdowns than a chain-smoking snowman.

The entire square has been decorated with hundreds of painted hearts to encourage social distancing, but it feels appropriate to my January Girl related train of thought too. Especially as I know she won't be the last time I fall, then fall apart.

Friday 10 July

One of my favourite retro YouTube videos is the drawing of lots to separate England and Ireland at the 1990 World Cup, after both teams finished the group stage with identical records. This was the biggest football competition on the planet, yet such matters were decided by two old dudes and a lady with electrified hair pulling Kinder Eggs from glass vases, in a what looks like a draughty hotel lobby.

In tribute, my homebrew version of Euro 2020 begins the same way. The play-off fixtures to decide the final four qualifiers were postponed due to the pandemic, so Lady S and I will draw our own lots to cement the finals line-up. Four pint glasses are sourced from the kitchen. 16 empty plastic egg shells, once home to LOL Dolls (don't ask), are each filled with a folded piece of paper containing a team name. Four shells go in each pint glass. Lady S dons a garish purple wig acquired on my best man's stag do to complete the abstract '90s vibe, and is then tasked with pulling one team from each glass.

Readers from Hungary, Slovakia, Scotland, and Kosovo, congratulations: you just qualified for Euro 2020.

Now I just have to motor through 51 matches of PlayStation football in three days. The game, *Pro Evolution Soccer 2020* (*PES*), automatically has the entire tournament set up ready to play: all I need to do is toss a coin before every match to decide which team I'll control. The only rule is that I have to try my hardest to win that fixture. Even if I'm, say, Croatia versus England.

This exact scenario unfolds five games in. I have seven jokes lined up in preparation for England's crapness, so naturally they score early through Harry Kane then defend doggedly for a 1-0 win. Balls.

Italy are shocked 1-3 by Turkey in the opening game, while Spain also start poorly with a 0-1 reverse to Sweden. Czech Republic are the first team eliminated following defeats to Scotland and Croatia, and remarkably the Spaniards are next to exit, losing 0-1 again, this time to Poland. These are the only two casualties of the tournament's first day.

Saturday 11 July

There's a supreme passage in the book I'm currently reading, Sue Townsend's *Adrian Mole: The Prostrate Years*, where Mole quotes his wife's explanation for leaving him:

"When I first fell in love with you, I thought you were fashionably geeky, but I've since found out that you're not fashionably *anything*, you're just a geek."

After today I fear the same fate awaits my next serious relationship. I rattle off another 20 matches of pretend football and love every minute, in the most shameless, way-too-old-for-this-but-don't-care manner.

Spain aren't the only surprise departure. Germany exit the tournament without scoring a goal. Cristiano Ronaldo and Portugal are dispatched in the first knockout round by one of Lady S's lot selections, Slovakia, on penalties. Croatia fall 0-2 to Poland, while a Belgium team starring Kevin de Bruyne and Eden Hazard suffers shootout agony at the hands of France.

It's a mixed day for the home nations. Wales can't emulate their semi-final run of 2016, eliminated with a solitary win over Turkey to their name. Scotland hold old enemies England to a 0-0 draw to sneak into the knockout rounds, only to be seen off 0-1 by Russia. As for my home nation, Kane and friends rattle off videogame performances I can only dream of in real life, defeating Czech Republic to top their group, then breezing past Sweden 2-0.

At the close of play eight teams are left for Super Sunday. Going by real-life pre-tournament betting odds, below are their chances of winning it all:

England 5/1
France 11/2
Netherlands 7/1
Italy 11/1
Ukraine 66/1
Russia 100/1
Poland 100/1
Slovakia 250/1

Sunday 12 July

I dearly hope you've not formed an in-house gambling syndicate and punted your last Monopoly notes on the tournament favourites. England fail to pass the Dutchies 'pon both the left and right sides until it's too late: Kane's 82nd-minute goal unable to prevent a 1-2 loss.

Plucky Slovakia are next to depart, falling 0-2 to Russia. A shame, as it's official football tournament parlance to describe rank outsiders as "plucky" at every opportunity once the knockout stages are underway. Plucky Cameroon in 1990. Plucky Bulgaria in 1994. Plucky South Korea in 2002.

Plucky Ukraine edge past plucky Poland 1-0 in game three. I'll stop with those antics before you tell me to pluck off.

Italy (computer) against France (me) is the tie of the round, but goes to penalties following a rancid 0-0 stalemate. Family keep telling me I seem much more relaxed after breaking ties with social media. Today I am anything but, cursing at every misplaced pass and wild shot. I feel like I've let a nation of 67 million people down as Benjamin Mendy drags the decisive spot kick wide to send La Marseillaise home. Zinedine Zidane, Daft Punk, Tintin, anyone who's ever appeared onstage in *Les Mis*: je suis vraiment désolé.

The quarter-finals are complete ahead of schedule, but I can hardly play the final of a feted football tournament in the afternoon. Instead, a new plan manifests itself. I shall postpone the last three games until the girls are in bed, and theme the evening around the four remaining nations. Netherlands, Italy, Russia, and Ukraine.

I know what you're thinking. 'Come on Wilson! You've planned this for months! You've orchestrated this entire tournament so you can chuck out another borsch joke!'

If only. Were that the case I'd have kept England in as an excuse to stock up on Doom Bar, and sent Poland through too – I'm quite partial to their respective section of the local supermarket. A cheeky Jezyki breaks all my gluten-free rules, and tastes all the more sensational for it.

Nope, this is unfolding in real-time. Which is how I find myself in a giant Tesco, in the middle of a pandemic, searching every shelf for a dish that might be considered Ukrainian.

The other nations come together easily after abandoning my dietary restrictions. Dutch pancakes, Dutch crisp bakes, Heineken. Pizza, salami, Birra Moretti. Vodka, inevitably. Russian fudge yoghurt too, although it later transpires that this is actually Scottish. But Tesco does not stock paska (Ukrainian Easter bread), or deruni (potato pancakes), or holodets (jellied broth of bone and cartilage. Yum). This makeshift plan is unravelling as swiftly as it came together.

After 20 minutes I ditch the idea. Figure I'll just not mention any of this in the book. Crack on with the semi-finals. Trudge to the checkout with a shopping trolley full of stuff that I can't put back now I've pawed it. The kids will at least enjoy the pizza. And vodka.

Then I see them.

Oh Wilson. You bell-end, Wilson. Two succulent loins, golden as an Odessa sunset.

Chicken bloody Kievs!

I'm still buzzing when, four hours later, the build to Holland vs Russia gets underway with some 2 Unlimited techno trance. Food choices are slapped in the oven. Heineken is cracked open. I unearth my Russian hat, bought especially for a 2009 New Year trip to Mosc... er, Massachusetts. It's immediately absurdly warm. Best do a voddie and Coke to cool off.

After a loud-enough-to-rouse-the-neighbours rendition of Russia's stellar national anthem, we are underway. No nerves now, just enjoyment: this isn't as great as Wembley would have been, but another unconventional Sunday night on the heels of Glastonbenny. Hilariously, after an entire afternoon's build-up, the match is over in 14 minutes and Netherlands are in the final, 1-0 winners.

Absurdity continues to reign. I search 'Ukrainian polka' on YouTube as part of the build for semi-final two, and am met with an accordion-led version of Katy Perry's Hot N Cold. It has 1.7 million views. I add four more. Then spend 15 minutes trying to sum it up in a single sentence. Or two. Now I'm into a third sentence and, as it transpires, there are no words.

There are Italian words to Jimmy Fontana's Il Mondo, and they make it the greatest love song you've never heard. I've still not finished my Heineken but open a Moretti anyway and drink in both beer and music. This also gets four plays, on 7" vinyl, the most beloved in my collection.

These listens aren't comedic. I'm not at Wembley, but I'm not in my living room either. I'm on a clifftop. Could be Cornwall, California, Clacton-on-Sea... I can't locate it. There's a lady. She's in a white dress, but this isn't a wedding. She's smiling, shyly. Pressing my palms to hers. Music in the distance from... a car stereo? A restaurant? A funfair? It doesn't matter. Everything else ceases to matter. *Il mondo, non si è fermato mai un momento.* She puts her arms around me and the world does stop, just for one moment, and it's the greatest moment, and...

Oh yeah. Digitised football. Italy break Ukrainian hearts in the 89th minute to win 1-0, with a goal so slapstick I'm amazed it isn't how England went out.

Having earlier saved a penalty, goalkeeper Andriy Pyatov collides with forward Ciro Immobile and the loose ball cannons in off defender Mykola Matviyenko's shin.

It's now 9.30pm, so I pencil the final – Netherlands vs Italy – in for 10pm. Eat some more eats, the chicken Kievs easing the pain of Ukraine's departure. Drink some more drinks. Then toss my trusty two-pence piece for the 51st, and final, time. Heads I control Netherlands. Tails I'm Italy. It's heads. I'm Holland.

10pm. Off we go. I score early, Memphis Depay bursting through the Italian backline to slot past Gianluigi Donnarumma on 19 minutes. With 20 minutes to go the same player doubles the lead and… truthfully, after all those listens to Il Mondo, I feel awful for Italy. This is the ridiculous extent of my soppiness. I find myself half willing the Italians to roar back, half wanting to avoid a contrived end result. Ciro Immobile nets on 80 minutes, becoming the tournament's top scorer in the process, but there the goals cease. It's all over. Controversy avoided. With a final score of Italy 1 Netherlands 2, the Dutch are European Champions, for the first time since 1988.

Italy's defeat means no ear-splitting renditions of Il Mondo (or timeless 1990 World Cup anthem Nessun Dorma) to round off the evening. It would, however, be rude not to open one more Heineken to toast the Dutch.

And one more.

And one more…

Monday 13 July

2 Unlimited were incorrect. When it comes to the amount of crumbed chicken, pizza, fermented yeast and hops a grown male should consume on a school – or rather homeschooling – night: yes yes, yes yes yes yes, yes yes yes yes, yes yes there is a bloody limit.

Tuesday 14 July

Complete Townsend's final, fantastic Mole book – the diary of a geek turning 40 with self-confidence issues, manchild tendencies, a cancer scare, a laughably calamitous love life and an unrealistically lofty view of his own painfully limited writing abilities.
Oh shit.

Wednesday 15 July

Two touching messages raise smiles amid the monthly check. "Hi Ben," writes tender-hearted, Bradford-City-devoted pal Rich on Twitter. "I noticed that you have been quiet on here during lockdown and I know it has been tough for a lot of people, so I just wanted to check that you are doing ok." I message him via WhatsApp to reply in the affirmative, and explain my Twitter disappearance, and ask how he's doing. Very well, thankfully.

"Hey Ben," writes Jo, a lass I grew up with in Streatham, via Facebook DM. "Been thinking of you today and not seen or heard of you recently. Hope you are OK and well. I'm always here if you need just a chat."

I scroll up to find an earlier message from Jo [whose name I've changed here] which I'd missed in my previous checks:

"Hi Ben. I hope you don't mind me messaging you but I think your posts are such an inspiring and difficult thing to do. I know it must take a huge amount of courage to put it out there. I know the stigma isn't as bad for women as men, although there shouldn't be any at all. I have suffered from depression and anxiety over the last 15 years and I am definitely not brave enough to share my experiences. It is a day by day thing and I don't know how I would cope if everyone knew what I go through as I really don't handle attention very well. So I keep my experiences to just the people in my immediate circle as I need their support. I really hope that by sharing your experience others get the help they need. As you know living with depression isn't easy but I hope you have more good days than bad."

I send Jo my number in order to catch up on WhatsApp. Much like my chats with Paul, this a perspective-changer. When I completed my CBT last year, who was there to embrace me with kind words and thoughts? A section of Facebook friends far larger than those who skipped a silly birthday party. I needed that post-CBT lift, and am honoured and humbled that Jo found my post uplifting in turn. Both instances demonstrate that behind petty political squabbles and macho posturing disguised as 'bantz', social media can aid people to tackle anxieties through the process of shared experience, particularly for those too shy to reveal their troubles.

When I go back in January, I know I'll still be prone to overshares – as do you, being halfway through a book filled with them. But my aim is to make them less about showy ego boosts like the Hulk Hogan interview, and more the raw experiences of fending off that indefatigable black dog.

Monday 20 July

In Exeter for my Uncle Dave's funeral. It's a send-off that features smiles as well as sadness, and a fitting tribute to a much-loved patriarch, husband, and sportsman. Dave was a successful amateur boxer and formidable snooker player, to go with his football and bowls obsessions, so it's little wonder sports-mad me grew up idolising him.

There is some embarrassment when family share anecdotes left by Dave's friends on Facebook and I admit that I've not read a single one. I explain why, and am wished genuine luck with the book, but it feels like I've let my cousins down. The first thing I will do on returning in January is take however is long required to digest them all.

Friday 24 July

Taylor Swift unleashed a surprise new album, *Folklore*, at midnight. You know I'm going to tell you it's exceptional, so instead of scribbling eight paragraphs (or tweets, as would have been the case this time last year) along those lines, I shall simply recommend three songs from it which might, just might, overcome any cynicisms you have regarding La Swift.

If you're already a fan, please feel free to smile and nod in agreement. Licensed cardigan optional.

Opener The 1 is a thoughtful ode to finding the right person at the wrong time, devastating yet somehow triumphant in the same breath – a Que Sera Sera for generation YouTube. Exile sees Swift duet with indie sonneteers Bon Iver to retread her country roots in tear-stained dirt-track solitude, ingeniously narrating both perspectives of a heavy break-up over a haunting piano backdrop. August is the ultimate in autumnal goodbyes, a brooding, sigh-told tale of teen romance unfulfilled.

Folklore's understated collection of plaintive ballads is a major departure for Swift, encapsulating the isolation of lockdown in hummable, memorable melodies. If this doesn't silence the cynics, nothing will.

Wednesday 29 July

Wilfried Zaha, the star player of the team I support (clue: rhymes with Bristol Malice), has criticised Twitter and Instagram (which is owned by Facebook) for not doing enough to curb racism on social media.

"For black footballers, being on Instagram is not even fun anymore," Zaha tells CNN. "You're not enjoying your profile – I'm scared to even look up my direct messages anymore. It could be filled with anything."

Earlier this month, a 12-year-old boy was arrested for making racist threats to Zaha, including an image of the Ku Klux Klan.

"I don't even have Twitter on my phone anymore because it's almost certain that you're going to get some sort of abuse, especially after games, because it happens so freely," says Zaha, who grew up in the South London area of Thornton Heath after moving to the UK from Côte d'Ivoire when he was four.

"I feel like with everything that we do in life, with everything we register to, we have to give some sort of ID. So why is it not the same with Instagram? Why is it not the same with Twitter?"

Facebook does offer a response to CNN. "Racism is not tolerated on Facebook and Instagram," it says. "When we find content that breaks our guidelines we will remove it and we will ban those who repeatedly break the rules. We take this issue seriously and invest billions of dollars in people and technology to help remove harmful content at scale. Last month, we also introduced a new safety feature that allows public figures to prevent people they do not know from sending them a message."

Friday 31 July

One month on, it's time to close the door on Glastonbenny. Little Blue is at nursery for the day, giving Lady S and I some long-overdue quiet time to go over my tent-based spending.

Alcohol was my biggest expense: 11 beers and three ciders at £4.50 each, plus four gin and tonics at £5 apiece – so £83.50 in total. Among other tallies I spent £6 on Coke, £10 on soup (healthy), £15 on cake (unhealthy), £10 on bagels (carbilicious), and only £4 on chocolate. 17-year-old Ben would be outraged at that last one.

The sum total of my gluttonous profligacy is £182.50. Which means the girls share £73 between them, and £109.50 goes to the main Glastonbury charities of WaterAid, Greenpeace, and Oxfam. The odd-ness of that number feels cloying so I round it up to an even £120 and then split it three ways.

What occurs next is a bonus Glastonbenny highlight. We visit each charity's website in turn, and talk though its aims and objectives, before paying in its £40 tranche. We watch a WaterAid video titled 'you can't have a rainbow without water', which feels particularly appropriate with our smudgy window panes still bedecked in the girls' NHS tributes. An Oxfam clip shows workers delivering water to a cyclone-ravaged remote village in Mozambique, using a curious-but-necessary mix of motorbike and canoe. Finally, Greenpeace introduces us to the dangers of palm oil, and plastic packaging – although there is a blip when Lady S sees which brands use palm oil and excitedly yelps, "can we get Pop-Tarts tomorrow?"

Questionable breakfast choices aside, it's a lovely hour of daddy-daughter time which I confess is as educational for me as it is her. We're diligent recyclers, but I had no idea that the plastic we get through each week only has a certain number of uses before that too becomes landfill fodder, or that our current recycling systems can't cope with the amount of plastic we send them. It's thought provoking, and Lady S later takes great pleasure in reeling off what she's seen to Mrs E.

Glastonbenny has been our secret, a necessary means of keeping this project going once the real thing was cancelled. Yet as a family it turned into something meaningful and unique, with a tangible end result.

End of month stats: July 2020

Weight: 14st 4lb
Twitter followers: 4,939 (-6)
Facebook friends: 833 (-1)
Instagram followers: 234 (+1)
Average sleep: 6h 21min
Books read: 3 – *Harry Thompson:* Penguins Stopped Play, *Sue Townsend:* Adrian Mole: The Prostrate Years, *Dave Roberts:* The Bromley Boys
Distance run: 56.4km
Time running: 5h 4min
Best 5K time: 24min 4s
Best 10K time: 55min 16s
Best half marathon time: N/A

AUGUST

Saturday 1 August

Whomp. Here we go again. Wake to find myself in the midst of another depression tsunami. Legs like ancient oaks which have been felled in the darkness, arms unliftable, numbness in my fingers, head a lead weight. Overnight I've become the most rubbish *Transformers* character imaginable. Craptimus Prime.

It's an inaction replay of my February lows. Towel rail assistance to the bathroom. Shower slumped against the wall. An eternity to get dressed as I try to redirect fallen trees into unyielding denim.

At least this time I can trace two sources. Uncle Dave's funeral two weeks ago was a memorable family occasion, but amid a quiet weekend the emotion of it has finally chased me down. That was then compounded by logging into Rightmove last evening to discover the words 'Under Offer' next to my dream house.

Outside of the KonMari mentions, I've not gone into detail regarding our move because it just isn't very interesting. Mrs E and I spent the entirety of lockdown preparing our house for sale, and it went on the market in mid-July. Shortly after I'd spotted the ideal place for the girls and I, and scouted it from outside, but couldn't view it in person until we were sold subject to contract. No offers have been made on our place, and now the dream house is gone.

Again, such a trivial thing on paper, but after a wobbly fortnight, sufficient to unleash that tsunami.

If there's a silver lining, it's that I revisit lessons from February and take hours, rather than days, to initiate positive responses. The first is to immediately confide in Lindo and Steve. Sure enough, their chat keeps me afloat, and goes from heavy subjects like life and death to trivial ones such as cricket (with apologies to those who consider cricket more important than life and death) as the day progresses.

The second is that I sling on my trainers and run. My knee has been playing up since Glastonbenny – hence the lack of July running updates – but the adrenaline required to withstand its gip for 10km helps obliterate my morning travails. In December, my runs were a time to mentally construct some form of reply to an election-related insult. This one brings clarity of thought, and a recognition that the best tonic for depressive episodes has been giving myself a fixed point on the horizon to look forward to.

So, after a brief chat with Mrs E, and inspired by my trip to see off Uncle Dave, I spend the evening arranging a mid-month break with the girls, to a remote B&B in central Devon. It'll be our first ever holiday as a trio – and my usual vacation routine of spamming Facebook with every movement will be off-limits. Nerve-wracking, but the plan has worked, with this morning's disastrous start temporarily overcome.

Tuesday 4 August

A spectacular arrival in the mail elicits my strongest temptation to tweet in months.

A couple of times per year I reminisce about the Sega Mega Drive on Twitter, and the posts usually garner a positive reaction from nostalgic followers of a similar vintage. So today's receipt of *Streets of Rage 4*, a videogame 26 years in the making, brings an overpowering urge to tweet sweet nothings.

The Mega Drive was a pop-culture icon in the early '90s – home to *Sonic the Hedgehog* and trigger point for the first real console war, up against Super

Nintendo and moustachioed plumber Mario. In the playground everyone had a side, and mine was Sega's black beauty, due to games such as *Sonic*, *Sensible Soccer*, and *Streets of Rage*.

The latter was the machine's seminal beat-'em-up. You progressed through levels pummelling odd-looking goons and bosses styled on Freddy Krueger and WWF wrestler the Ultimate Warrior, using punches, kicks, weapons, and elaborate special moves. Released in 1991, *Streets of Rage* and its sequels *Streets of Rage 2* (1993) and *Streets of Rage 3* (1994) became cult favourites for their pick-up-and-play controls, gritty environments, loveable protagonists (red-skirted brunette Blaze brought a world of confused yearning to lads going through puberty), and atmospheric soundtracks.

I was 14 when *Streets of Rage 3* came out, and like thousands of gamers worldwide have been waiting for a sequel ever since. Now it's here. Naturally I've forked out £45 for the signature edition, containing a wealth of geeky paraphernalia.

The game is splendid. Chunky character models, meaty combat, thrashable enemies, a soundtrack that enjoyably apes those originals, levels that feel old-school without resorting to cliche: cargo ship, skytrain, Chinatown. It's everything I've wished for over three decades.

Yet – and I can't believe I'm typing this – the extra gubbins leaves me cold. When I pre-ordered in May I couldn't wait to get my hands on an official keyring, art book, numbered collector's certificate, set of enamel pins, '90s-style bandana, and double soundtrack CD. Three months on, deep into the process of KonMari-ing, it feels like filler. It's been a similar story with my Funko Pop figure horde: in April I joked that I'd never be parted with a special Hulk figure. Yet over lockdown I sold a third of my collection, and none of it has been missed. It's made me consider whether there's a more general connection between materialism and social media, and is a topic I plan to revisit.

No time for that now though. I have some serious goon-whacking to do.

Wednesday 5 August

There will be no Bristol Half Marathon for me, as the event has been cancelled. But hope comes from an unlikely source, all of 315 miles away. Newcastle's Great North Run on Sunday 13 September will be my first ever official half marathon – and I won't need to travel any further than my front door in order to make the starting line.

Like Bristol, the Geordie event has been canned due to the pandemic. However, it's taking place virtually. "With our partners ViRACE, we are creating an app to bring you an innovative virtual experience with audio clips from the event so that you will hear the sounds of the Great North Run," reads the official website. "From an upbeat warm-up led by the legendary Roy Gayle, to chants of Oggy Oggy Oggy, and the iconic roar of the Red Arrows fly-past, we are making it feel as much like the real event as we can."

Response to the announcement is so popular that I have to join a virtual queue of 41 people to sign up. It's free to enter but I can't resist the option to purchase a finisher's medal for £15. So I've no option other than to complete the race now, even if doing so leaves my knee in tatters. No pain, no... brain?

Thursday 6 August

The inevitably manic yet always welcoming toddler group I attended in January is shutting its doors permanently due to the pandemic.

It's a sad feature of this ghastly year for so many. The group forms part of a nursery which has been running for 51 years, and is also now finishing up. Half a century of history curtailed with a finger-click.

There's a closing down sale today, which I attend with Amber – the friend who recommended *Eleanor Oliphant is Completely Fine* at that January session. It's full of bittersweet reminiscing. I've got to know the owner, Mariah, since first attending in 2014 and she is heartbroken. Toys my girls cherished and/or squabbled over for years are being offered in desperation for 10 or 20 or 50p, but the house move means we can't purchase on sentiment alone. There will be no Sunnyside Daycare rescue hopes for these much-loved playtime stalwarts.

The closure cauterises one of my parenting foundations: I attended that group almost every Wednesday for half a decade. While social anxiety meant my first port of call once the girls found an activity was Facebook or Twitter, upon reflection all my lasting parental friendships are tied to it too. Names sprinkled through this book, such as Lindo and Sam and Amber, are only here because of bonds developed on those Wednesday mornings. So while the girls loved it, looking back I did too – and for the people, not just the chance to browse social media over a morning cuppa.

Sunday 9 August

I'm not the only Twitter blue tick who finds social media unnerving. *Secret Diary of a Call Girl* star Billie Piper – a better singer, actress, and vessel for the entire time vortex than I can ever hope to be – tells another Benji Wilson, this one from the *Sunday Times*, that her career would have been an even bigger challenge if it had launched in the era of Twitter and Facebook.

"I wouldn't have wanted to be a famous pop star now," says Piper. "The social media element of it all is terrifying because it's continuous, it's in your bed, next to your bedside table every night."

"In my pop career there were moments that were horrible to experience as a teenager, but they came and went," she continues. "But the thought of having that constantly on your person – I wear my phone round my neck like some weird slave – and with one simple click you're able to see what millions of people think about you or other people, or just about anything… I would argue that it's got worse."

"Everybody has an online profile and everything you do on some level could be seen to be incriminating, even if it's actually quite innocent."

Thursday 13 August

Little Blue's final day at nursery. For all the personal progress made this year, it's a tough one not to be on Facebook for. I've mostly enjoyed my new-found privacy, but on this day I would like to post something public to commemorate her growth since being packed off elsewhere for eight hours a week while still in nappies. We're not organised enough to have made physical scrapbooks, or arranged the girls' photos in a digital way, so cycling through Facebook and picking out the highlights for a round-up post would have tied up her nursery years neatly. Instead it's an occasion I mark with a few tears at pick-up time and a few glasses of orange gin in the evening.

It's a cliche, but they really do grow up too fast. And for all Facebook's drawbacks, it's very effective as an instant way of reminiscing on those formative years.

Saturday 15 August

Tradition dictates that I spend today assembling what Mrs E calls the 'Benji Entertainment Centre', ahead of taking the girls to Devon. That cliche about ladies packing three wardrobes' worth of clothing for a single week's vacation? I'm fifty times worse. But it's nothing to do with fashion. Instead I must ensure that my child-free evenings feature at least five separate options for off-duty enjoyment.

These accoutrements have evolved over the years. A laptop and iPad have always been the bare minimum, along with a handheld gaming console. PSP, PS Vita, Nintendo DS, even an old-school Game Boy have all ventured south-west to Cornwall. A library of five magazines and three books, a minimum of two board games, my guitar, notebooks and pens with which to scrawl lyrics or future work ideas. iPod, portable dock for blaring tunes out loud in the day, noise-cancelling headphones for doing so once the kids are asleep.

Most ridiculous of all was the year I took my PS4 and a jumble of cables and controllers to a tiny Padstow cottage, and Lady S's godfather Dave and I spent every evening hammering *Call of Duty* and *Rocket League* rather than indulging our wives and families, or enjoying sunset scenery. It's a miracle that Mrs E didn't file for divorce there and then.

None of this for our upcoming trip westwards. Coming off social media has simplified my life, right down to holiday essentials. I pack the MacBook to write on, the iPad to game on, and two books. That's it. Oh, and some clothing. I'm proud of the weight loss brought about by leaving social media, but Devon is most certainly not ready for this jelly.

Lightly packed, I squeeze in the monthly @ replies check. Total silence, other than being tagged in a brief debate among Palace fans regarding Taylor Swift's new album.

"Nice," says @RoDuSu.

"No album is nice – either good or bad," counters @CrystalMick.

"It's not good or bad but shitting brilliant," is what @BenjiWilson would reply, if he could.

Sunday 16 August

"Anyone need the toilet before we come off the motorway?"

Little Blue: "No Daddy, I'm fine."

Lady S: "No Daddy, I'm fine too."

Exeter services whizz by the right-hand window in a 67-miles-per-hour blur.

Lady S: "Actually Daddy, I'm busting."

Never doubt your child's abilities to trash any and all notion of forward planning, in-the-moment flexibility and/or consistent behaviour when it comes to toilet stops. "Why didn't you just pull in at Exeter services and make them go?" I hear you ask. Ha. Haaaaaa!! Good one. Just as a watched kettle never boils, so a pressurised child never tinkles, until you're 10 minutes down the road and you hear a nervous "oops" alongside what sounds like a leaking tap, and your upholstery is doomed to reek of urine until the next Big Bang.

Nine minutes and 57 seconds beyond Exeter services, we pull over so Lady S can have a wild wee behind an SOS phone unit. Wait, that's not what the white-on-blue 'P' stands for?

Our first hours on holiday proper are drama-free. Superb, in fact. We're staying at a pub-cum-B&B called the Waie Inn, in the tiny village of Zeal Monachorum, 20 minutes west of Exeter. Population 1,660, the village's name translates to Cell of the Monks, making the pub an outpost within an outpost – and a phenomenal one. Our family suite comprises a Tardis-vast triple bedroom, sizeable bathroom, and ample living room with two sofas. Green, sheep-dotted views stretch in all directions. We get the swimming pool to ourselves for an hour a day at no extra charge, and also on site for the kids are a skittle alley, playground, two ginormo-slides, a football pitch, and all sorts of space to roam. The cost? £80 a night. In the height of summer. There must be a catch.

Well, there is a small personal catch: I want to bleat my excitement all over Facebook but can't say a thing. It's 15 years since I did a holiday or multi-night work trip without spending the first evening 'checking in' online and unveiling initial thoughts alongside a photo blitz. I don't know what to do with myself for the first half hour once the girls are down.

So: I brew and drink complimentary PG Tips, then brew and drink complimentary Tetley, then text some pics to Mrs E and my mum, then lie back on the sofa for some Freeview TV, and eventually spend two hours watching the film *Dodgeball*. Even the unskippable ad breaks. With no restlessness, no second-screen videogames, no Benji Entertainment Centre, no more urge to blurt on social media once those tricksy first 30 minutes have been negotiated.

It's weird. Surreal. Sober. Again breaking a two-decade holiday habit, I've not even thought to order a beer. In a pub, with room service. Being off social media for so long really has changed the way I'm wired. In all areas other than my bladder, which is reacting the same to all that tea as it did many a Cornish night on the Doom Bar. Still, at least I don't have to go behind a phone box on the A30.

Monday 17 August

Spend a blissful day on the outskirts of Drewsteignton at Castle Drogo, the final castle to be built in England and the first building constructed in the 20th century to come into the National Trust's care. Opportunistic restoration work renders the castle itself inaccessible, but we nonetheless pass carefree hours wandering its impeccably maintained gardens, spotting flowers whose names could easily double for Harry Potter spells: Hydrangea. Wisteria. Verbascum chaixii. All that's missing is an appearance from the actual Khal Drogo, though I decline to share this critique with the girls. Twitter can know of my Jason Momoa mancrush, but its post-watershed nature means they must not until at least 18.

Tuesday 18 August

The human brain's ability to faultlessly stash information that nine-year-old you considered pertinent, yet is quite useless, never fails to amaze me. Without a crib sheet I can't recall how to work the washing machine, and am mocked on a nightly basis by Lady S for wandering up the stairs to fetch something, then coming down without the item I went up for. But the location of an Exeter newsagent from which I once bought a sickeningly sugary packet of Nerds (half cola, half grape)? Stashed away in the memory bank until my dying day.

Traversing my mum's city of birth, to which my brothers and I would schlep off on holiday every summer, my hippocampus reverts to what is best described as '1989 mode'. I am indeed nine-year-old me, without any need for maps, instinctively aware of the location of all toy stores, sweet shops, and videogame emporiums within a two-mile radius.

We spill out from the car park onto Sidwell Street, directly opposite the Pram & Toy Shop (now a Sainsbury's, but not in my memories) where I used to buy all my Subbuteo teams. One squad per Devon trip, permissible because they were £1.50 cheaper than our local toy store in Streatham. Naturally their affordability was down to never having any famous teams in stock – no English teams at all, for that matter – but goodness did I play out some monumental pretend-football tournaments between the likes of Austria Vienna, Standard Liège, Nice, and Stranraer.

Except when, God forbid, Vienna and Stranraer both made the final – a Biblical calamity given that a single set doubled for both teams.

Next, in the city's ageing Guildhall shopping centre, what was Woolworths now has a Wilko sign above its doors. Regardless of the name, for me it was the entry point to the Wilson household for many a classic Mega Drive game and thus triggers retrospective delight.

A few doors down we come to what was WHSmith, and is still WHSmith. I am fleetingly tempted to take the girls inside, before I remember that no one has been inside a branch of WHSmith since 1999. [If you happen to have purchased this book in WHSmith, please note that I am joking. Also, did you get a new haircut? Suits you! Very smart.]

Further towards the River Exe we find the local branch of Toymaster beckoning: the Darth Vader to Pram & Toy Shop's Luke Skywalker, where I once paid 50% more than the going rate for some WWF wrestling figures – the Nasty Boys – because I'd never seen a two-pack before. At a wallet-combusting £28 for the modern equivalent, I'm almost impressed to see some element of consistency retained from my teens.

An abiding memory of my football-obsessed youth is that while all the boys I went to school with in South London were Liverpool fans, these Devonian streets teemed with Manchester United shirts. Wondering whether times have changed – the commute from Exeter's St James Park stadium to Old Trafford is 246 miles – we pop into Sports Direct. I'm trying to avoid purchasing souvenirs with a house move imminent, but not averse to buying the girls Exeter City shirts to mark their first visits.

The polite-if-flustered member of staff I speak to inside Sports Direct curtails these plans. The chain boasts of being the UK's number one athletics store by way of a spirit-sapping advertising jingle, yet does not stock any replica kit of the club just a few minutes down the street. I can choose between polyester creations belonging to Arsenal, Manchester United, Newcastle United, Real Madrid or – for a penny short of 60 quid! – Italy, but for an Exeter City equivalent, "you'll need to go to the club shop," she wearily informs me.

Bah. Enough shopping. My grandparents lived amid a steep row of terraced houses behind Exeter's imposing jail, and I loved walking back to theirs (new Mega Drive game and Subbuteo squad in hand) along an elevated, tree-lined path adjacent to the platforms of Exeter Central. We retrace those steps today and the girls enjoy watching trains depart for Paignton to the west and Waterloo to the east just as much as I did, waving at the few passengers on board in these curious times.

There are many ways I hope my daughters don't grow up like their father: paranoid, insecure, constantly searching for acceptance, and battling depression. But these parts, the enjoyment of life's simple pleasures, even in a world of daily technological advances and third-party pressure to 'be cool'? They're the strands of me I hope they have inherited, and never relinquish.

Wednesday 19 August

Another day trainspotting, this time from the beach at Dawlish – whose station looms directly over the sands. At least, that's how I've imagined it for the past week.

Two problems: monsoon-like rain which drenches us every time we're out in the open, and a rough tide whose every wave slams hard into the train line's protective sea wall. 6,000 tonnes of concrete, erected as part of an £80 million restoration project after the line collapsed into the water in 2014, bat back roiling waves effortlessly. One largish human and two much smaller ones are unlikely to prove so resolute.

I've been obsessed with this stretch of railway since I was Little Blue's age. 36 years on I'm yet to find a journey I enjoy more. Opened in 1846, the Riviera Line runs from Exeter down to Paignton via Basil Fawlty's hometown of Torquay, packing in crossings of a viaduct and lifting bridge, a brief rattle through the parkland of Powderham Castle, adventures in tunnels carved beneath red sandstone cliffs, and 75 minutes of indelible scenery.

Twice per week during childhood holidays we would depart Exeter Central waving carrier bags stuffed with buckets, spades, and jelly sandals, and gaze out of the windows in awe. After the stations of St David's and St Thomas the entire line hugs water, first the Exe Estuary as it passes through Starcross, then the Channel with stops at Dawlish Warren, Dawlish, and – after burrowing through five tunnels within the space of a mile – Teignmouth. As with Exeter yesterday, childhood visits mean the layout of all three of these locations are seared into my memory like an internal GPS.

I tap into that intel now to unearth replacement activities for our abandoned beach day. Dawlish's arcade is an easy win – which quickly turns into a dramatic defeat, as Little Blue spends her grabber machine budget failing to ensnare a cuddly Cinderella, and embarks on a tantrum which makes the tumultuous ocean over the road look calm. The old-school sweet shop a few doors down lifts her mood, and mine when I discover they sell white mice – a staple of my visits three decades ago. I buy a £3 bag to last the rest of the holiday. It'll be empty by the time we're back at the B&B.

The centrepiece of Dawlish is its brook, which starts six miles away in the Haldon Forest, cantering through the town across a series of weirs before running under the railway line and into the Channel. Strings of flags and coloured lights lend it a picture-postcard feel even on this turbulent afternoon, and we cross its bridges multiple times to admire it from every possible angle. Lady S is especially overjoyed at the sight of two black swans. Introduced to this stretch of water in the 1940s by GRS Pitman, a game warden seconded to Uganda, they've been resident ever since.

I'm capturing these experiences on my phone, but with a different attitude to past trips. I'm not looking for pics that are perfectly framed for Insta, or sufficient to form a time-of-our-lives Facebook gallery. Instead I'm just grabbing moments. The girls holding hands while peering into the surging brook, or pointing and smiling together at the contents of a small water-side aviary, or animatedly making food choices inside the delightful, one-of-everything-please Gay's Creamery. Again I send a few to Mrs E and my mum, but otherwise enjoy the knowledge that these personal, private moments will remain ours alone, even when we reflect upon the photos in two decades' time. That was an entirely alien notion at midnight on 1 January.

Thursday 20 August

More exploring, more photo opportunities, still no temptation to share any outside of immediate family and select friends. My dad converted to the North Devon quiet life a decade ago, so we visit him at lunchtime and then cross the border to Bude for an afternoon on Cornish sands. The girls get the beach time they missed out on in Dawlish, and I fend off gale-strength winds to finish a book I only started on Sunday, *Football Against the Enemy* by Simon Kuper.

With no Benji Entertainment Centre, I've used this week to properly action Joel's principles of reading wherever possible. Four pages at the breakfast table while the girls debate favourite Disney princesses, then another four while they argue about having both chosen Cinders. Six pages during morning ablutions – sorry for the level of detail – and another four around a sit-down lunch. 15 pages as they warm down from the day's activities with late-afternoon telly, another four over dinner, and then 10 with a pint while they amuse themselves in the playground. They're in bed late, but after 9pm I bung a film on and keep reading, aiming for 20 pages a night.

A year ago we took a weekend's holiday near Minehead, and then a week in Penryn, where all similar instances of downtime would be spent cycling social media in order to post holiday pics or keep up to date with the world. It meant endless stress, always searching for the ultimate vacation snapshot or feeling like I was missing out on key sports news. In contrast I've spent this trip feeling relaxed, using reading as my sole chillout tool, and the girls have behaved as well as I've ever known them to.

Essentially, I've spent countless summers attempting to document and share the best holiday ever, despite the fact that trips away with children are exhausting and combative and the very opposite of relaxing. Because that's what social media conditions us to do. Without it, I've given up trying to fulfil preconceptions, and just enjoyed each day as it comes.

It's been wonderful. I don't want to go home. The girls express similar emotions. We've bonded and explored and it's been so uncharacteristically laid-back. We share Slush Puppies – another favourite from my youth, successfully passed on – from the Crooklets Beach Cafe as the sun sets, and I know that this project has spawned a new summer tradition: just the girls and I, in Devon, for a week, with all social media formats set to 'off'.

Friday 21 August

One garden centre, two Fruit Shoots, three pee stops (none at the roadside, hallelujah!), four Taylor Swift albums, five hours, and 17,000 muttered curses at standstill M5 traffic later, we are home.

Wednesday 26 August

The final week of the longest summer break ever – Lady S has been off school since 20 March – affords the chance to KonMari our extensive board game collection. The girls are too young to understand that Monopoly should really be called Monotony, so that's first on the charity shop pile. We have fun sampling others. Escape From Atlantis, in which you race to save your pawns from a slowly sinking island, is a classic from my childhood which Lady S quickly falls in love with, and so is kept off the cull list. As is Ghost Castle, a spooky dice-roller with glow-in-the-dark skull and 'working' axe and coffin. This was the most-wanted game of every '80s kid, to the point that complete editions fetch 60 quid on eBay.

Both daughters enjoy it so much that I am not permitted to cash in.

We go further back in time to revisit the 1977 MB Games edition of Hangman – which is littered with complications when playing with a four- or seven-year-old. The idea is to guess a word set by your opponent in 10 turns or less, with each failed turn adding a body part to the hanging man, depicted on a vertical square board. Once the picture is complete, he is dead, and you've lost.

Explaining this notion to two squeamish under-eights who've only just adjusted to the mild peril of Ghost Castle is not my greatest ever parenting decision. If they don't sleep for the next week I only have myself to blame.

They guess my word correctly – 'Violet'. It takes eight turns, for a cute reason: in their innocence they pick all the exciting letters such as X and Q and Z first, only resorting to vowels once those are exhausted. Fearing high-score humiliation in their teenage years I wordlessly ferry Scrabble into the chazza shop pile.

Next it's their turn to pick a word. Or rather, Lady S's. Little Blue has already wandered off to dig out Lego. I gently remind Lady S that she needs to spell the word out in front of her correctly, then place it on the board backwards – so that it appears the right way around to me on the other side, if and when I correctly guess individual letters.

In the early rounds I correctly select L, A, and S, and wrongly plump for E, I, O, and U.

In round eight I opt for C.

My seven-year-old daughter interprets this as K.

I let it go because, as soon as that letter is unveiled, I know there's no way I can 'win' this game.

In front of me I now see: LK_A_S. Is it a *My Little Pony* character? A Greek Thundercat? Some YouTube monstrosity I am yet to discover but which is already imprinted on her brain?

My last few letters are frittered away until I am hanged. Lady S sets off around the room in a celebration so elaborate I wonder if she's been secretly watching my Crystal Palace season review DVDs.

"Go on then, show me the word," I smile.

She slowly reveals the last two letters to spell… LKRAPS. So much for my attempts at homeschooling.

"Ill crabs? Lock wraps? Daddy doesn't understand, darling."

"Silly Daddy," she laughs, back to cartwheeling round the room. "It spells 'Sparkle'!"

Hangman skips the charity shop pile and is reconsigned to the bin.

Saturday 29 August

Chadwick Boseman, the *Black Panther* star mentioned briefly in January, has died of colon cancer aged just 43. In a year of bombshells this one feels thermonuclear.

Boseman had been suffering from the disease in secret for four years and still kept in remarkable shape for the filming of his most-renowned role, as well as *Avengers: Infinity War* and *Avengers: Endgame*, between surgeries and bouts of chemotherapy. It's no exaggeration to call him an icon. *Black Panther* was the first triple-A superhero movie to have an African American director and predominantly black cast, and Boseman excelled in its central role.

I don't need to sign into social media to read the many very-much-merited tributes. They're widely disseminated on sites such as the BBC, and stretch all the way up to another pioneer in breaking down barriers of race.

"Chadwick came to the White House to work with kids when he was playing Jackie Robinson," writes Barack Obama, in reference to the baseball film *42*. "You could tell right away that he was blessed. To be young, gifted, and Black; to use that power to give them heroes to look up to; to do it all while in pain – what a use of his years."

Monday 31 August

Across August, in an attempt to jumpstart the restaurant business following three months of enforced closures, the government has enacted an 'Eat Out to Help Out' scheme. Dine in a pub or restaurant on a Monday, Tuesday, or Wednesday and you get 50% off your bill, up to a value of £10 per head. The scheme finishes today, so Mrs E and I take the girls into Bath for an end-of-summer pizza or three.

Six miles into a seven mile journey, I discover that I've left my phone charging at home.

There follows much passive-aggressive head shaking, and a frustrated thump of the steering wheel, before I click that this is actually a good test of how far I've come. I wrote in January that my phone was a fifth limb, so obsessed was I with checking social media at all times. Can I go without it for a trek around Bath's Roman cobbles and long lazy lunch?

I'd like to say yes. The real answer is 'sort of'.

There's no temptation to Facebook or tweet before, during, or after the meal. Those instincts are well under control. But eight months offline hasn't changed my attitude to food porn: stick a gluten-free pollo ad astra under my nose with accompanying Peroni and I still feel an urge to photograph and share. [Mrs E rolls her eyes when I ask to borrow her phone so I can sate this addiction.]

I'm also on edge about what news I might be missing via text or WhatsApp message. Close friends and family know I'm off social media now, so use those formats to update me on football transfers, gaming gossip, or what they've been up to during a weekend. Four hours after departure, I arrive home bricking it about all the life-changing developments I've missed.

Through the door.

Phone on.

Zero messages. Ha!

Mobile mini-drama aside, it's another green tick for this project. Eight months! It's 244 days since I last whipped up an acerbic tweet about Crystal Palace, or Instagrammed a pic of the kids [or a massive pizza], or got pulled into a Facebook debate about Jo Swinson's political abilities. I'm pleased with that. During the entirety of 2019 I'm not sure I managed 244 seconds without doing any of those things. This assessment does raise one important question, however.

Whatever did happen to Jo Swinson?

The monthly tracker contains some disappointment. A calorific holiday has seen me pile on a few pounds for the first time this year, the running times have dipped due to injury, and I've still not managed eight hours' sleep. They're things to work on, much like my blasted mobile addiction. On the upside, at 66%

completion this project has concentrated and calmed my mental health, inspired a genuinely relaxing holiday with my kids, and bolstered personal friendships.

Personal friendships which are tested minutes before midnight, as I use WhatsApp to spam my nearest and dearest with uncensored photos of Italian meat and beer.

End of month stats: August 2020

Weight: 14st 7lb
Twitter followers: 4,936 (-3)
Facebook friends: 834 (+1)
Instagram followers: 235 (+1)
Average sleep: 6h 2min
Books read: 3 – Caitlin Moran: How to Build a Girl, *Louise Wener*: Goodnight Steve McQueen, *Simon Kuper:* Football Against the Enemy
Distance run: 94.5km
Time running: 10h 13min
Best 5K time: 27min 4s
Best 10K time: 56min 59s
Best half marathon time: N/A

SEPTEMBER

Tuesday 1 September

I kick off the final third of the year by announcing my decision to step down from the PTA. My list of accomplishments as chair makes for quite the glittering read:

- School discos: one (started 25 minutes late due to a technical hitch).

Er, that's it. Okay, that and a handful of Facebook updates on relevant matters during the stay-at-home months. Which is one of the reasons for stepping down: a rule of this project was that I could log in intermittently to post essential info on the PTA group. But the longer it's gone on, the more signing in has felt against the spirit of the book. With a third of it to go I want that necessity gone.

Most school parents would understand if I said I was taking a break from the role and planning to return in January. I can't do that. With our house finally on the market, I'll soon be a single parent three-and-a-half days per week: Mrs E and I have agreed to split time with the girls equally. I need to focus solely on them during that time. The lessons learned about short-changing them by exhausting myself with political discussion also apply to the PTA.

I've been on the committee for nearly three years, and enjoyed much of it, but it's been a 24/7 concern that I've found it impossible to disconnect from. The girls and I need a clean break. To self-preserve and keep life simple. Andy S used those words to me in a text at the end of January. Between the Devon holiday and decisions such as this, it's finally dawning on me that he was 100% right.

Saturday 5 September

Wake up in another man's bed. Not Steve's, nor Andy L's, but that of Matt, the good friend whose 40th birthday I missed in May. We've finally managed to cram in some belated celebrations in a spit-and-sawdust boozer five minutes' walk from his house. No social media, minimal phone use, just conversation and laughter and a considerable dose of liquidised hops.

To clarify, Matt isn't in the bed with me. This is his spare room. A spare room housing a Super Nintendo and a copy of *Street Fighter II*. Bringing to mind my all-time favourite piece of gaming trivia: the bizarre naming conventions of its three end-game bosses.

One of *Street Fighter II*'s most recognisable characters is a boxer clearly based on Mike Tyson – the original game was released in 1991, at the height of Iron Mike's fame. In Japan that character was named M Bison. But when the series was prepped for international release, makers Capcom apparently feared being sued by the world's most famous pugilist, and so switched three character names around.

Boxer M Bison, inspired by boxer M Tyson, became Balrog.

Masked, claw-handed Spanish warrior Balrog became Vega.

The biggest evil-doer of all, red-suited, army-hatted endgame boss Vega, took on the mantle of M Bison. Under that guise he has become as iconic a villain as you'll find in any pixellated universe. The foe every gamer, casual or hardcore, loves to hate.

Except in Japan, where 29 years on, he's still known as Vega.

I love that story. I also love waking up with a hangover that isn't swamped by paranoia and anxiety and depressive thoughts. Matt and I spend the morning reminiscing on our collective 80 years on this daft rock and I feel energised and truly content. I'm not worried about how much of a pillock I made of myself on Facebook or Twitter at 1am because I know I wasn't on there. I'm not forced to follow up with Matt on half-heard conversations, missed while I spent half the night on my mobile, because I was paying attention 95% of the time. Again, life just feels simpler. Streamlined. There's less noise going on in my skull 24/7.

Matt says I seem happier, healthier, and more relaxed than at any time in the decade he's known me. I return the compliment – with a young child he too has rejigged his priorities in these unusual, pandemic-affected times, and found that he simply doesn't have time to tweet or Insta as much as in his pre-baby days. Perhaps we're both simply too old to keep up with the social media rat-race. If that means days like this, swapping out 280-character updates in favour of lazy catch-ups over sugary tea and mountainous bacon sandwiches, then bring on the twilight years. Especially if they feature a Super Nintendo and *Street Fighter II*.

Monday 7 September

Last Thursday, after 167 days at home, Lady S finally returned to school. Today she is joined by Little Blue. I'd like to say I spend my youngest's first day in formal education getting emotional and/or outrageously drunk, but actually it passes in a misbelieving daze. Both daughters' births feel as if they occurred days ago, yet the eldest is more than a third of a way towards adulthood, her little sister in uniform mere weeks after being in nappies – or at least it seems that way.

It's a new new normal when I'd only just got used to the old new normal, and in addition to taking on more work I'm aiming to crack my monthly book record. If you're still looking at the tracker you'll know three is the most I've managed. Five is my September target. Today sees the first one ticked off: *A Civil War: Army vs Navy* by John Feinstein.

February's Super Bowl has already breached this book's critical limit on American football, so I shall keep the summary succinct: 1995, two rival varsity teams, well-woven personal stories of individual players, a tale that makes you want both sides to win the big game even though only one can. Essential if you're into US sports. Ignore if you can't tell a quarterback from a cornerback.

Tuesday 8 September

Going through old videotapes ahead of the move. This is less a KonMari job and more a complete cull; I can't believe how ruthless I'm being. Again, this indubitably would not have happened without stepping down from social media.

Some of these 'gems' I've had for decades. *Kylie The Videos 1*, featuring Miss Minogue's first four promos from way back in 1988, is straight in the bin after 32 years travelling the UK with me. So too the imaginatively titled *Kylie The Videos 2*. *WWF SummerSlam '92* is a poignant one to get rid of, as I vividly remember purchasing it at the Exeter branch of Woolworths mentioned last month, and being allowed up late to watch its entire 180-minute duration at my nan's. But get rid I do. Every Crystal Palace season review from 1990 to 1997 gets dumped on eBay for peanuts, and some home-recorded classics from my youth (*Kissyfur*) and teens (*Fantasy Football League*) are unceremoniously trashed.

Most of these tapes have lived with me in Clapham, Streatham, Carshalton, East Ham, Clapham (again), Balham, Bath, and our current West Country village. A year ago you'd have had to knock me black and blue in order to consider parting with them. Now? It's more filler I no longer need. Three decades' worth of unnecessary burden, detached and disposed of without a second thought.

Friday 11 September

Meet up with Mel, nanny to the stars, to fact-check the Chesney Hawkes shepherd's pie story.

Mel delivers the most awful news. Sue, the friend at the centre of that tale, passed away in April at the age of 49. She had been in hospital since last August following a double lung transplant.

It's an upsetting tale, yet Mel's focus is on sharing heart-warming stories of her friend's bravery. Sue developed cystic fibrosis as a baby and was told in her teenage years that she wouldn't make it to 18. Instead she fought on, through transplants and intense treatments, for another three decades. She would have been 50 on 13 August, and Mel shows me a WhatsApp group in which more than 30 friends celebrated her big day by posting photos of Sue's two favourite things: dogs and booze.

There's a photo of Sue with Chesney too, to which I can only raise the widest smile. The pair kept in touch from afar and had a mini-reunion in person shortly before her double transplant, following Hawkes' performance in the lead role of *Joseph and the Amazing Technicolor Dreamcoat*.

Their prime method of maintaining regular contact over the last decade? Facebook.

Saturday 12 September

Great North Run weekend. At least, officially – 'great' does not feel appropriate as I nurse a swollen knee that feels as if it may implode at any distance greater than 10K.

Still, I'm determined not to wuss out. Instead I refocus my attention to the March prep which turned out triumphantly. A trip to the shop to nab energy gels (loved the Haribo, but these feel like a more grown-up choice) and sports drinks, lots of water intake throughout the day, a light carb-loading dinner of chicken and jacket potato. The new football season kicks off today, and Palace edge past Southampton 1-0, but my focus on giving myself the best chance tomorrow means I forsake *Match of the Day* for two of the dirtiest words in my vocabulary: "early night."

Sunday 13 September

Wide awake at 5.08am with a pressure headache, a gurgling gut, and a seven-year-old next to me breathing with the calm of an Atlantic Ocean tropical storm. Textbook race day build-up.

I manage to bed down again for an hour once the entire household is up, and it turns the morning – and weekend – around. The race is at 9.30; by 8.30 I am bedecked in running gear, pockets overflowing with gels and a couple of Haribo-based treats, and banging out the inspirational race day tunes. Alright, Bryan Adams' *Reckless* album. Slowly I go through my warm-ups, and the nerves in my stomach progress into little rocket shots of adrenaline.

Despite my race being a social media secret, select friends do know, and my phone repeatedly pings with spirit-soaring good luck messages from Lindo and Amber and Amelia and even January Girl, who I've had intermittent, friendly contact with since the lifting of lockdown. By 9.20 the concerns of yesterday are long gone. I am gunning for my football-less cup final.

The Great North Run usually spans a route from Newcastle Upon Tyne to South Shields, and its inaugural event took place on 28 June 1981. Mo Farah won it six years in a row from 2014 to 2019, although the course record is held by Kenyan runner Martin Mathathi, who clocked a time of 58:56 in 2011. A fellow Kenyan, Brigid Kosgei, broke the women's record by winning last year's race in 1:04:28. I'm aiming for a more modest time of two hours flat.

I set the official viRACE app going and Geordie legend Brendan Foster pops into my ear to deliver a pep talk. There's a quick warm-up, and then a wave of crowd noise to set the scene of a packed start line. It works. It really works. 9.30 comes and I burst out of the front door feeling like I could sprint to the real Newcastle by mid-afternoon without a single additional inhaler puff.

I fly through the early stages. To hit my two-hour target I need to complete each kilometre in five minutes 41 seconds, or less; the first is blitzed in 5:11. It's too fast, but having Newcastle United anthem *Local Hero*, and the cheering of

Ant and Dec, and the sound of the Red Arrows injected directly into my skull proves too uplifting to temper my frantic pace. Alan Shearer pops up at the end of mile number five, to crack an uncharacteristically humorous one-liner about not being given mile number nine.

I'm laughing and smiling. I'm loving this. My first ever proper race, a distant pipe dream when this mad year got underway, a prospect I bottled when it was possible on my own doorstep. I'm 10km in, then 12km, then 14km. It is affirmation of this project. I am jubilant, cruising, high on a mountain top with arms open wide in triumph. 7km to go. Easy.

Then the crash comes.

No warning, sudden, emphatic, matchstick man versus articulated lorry. As suspected, I've burned myself out completely with that exuberant opening burst.

I'm still moving, but after 15km I can barely feel my legs. They are flabby pools of half-set jelly, liable to liquify and flood the pavements of Radstock at any moment. A Midsomer Murder of my own making. The one area I vaguely sense is the soles of my feet, because it's impossible not to: two lumbering, oversized horse hooves, still bathed in the 2,000-degree heat which forged them. My breathing is heavy, my arms sore and cumbersome. Pins and needles in my neck should be the scariest symptom of all, but I'm too knackered to pay them any mind.

Mo Farah and Gabby Logan and Sue Barker are dropping 'nearly there! you can do it!' missives, but I can't hear them. I zone out completely. Later I'll revisit my run playlist and have no recollection of hearing the Manics' Motorcycle Emptiness, or Otto Knows' Million Voices, or even my old Italian favourite Il Mondo. But they all played during an anguish-filled, out-of-body-like half hour. I know because iTunes has them time-coded.

Somehow in this trance, determination and stubbornness and resolve kick in. Elephantine right leg clubs a step, rhino-like left one thunders another, and on the interminable trudge goes. 18km. Broken. 19km. Cooked. 20km. Finished, completely finished, bust right knee hanging on by a single sinew. 21km. Done. As in, I am done. But somehow, by some miracle, the race is too.

I've really done it. I've completed the Great North Run.

I can't manage a single footstep more. At the end point I'm teetering along a disused railway line, flanked by pretty trees atop a grass verge. As soon as the app informs me that my race is run, both legs give way and I keel over onto the verge, graceful as a hurricane-struck redwood. I turn over onto my front and before even realising that it's happening – look away now, ladies – piss myself.

For the first time since I was, I dunno, four years old.

Seriously, it's Niagara Falls down there. Toilet accidents aren't outlandish in the running world – Paula Radcliffe's roadside poo during the 2005 London Marathon is often recalled as fondly as her sparkling race achievements. My wild wee is a complete shock, though. There's been no internal alert that I might want to look for a restroom once past the imaginary finish line. Just an oceanic release. Of nerves and pressure and energy and metabolised Lucozade Sport.

I lie prone for five minutes, then pull myself up into a sitting position and remain there for half an hour. My time is just under one hour 59 minutes – not the PB I managed in May, but still a solid showing, especially as I had minimal clue what was happening for its final quarter. I update the kind friends who messaged earlier, allow some feeling to return to my legs, ensure my post-race flood is no longer evident, and traipse up the steep hill home. It's usually a 20-minute walk. It takes me 42.

For the rest of the day I can barely move. While letting my exhausted backside and deadweight limbs imprint themselves into soft bedsheets I read an entire book in one sitting (well, laying) for the second time this year, Michael Palin's eye-opening *North Korea Journal*. The legs are gone but I do at least manage to crawl from bed to bathroom every couple of hours and avoid a repeat of this morning's waterworks. Despite that climax my first race day has delivered far more good than bad. As the famous sporting saying goes: urine some, you lose some.

Monday 14 September

Uh-oh. Spoke too soon about the excellence of viRACE. My official time auto-submitted by the app to the Great North Run website is two hours 51 minutes. Had I known it was going to be so wildly incorrect I'd have hunkered down for a lazy pavement sunbathe at the 15km mark, then strode those murderous final miles, perhaps stopping off for a lunchtime pint. Or Cornetto. Or pint-dipped Cornetto. You can have that one for *Dragons' Den* on me.

Thankfully I had the sense to record the run on Strava as a back-up. The time still isn't quite right, owing to a random pause, but 1:59:04 is significantly closer to my real finish than almost three hours. I appeal the result, feeling like a bronze medallist who's just been denied his podium place by a false-positive drugs test. Using a pee sample extracted from a grass verge.

Tuesday 15 September

Today throws up the most frantic monthly messages check of the year. Little Blue starting school has seen me added to the reception-class Facebook group – I'm grateful for the invite but feel bad about not being able to interact until January. Especially as pandemic restrictions mean playground socialising is kiboshed for parents.

There's a post from a friend, Sarah M, sharing news of Steps touring – a mammoth development in the world of uncool-but-excellent pop. And another from a mummy mate, Leanne, sharing a memory of tiny Little Blue, and slightly-less-tiny Lady S, hanging with their assorted various-states-of-tiny friends three years ago.

The big development is a message from an old Palace pal, Ann-Marie, checking up on my whereabouts. As per the rules I pass on my number and invite her to carry on the conversation away from Facebook. Within minutes she messages on WhatsApp, and we spend the rest of the day reminiscing on our years drinking around Selhurst Park, and shared music taste (more uncool-but-excellent pop, namely McFly), and what we've been up to since last having any sort of contact. In 2008.

For 12 years we'd been Facebook friends without ever messaging one another. It's more than 4,380 days since we exchanged a single word. How absurd is that? How many more friends is that true of on my Facebook account, and on yours? We'd probably have gone at least another decade in a state of polite silence too, had Ann-Marie not noticed my absence and messaged to ask how I was doing. I'm grateful for her having done so, and make a mental note to check in with similarly detached friends once my self-imposed ban is lifted next January.

Friday 18 September

60% through the month, 60% of the way towards my reading target. Today's ticked-off tome is pertinent: *Twitchhiker* by Paul Smith. Written in 2010, it's the speedy, unpredictable tale of a British journalist being carried around the world in one month, entirely reliant on the generosity of his Twitter followers. Smith is not allowed to pay for any transport or hotels, and can only plan three days in advance, leaving kind strangers found on the internet to shift him from Gateshead to Paris, Frankfurt to New York, and on to New Zealand. The Twitter of the book is sadly a different to the one I've experienced in recent years, as evidenced in the foreword by Jemima Kiss:

"Twitter's network is largely idealistic and optimistic, perhaps because no one would want to follow anyone as tediously rude or unconstructively negative as your average internet troll. Twitter is also still small enough that users feel a kinship with fellow users, in the same self-congratulatory finger wagging way as VW Beetle owners."

Don't think you'd find Billie Piper, or Wilfried Zaha, or irrelevant old me, agreeing with that description now.

Still, the book is a great read, and my 25th completed this year. Smith does encounter some negativity, including New York journalist Jeff Koyen offering $500 should someone deliberately lead him to his death. Generally, however, the tale is a triumph of human kindness and largesse, all brought about by kinship fostered on social media. It calls back to a time when Stephen Fry and Jonathan Ross made Twitter feel like *the* chilled-out place for humorous and pithy discussion – when Smith's book was written the format's limit was 140-characters.

It's natural to wonder, then, whether the increase to 280 characters in November 2017 directly correlated to people being crueller to one another, with more space available to unleash abuse.

Surprisingly, no. The increase in characters actually saw tweeters shorten their posts. TechCrunch's Sarah Perez ran the numbers a year after the jump in character length: "The most common length of a tweet back when Twitter only allowed 140 characters was 34 characters. Now that the limit is 280 characters, the most common length of a tweet is 33 characters. Historically, only 9% of tweets hit Twitter's 140-character limit, now it's 1%."

Two things that did increase in the year following Twitter's revised character limit were usage of the terms "please" and "thank you", by 54% and 22% respectively. I like to think that this means a subsection of Twitter which passed me by entirely were at least enshrouding their cruelty to celebrities and strangers with don't-wish-to-really-offend Britishness: 'I vehemently disagree with you. Go fornicate with yourself, mother-fornicator. Thank you. Please.'

Tuesday 22 September

Book four ticked off. It's a 50p charity shop find, which proved irresistible given the Suede overtones of this book's January chapter. Much like his lyrics, Brett Anderson's autobiography *Coal Black Mornings* paints fascinating pictures of life growing up in satellite towns, his language full of surprise and colour and descriptive flourishes.

Anderson's description of wearing a facade to placate others, rather than simply be who we are, feels particularly apt: "Before I had the maturity and confidence to find myself, I think, I was playing with the idea of becoming someone else; trying on the clothes that didn't really suit me and developing those brittle layers, that fragile emotional shell that many men wear all their lives as they strive to become an almost fictional construct – an amalgamation of other people's traits garnered from idols and parents and peers."

Wednesday 23 September

Katie 'Lindo' Castle is a fucking warrior.

Until lockdown intervened I'd spent almost every Wednesday morning for six years with Lindo – her maiden name – hanging out at the toddler group mentioned elsewhere. Over that time she became one of my closest confidantes, and a regular weekend drinking buddy.

With our ragtag posse of four now at school, today sees the start of a new tradition we're hoping to carry forward for another six years, and beyond: A gin breakfast. At nine in the morning we're in the local JD Wetherspoon enjoying an unlikely yet great bacon sarnie and Gordon's combo.

However, it's not her ability to drink me under the table in any scenario which I find inspiring, impressive as it may be.

At the age of seven Katie suffered a stroke. For two-and-a-half decades she has powered on, despite living with brain damage and spasticity down her entire left side. Each Wednesday for more than half a decade I've watched her control tantrums, change nappies, paint, draw, feed, and carry out all the other frenzied minutiae of parenting on one hand and one leg. When others have faltered, like yours truly with his mental health woes, she's been a phone conversation or

WhatsApp message away. Yet she's never, ever asked for anything back. With every right to feel hard done by, Lindo soldiers on, seemingly unscathed.

Except she isn't unscathed. Over the past two years the pain and fatigue of parenting, of 25 years coping with disability, have caught up with her. The closer I've got to know her, the more she's told me about the broken afternoons where she feels too tired to walk to the toilet, the exhausted evenings where her husband Jon has to carry her up to bed, the cloudy future where she may need to have holes drilled in her skull or utilise a wheelchair.

Being unable to do more for her at this time hurts. She's in the high-risk category for Covid-19 so I can't even hug her. But I can listen. Today I listen as she tells me about how social media has changed her life – for the better.

"Two years ago I joined a Facebook group called Different Strokes. It gave me an identity. Before then I used to stand in my kitchen and think, 'what do other disabled parents do to survive?' Jon and I attended a weekend group with lots of members and it was the first time I had met another stroke survivor. Ever. I was so apprehensive about going, but it was wonderful. To realise I wasn't the only person suffering, to meet people struggling like I am who understand how hard it is to put a brave face on things every day. Every. Bloody. Day."

"I still get low so often," she continues. "But if I go into that group or another one called Mums Like Us and post how I'm feeling, there is always someone there who knows how it feels and gives me a lift. I could not do what you are doing. I would lose my support network."

I should say something. Friends mock me endlessly for my talkativeness. But I have no words. Katie is bludgeoning my preconceptions and I'm delighted for her to do so.

"Don't get me wrong, social media is hard work," she says. "I live in a comparison state – constantly gutted when my friends post photos of their kids doing after-school clubs or playground trips, when all I can do at that time of day is put them in front of screens. But the positives outweigh the negatives. Have you heard of Nina Tame?"

"No," I confess.

"She's incredible. On her Instagram she calls herself 'the disabled step-mum you never knew you needed'. Her content is both funny and heartfelt – stuff like why you shouldn't ask a wheelchair user if they can still have sex. That it's okay to have limits, that I shouldn't feel like I have to explain my arm every time I meet someone new. Again, she inspires me daily. I wouldn't have that if I switched my social media off."

"I do have a great support system in real life, and I'm grateful for my friends and family," continues Katie. "But having people of similar ilk to interact with on Facebook is extra special."

It's further evidence that the view of social media with which I began 2020 is myopic and privileged: able-bodied middle-aged white guy thinks Facebook is bad, so tells the world they're all better off without it. That's wrong. I was wrong. Much like Paul's tales of using that space as a means to keep up with family around the world, it's a critical element of Katie's daily existence, just not a flawless one. Nuance. It's all about nuance, and balance.

"I'm a little bit speechless, Linds," I sputter. "Thank you for opening my eyes."

"Drink your gin and don't be a soft twat, Wilson," she responds. Normal service resumed.

Friday 25 September

A lovely social media story makes the BBC news home page. At 94 years of age, national treasure David Attenborough has broken the official Guinness World Record for the fastest time to amass 1,000,000 Instagram followers.

He reached the milestone in four hours 44 minutes, overtaking *Friends* star Jennifer Aniston's time of five hours 16 minutes, achieved in October 2019.

The small caveat is that while the account is in Attenborough's name, he's not the man pressing the 'submit' button on his posts. "Social media isn't David's usual habitat," admit collaborators Jonnie Hughes of the BBC, and Colin Butfield of the World Wildlife Fund. "So while he's recorded messages solely for Instagram, like the one in this post, we're helping to run this account."

Still, they've been honest about it, and it's David Attenborough. I think we can agree he gets a free pass.

Saturday 26 September

Clock something massively exciting while doing the weekly shop at our nearest Tesco Superstore: a bespoke display of all-new Funko Pop figures. Imported ones, from the San Diego Comic Convention. £15 a pop (literally), guaranteed to sell out over the next fortnight.

Massively exciting, that is, if this were 26 September 2019.

At that time I'd have photographed the display to share on Twitter, before asking my follower base which to pick up. Then grabbed at least one: if not to showcase at home, then to rise in value and sell on at a profit somewhere down the line. One year ago I plumped for Wong from *Avengers: Endgame* from this exact store, as it ticked both boxes. It'd look nice on a shelf and be worth £30 or more come 2023.

Today: no reaction at all. The four characters are Goku from *Dragon Ball Z*, Clawful from *Masters of the Universe*, Marvel's Nightcrawler, and Wizarding World Harry Potter. If those names read like gobbledygook to you, then 1. You need to brush up on your JK Rowling books, but more importantly 2. Here's the thing: they read like gobbledygook to me too. I'm just not interested.

Much of my collection is now boxed up ahead of the house move, but I now know with clarity that once in the new place, it'll be sold off as I unpack. I don't need the clutter or noise, and the money will be handy. It's been a year of changes, and moving on from four decades of hoarding feels like a transformative one.

Monday 28 September

Receive my Great North Run finisher's medal, and the news that my appeal has been successful – and with the original, correct time of 1:58:54.

I officially finished 2882nd in the 2020 Great North Run.

With no Mo Farah competing this year, it's only fair to congratulate the runner who finished 2881 places ahead of me: Inverness resident Graham Bee, with a time of 01:11:26. He too was sensible enough to back up his run on Strava – after, "[Of] course the Great North Run app died with a mile to go."

Wednesday 30 September

Book target achieved – but only just. Minutes before midnight I finish up *Within the White Lines* by Ruth Fox, a young footballer's tale of using sport to overcome depressive habits such as cutting herself.

It's an affecting story. At the back end of 2017 Fox wrote a suicide letter in readiness to end her life. But she found a new resolve from playing football, and writing a book, and in May 2018 was named Cambridge United's Community Hero of the Year. She's now with Ives Town, sharing thoughts on depression with nearly 9,000 Twitter followers, many of whom are young ladies who've suffered similarly and been inspired by her story.

There's a social-media related tale behind me owning Fox's book in the first place. I am, you may have registered, somewhat competitive. Shortly after sharing the story of my CBT on Facebook in 2019, I'd been involved in an especially combative five-a-side football match against a team containing a pal named Fran. While good mates off the pitch we'd spent years playing for rival squads on it, and would often chirp away at one another during games, only to hug it out at the final whistle.

On this night my team had been unbeaten for six months. This naturally caused Fran to raise his game in a confrontational manner which I felt overstepped boundaries. As captain of my team I passed on my objections on multiple occasions; he responded by smashing home the decisive goal with two minutes left to play. Final score: 1-2. We'd lost for the first time in the calendar year.

Sportsmanship – and old fashioned Britishness – dictates that in such circumstances you puff out your cheeks, shake your opponents' hands, and save any temper tantrums for the drive home where no one else can hear.

You do not make a scene by shunning those handshakes and kicking the cage surrounding the pitch multiple times. While using curse words to question the opposition's legitimacy at birth. Unless you are me.

Worst of all – I've had many cringeworthy moments in my life, but this may be the lamest – when a good friend (Fran) approaches to calm you down following such antics, you do not ask, "How can you behave like that when you've seen all the shit I've just been through?" Except, well, I did.

"What shit, Ben?" asked Fran.

"Facebook mate. It's all there. As you know full well."

"Ben, I left Facebook months ago…"

And he had.

It was the arrogant, buffoon-aping equivalent of "don't you know who I am?". I'd assumed that sharing an important personal breakthrough on Facebook imprinted it on every acquaintance's brain. Because I was on social media 24/7, soaking up every last image and thought shared by friends and family, surely it was the same in reverse? No, you idiot. No. People have lives. Lives that don't revolve around your banal Facebook updates. Lives that sometimes lead to them leaving social media formats completely. You presumptuous plank.

That revelation was a baby step towards making changes which continue here. The following night I messaged Fran a grovelling apology and outlined the ups and downs of CBT. He could have held a grudge, or gloated about the previous day's scoreline. Neither happened. Instead he told me he was always available to discuss mental health struggles, whether over WhatsApp chats or a post-football pint. And he has been.

Nine days following my cage-whacking tantrum we arrived for a Wednesday night kickabout at the same time. "Wait for me after the game, dude," Fran requested, and so I did. We walked back to our cars together, and at the point of departure he handed me a paper bag. "I meant what I said, mate. Always here for you. Don't open it 'til you get home."

Inside the paper bag was a book. *Within the White Lines*, by Ruth Fox.

End of month stats: September 2020

Weight: 14st 2lb
Twitter followers: 4,934 (-2)
Facebook friends: 834 (NC)
Instagram followers: 234 (-1)
Average sleep: 5h 59min
Books read: 5 – John Feinstein: A Civil War: Army vs Navy, *Michael Palin:* North Korea Journal, *Paul Smith:* Twitchhiker, *Brett Anderson:* Coal Black Mornings, *Ruth Fox:* Within the White Lines
Distance run: 103.4km
Time running: 9h 37min
Best 5K time: 23min 51s
Best 10K time: 50min 12s
Best half marathon time: 1h 58min 54s

OCTOBER

Thursday 1 October

Next time you apply for a job you'll likely spend hours preening and polishing your CV.

What you may not consider is the need to spend just as much time tidying up your social media accounts.

I'm catching up with my boss, Sam Loveridge, global editor-in-chief of GamesRadar – the UK's biggest gaming website. While social media had little bearing on my path to the *OPM* editor's chair (aside from that poxy Myspace top eight), she's had to grasp and navigate all the major formats across a seven-year ascent to Khaleesi-dom. In an environment that still skews narrowly towards men, too – a 2019 study showing that in the US 54% of gamers were male, compared to 46% female.

I've called to discuss how her findings compare to those of Ruth Fox, but a revelation about social media as a resource tool feels even more pertinent.

"Social media presence is definitely something I look for in recruiting for the site," says Sam. "When you get down to your shortlist of 20 you always look at their social media. You can instantly tell whether someone is going to be a good fit, whether they're carrying red flags. People forget that Twitter is your brand. What you retweet, what you engage with, what you Like: *anyone* can see those traits. Only today, someone made an anti-GamesRadar comment, and a couple of our freelancers Liked it. Whatever your job, the things you interact with on social media can colour someone's perception of you. A Like in the wrong place can be costly when everything is so public."

It's a fascinating discovery, particularly when applied to Twitter, a format where active debate with both friends and strangers on any subject can quickly become heated, as I know from impassioned post-match discussion with fellow Palace fans. A CV can be carefully edited and tweaked and filtered before submission. Tens, hundreds, thousands of tweets and Likes are much more difficult to undo – yet immediately accessible to any potential employer.

As for my original point, Sam – like Fox – does have kind words to say about Twitter – particularly in the wake of a pandemic. "Followers have been interacting with us more, asking genuine questions, enjoying the discourse. People being home and having more time to think about games has meant they have more queries for us. It's definitely better than this time last year. People have been more open, more engaged, more constructive."

She is largely positive about Instagram and Facebook too, reserving her criticism for a site I considered broadcast-only when it first appeared on these pages. Little of my work is video-based, so I've rarely had to dip into the realm of YouTube comments. That isn't the case for Sam, who has found the more pleasant attitudes of other formats remain absent from YouTube.

"It's toxic," she says. "I recently did a video on the new Xbox Series X console. The very first comment was, 'Why have you let a woman on here? She clearly knows nothing.' I formed a logic-based counter-argument, but then thought, 'Why am I wasting my time on someone so closed-minded?' I had to tell myself to leave it. But that kind of response happens constantly. Most YouTube comments tend to be nasty ones."

One home-based critic went further than a nasty comment, in a manner which Sam struggled with at the time but finds amusing upon reflection.

"I'd gone to a conference and was writing about *Battlefield 1* having female soldiers," she says. "I said how refreshing it was to play a big, triple-A multiplayer game and hear a woman's voice – a woman panting! Somebody didn't realise 'Sam' was short for 'Samantha'. So they made an entire YouTube video saying how stupid I was. I had to mute all of the words to do with

'*Battlefield*' on my feeds for a bit, because the replies got so bad. It blew my mind that people would be annoyed by the notion of a man enjoying playing as a woman."

Even so, Sam's social media experiences are more positive than negative – and like Lindo, the sense of a specific, like-minded community often provides solace: "*Animal Crossing* got me through this year. It became my social space. I met new people through trading items. It became a wonderful global bubble where everything was peaceful and serene, away from the ongoing bad news. That spread across Instagram, and Twitter, and Facebook, and random apps that sprang up for trading turnips and God-knows-what. It's been my lifeline. I've spent 800 hours in that living, breathing world generated by social media."

Friday 2 October

US president Donald Trump and first lady Melania Trump have tested positive for coronavirus.

In theory this is a major story to be absent from Twitter for. Yet events like the deaths of Kobe Bryant and Chadwick Boseman demonstrate that social media is inescapable in this era of blanket news coverage. In the wake of Trump's diagnosis, *The Guardian* launches a blog tracking developments, most of it devoted to tweets from the president, UK leader Boris Johnson, American political commentators, and opinionated celebrities. It's Twitter without even having to look at Twitter. If you have an active internet connection, there's no way to truly, permanently curb social media.

Trump is being treated with Remdesivir, a drug widely used to accelerate recovery from the disease. In the hands of the nation's best medical experts I suspect he'll shortly be back to campaigning for the US election on 3 November.

Sunday 4 October

"Harry, what's happened to Ben's head? Harry?!"

I'm in a marquee by a West London football pitch, that's acting as a makeshift post-match changing room, and my mum is panicking about an apparent cranial injury. Unbeknownst to me I've picked it up in my 11-a-side team's first match since lockdown. Except I've not taken any bumps to the skull, and survived 90 minutes of haring around without any obvious damage up top.

Mother, however, is in quite the tizz.

"Harry! Quick!"

Harry, you may recall, is my littlest brother, as well as strike partner for the day. He wanders over.

"Errr, mum... I think that's psoriasis."

Harry is correct. Mum has spotted one of the two mounds of flaking skin that finally became visible to the world upon shaving my head. In that one moment, the ridiculousness of me playing a character my entire adult life, rather than simply being myself, swings into full beam. These patches of dead cells have been hidden under my slowly thinning hair for more than half my lifetime, but I've kept them secret from even my own mother. *Live the lie, Benjamin. On social media, in the pub, to your own family. Don't show weakness. Ever.*

Sod that attitude now. I'm 40, and it's exhausting.

"Yes mum, it's psoriasis," I confirm. "No idea how you didn't spot it at Uncle Dave's funeral? I've had it since my mid-teens. It looks horrendous but it's me. No hiding it anymore."

It's the end of a bizarre but positive return to organised sport. We've won the match 2-1, Harry laying on the winning goal by drawing the keeper then gifting me an easy tap-in. There's more personal glory too, with the news that I won last year's Goal of the Season award. All of which would have made for quite the shameless Facebook boast post a year ago.

This time out I'm happy to keep celebrations to my team-mates and family – Lady S is in London with me for the trip. Indeed I can't get carried away: Mrs E later requests her highlight of the day, and the answer has zero correlation to football.

"I got sausage, mash and beans after the game, and then Burger King on the way home," beams Lady S. "Two dinners!"

She is, unequivocally, my daughter.

Tuesday 6 October

Donald Trump is out of hospital – and downplaying the threat of coronavirus, again in a tweet shared by every major news outlet. "Flu season is coming up!" he writes. "Are we going to close down our country? No, we have learned to live with it, just like we are learning to live with Covid."

As I write this the US has 7.4 million cases and 210,000 deaths. According to the BBC, the flu caused between 24,000 and 62,000 deaths in the US from 1 October 2019 to 4 April 2020. Of all the social media posts I've seen amplified in news stories across the year, this feels like the most irresponsible. That might prove costly on election day.

Sunday 11 October

It's 3am and I'm at war with a foam wrestling toy.

A few years back Lady S collected WWE Brawlin' Buddies – chunky foam wrestlers who speak or yell when bashed against one another. Which is to say, I chose to buy them under the auspices of her collecting them. In fact she showed zero interest in any character other than The Rock, because he sounded like Maui from *Moana*.

In preparation for our house move these hulking masses of talking fluff have been pulled down from the attic, and are all low on battery. Bashing them together causes either total silence or low groans of pain, as if in the throes of existential sadness and/or foam-wrestler gastroenteritis. Those ailing murmurs are a little unnerving, so before the girls' bedtime I parked them in the study with the idea of sorting them after dark.

I forgot. (i.e. got distracted by playing Saturday night *FIFA*.)

In the night, insomnia raging as is standard, I become aware of voices outside the house. Well, one voice. Saying the same thing, over and over. In a slow slurring drawl.

"Youuu can'ttt seee meee. Youuu can'ttt seee meee. Youuu can'ttt seee meee."

I'm too much of a simpering manbaby to watch horror films, so have no cultural reference to drop in here. What I can tell you is that I'm sufficiently unnerved to turn the main bedroom light on, then perch on the edge of the bed in a state of must-protect-my-family alertness.

"Youuu can'ttt seee meee. Youuu can'ttt seee meee. Youuu can'ttt seee meee."

Hang on. It's coming from the next room. FFS, Wilson. It's a talking wrestling figure! It's John Cena! Just remoulded in cushion form, and nursing some early hours foam-wrestler gastroenteritis. Okay, that's not so bad.

"Youuu can'ttt seee meee. Youuu can'ttt seee meee. Youuu can'ttt seee meee."

I stagger into the study and sift through the box holding the wrestlers. Except – true to John's word – I genuinely can't see him. Unlike the other Buddies, John is tiny. John, I discover after turfing out every one of his mates, is a mini Brawlin' Buddie. A mini Brawlin' Buddie who still has his tag attached. A tag which reads, 'this product contains batteries which are not replaceable.'

"Youuu can'ttt seee meee. Youuu can'ttt seee meee. Youuu can'ttt seee meee."

The senior Buddies all have slits down their back, held together with Velcro, from which you pull out a small white case in order to replace the battery. As he yaps away at me, I can feel that John's innards have a similar, smaller pack. Yet there's no way to get to it. He's fully sealed. No slit. No Velcro. I'm going to have to perform 3am surgery. On a cuddly toy.

"Youuu can'ttt seee meee. Youuu can'ttt seee meee. Youuu can'ttt seee meee."

To the kitchen. John is placed flat on the counter, face down. My intent is to save him if at all possible. I make a clean cut along what would be his spine, then begin to pull out foam. Then more foam. Then all the foam. There's a line in the TV show *Lost* where main character Jack is discussing a botched attempt at spinal surgery on a 16-year-old girl, in which he made a small mistake and her nerves spilled out "like angel hair pasta". This is like that. With foam.

"Youuu can'ttt seee meee. Youuu can'ttt seee meee. Youuu can'ttt seee meee."

Finally I reach the white case housing the battery. This is a well-made child-friendly toy, so I can't just yank it out. I have to use scissors to cut the wiring that holds it snugly in place, behind Cena's chest. I presume this will also short-circuit the toy. One snip, and the procedure is over. And…

"Youuu can'ttt seee meee. Youuu can'ttt seee meee. Youuu can'ttt seee meee."

Well, at least the case is out! Again, the toy's impressive robustness means there's no easy way to get inside the little white box. I try stomping it on the dining room carpet – but that's exactly what the toy was built for. My hippo-heavy clomp muffles the sound, but that's all. I'm going to have to get inside.

"Youuu can'ttt seee meee. Youuu can'ttt seee meee. Youuu can'ttt seee meee."

There's a small lip in the edge of the battery compartment. Using a butter knife I press hard into the lip, pulling it away from the rest of the box, and finally it comes apart. While still talking! John is one determined little guy. It's time to end this though. Inside the case is a tiny battery, connected to a small green chipboard. I snap, then wait.

Silence. Peace. Tranquility. Phew.

Alas, John can't be saved. I spend the rest of a patchy night racked with guilt as teeny Cena acclimatises to his new home: the kitchen bin. At least I've cured his foam-wrestler gastroenteritis.

Thursday 15 October

A near-silent monthly check. There's one Facebook work enquiry regarding *FIFA*, which I respond to via email. One new follower on Instagram. Nothing whatsoever on Twitter, where my last @ mention was on 28 August – and intended for the *Sunday Times*' Benji Wilson.

Like foam John Cena, I am at peace. Particularly as this evening's PTA AGM passes with no objection to me officially stepping down.

Curiously, there's also complete silence when I mention being content to provide future DJ duties.

Friday 16 October

Friday evenings have become my favourite time to run. There's an element of relief to having survived another school week, a sense of achievement in kicking off the weekend with an endorphins boost, and an air of maturity in spending Friday nights doing something good for the body and soul, rather than dousing it in gin.

So I douse it in gin on Saturday nights instead.

It's unseasonably balmy out, so I set off with only one aim: jog towards the sunset for however far my legs can manage. I barely register my pace, preferring to focus on enjoying my usual running tunes and the mild winter conditions. I trek through comely villages and scenic woodland, and by the time the sun has disappeared beyond the distant Mendips, I'm up to 14km with plenty in the tank. A little while later, now in pitch darkness, this random ramble has turned into my fourth half-marathon of the year. The time of two hours and nine minutes is my slowest, but I don't care: much like building the girls' YouTube channel, I'm finally understanding that not every element of life has to be about numbers and competition. It's okay to just 'run'. It's okay to just 'do'. It's okay to just 'be'.

Sunday 18 October

37 miles separate Crystal Palace's football ground of Selhurst Park and the Falmer Stadium where Brighton & Hove Albion play their home games. Yet theirs is one of the most heated rivalries in English football, and today is the first meeting of the 2020/21 season.

The 'M23 rivalry' developed in odd circumstances. As both sides chased promotion from the third division in 1976, a heated derby clash threatened to spill over because of nicknames. Boys will be boys, and all that. Palace had recently changed their moniker to the Eagles; in response, Brighton chanted "seagulls!"; Palace supporters in turn threw smoke bombs. Brighton won, and soon took on Seagulls as a permanent nickname.

Matters escalated the following season. A scrappy cup replay at Chelsea's Stamford Bridge ended 1-0 to Palace after a successful Brighton penalty was ordered to be retaken, and missed. At the final whistle Brighton manager Alan Mullery flicked V-signs at Palace fans, before entering the opposition changing room, throwing £5 on the floor, and telling manager Terry Venables: "That's all you're worth, Crystal Palace."

Thus a rivalry was born. Historically, then, this is a day I spend not only on Twitter, but also both sides' main fan sites: cpfc.org and northstandchat.com. Win, lose, or draw, if I'm unable to attend the game in person then the internet usually proves a reliable source of nervous excitement beforehand, and elation or fury afterwards.

Ahead of today's game, a 2pm kick-off on Sky Sports, I forsake such matchday traditions. Instead of venturing to the pub or immersing myself in Twitter build-up, I enjoy a cooked lunch with the girls, then pad around Tesco with a seven-year-old in tow. In fairness, the supermarket's carrier bags do a passable impression of Albion's traditional home kit.

Home just in time for the match, I'm nervous as with most fixtures against the not-that-old enemy – but in a controlled, unflustered manner. Eight years ago, a

Brighton player was sent off in a clash at Selhurst for which I had front row tickets alongside Naveed. As the opponent in question strolled past en route to an early bath, I blasted his ears with every curse word in my vocabulary, plus a few made-up on the spot. ['Thundertwat' would not pass for being kind, nor tally with my revised perspective on those in the public eye.] When the same player is shown a red card today I simply shrug and enjoy the prospect of him sitting out Brighton's next three fixtures. 2012-me would be dismayed at such a sterile reaction.

In truth, it's a sterile match. Devoid of fans due to the pandemic, devoid of attacking intent from Palace. We eke out a 1-1 draw through another soft penalty; even the last-minute Brighton equaliser can't tempt me to reach for the laptop in anger or frustration. The match ends and I get on with my day, playing with the girls and taking in a sunset walk around the village. Within two hours it's like it never happened.

Football has always been the axis upon which my world revolves. I hardly missed a Crystal Palace game through the noughties, attending every match home and away at ridiculous expense in the club's 2003/04 season. Yet in the last 10 months, this mentality has evaporated. Being offline has shielded me from toxicity, but it's also stifled my passion. That's healthy, but saddening, too. Escaping social media has made me the type of fair-weather fan I spent two decades openly criticising. Hand on heart, I cannot say whether that's a positive or negative takeaway from this year of recalibration.

Tuesday 20 October

I thought I'd done fairly well negotiating nine months, 19 days, and 13 hours without social media. Until, searching for experiences similar to Rohit Neralla, I uncover the name Rosie Leizrowice. She's a content strategist who went four years without social media, before rejoining Twitter in June.

"During my teens, I had such an unstable, malleable sense of identity that I found having digital profiles that were supposed to reflect my personality excruciating," she writes of her decision to delete Tumblr, Snapchat, Facebook and the rest. "Getting to grow up a bit without as much scrutiny, imagined or real, feels healthier. I like people I meet getting to know me as a person, not also through a profile."

Time and focus were further issues: "I got distracted with ease and struggled to feel present in any situation. I'd zone out for hours while scrolling, or miss out on sleep… I always find myself piling up projects to do, books to read, things to study. Spending what often amounted to hours a day on something I didn't really enjoy seemed silly."

Leizrowice walked away successfully for close to half a decade. She found that being off Insta led to her spending less time and money on her appearance, while evading Facebook restored the alone time required for those books and projects mentioned above. There were downsides too: elements of loneliness, missing out on local events through not knowing about them, and occasionally feeling like she didn't know what was happening in her friends' lives.

Four months ago Leizrowice returned to Twitter. In an intriguing decision which mirrors the positivity of Ruth Fox, she chose the format as an ideal space "for incubating ideas in public, for generating writing ideas, and for practising condensing thoughts". Here's where her experience differs from mine: "While I can't imagine using Facebook or Instagram again because both made me kind of miserable about my life, Twitter never seemed as bad."

Critically, she's made her own ground rules, and they're something I can learn from. "I won't install it on my phone. I will use StayFocusd [a productivity management tool for Google Chrome] to restrict the time I spend on it each day. I don't want to think about followers or Likes or other metrics because that's what caused a lot of the strife the first time around. It won't get too personal."

Me not taking stuff personally? Ack. That's going to be one of the biggest challenges if and when I do make a social media comeback. Still, Leizrowice's story is inspiring, and gives me faith that even a Twitter return may, just may, be achievable.

Wednesday 21 October

The battle against mental health is one you never win. It's impossible to truly kill off the black dog. Those Hollywood films where the antagonist meets his maker, only to spring back to life and chew a second round of bullets? Depression is like that. Except there's always another round of bullets that need to be lined up somewhere in your future. And another. And none of them are ever enough to destroy this inaudible, unrelenting foe.

I'm reminded of this today by a text message from the girls' school. I shall paraphrase for brevity's sake: "Dear Ben and Mrs E. I've just spoken to our speech and language therapist. Little Blue's assessment has come out with severe language difficulties because she was very literal. The therapist will observe Little Blue in the classroom during the next half of term to gain more information."

I've felt in full control of my mental health since that early August lapse following Uncle Dave's funeral. Reading the message triggers the bursting of a dam.

Have you seen the modern remake of *Sherlock*? One of the best bits of that show is the way words and clues flash through his brain at whirlwind speed, and are visually represented on screen. This is much the same, but I am not Sherlock Holmes, nor Benedict Cumberbatch. I am Benjamin Broken.

Some of the phrases flash by in an instant and are gone again. Homeschooling. House move. Psoriasis. Lazy eye. Others linger, longer, daring me to examine them more closely. Coronavirus. Lockdown. Isolation. Loneliness. Autism. But I can't place them in any sort of order, can't control them. I have to go upstairs and lie down and let them overwhelm me, feeling anxiety rush through every vein and every synapse, before I'm able to finally push them away.

It's debilitating and derailing – the process takes half an hour, but I feel emotionally spent for the rest of the day. Other parents are chipper at school-pick up, celebrating the onset of half-term with their little ones, but I am a shell, desperate to get home and hide away. Yet when they saw me six hours previously, I was fine. Genuinely fine.

It's why there are no easy answers where mental health is concerned. It's yet again why 'man up' is such an insulting command. Little Blue could be on the autism spectrum, or it could all be a false positive. We'll love her either way, and news isn't apocalyptic. But my inner reaction to it, and its ability to cleave open so many old wounds, most certainly is. It's something I know I'll have to work on for the rest of my life. Staying away from Twitter might make me less likely to suffer mental health relapses. But I'm learning, and accepting, that I can't outrun them forever.

Friday 23 October

Bump into an old work colleague, Kate, on a half-term supermarket run with Lady S. Kate was office manager during my *OPM* days, and this random meeting feels almost *Truman Show*-like in the way it calls back to my past: she was the lady who booked my flights and hotels for the E3 disaster trip. Before today I've not seen her in real life for seven years.

We catch up and swap stories of lockdown and this crazy year, in far greater detail than our single-sentence Facebook comments to one another over the last decade. Kate seems intrigued by this project – and catches me on the hop with an instinctive query:

"How much time do you think you've earned back by giving up social media?"

It's a stimulating question. I spend the evening tallying the answer. My conservative estimate is that I averaged 75 minutes per day on social media before walking away: 10 scrolling Insta, 20 arguing politics or football on Facebook, 45 or more tweeting or firing off @ replies. Some days, such as those involving Palace fixtures or during the election, it'd be closer to two or three hours.

The result this turns up is startling. There've been 296 days since 1 January. 296 times 75 is… 22,200 minutes. 367 hours. *Three hundred and sixty seven hours.*

I've got more than 15 days of my life back by leaving social media. A figure so large I cannot process it. I'm looking forward to tallying the final, definitive number at year's end.

Saturday 24 October

I've hit my target weight for the year. After a 5km afternoon run I tiptoe onto the bathroom scales and see the numbers 13:13 peering back up at me. It's the first time I've crept under 14 stone in nearly two decades, and a mammoth turnaround from the year after we had Little Blue, in which my heft edged towards an unhealthy 17 stone.

It's a personal milestone, but the key part for anyone wishing to do similar is that there's no trick of the light in play. I've not secretly been on crash diets as part of the book-writing process, and I've still guzzled a disgusting amount of fizzy pop. Ask me to give up booze, or carbs, or social media, for a little while

214

and my will power holds fine. Order me to stay off full-fat Coke for a week and it just cannot be done.

There is one caveat: I switched to a diet called FODMAP two years back, to aid issues with irritable bowel syndrome (this book is one sexy confession after another, eh?) and fibromyalgia. The plan cuts out gluten, most dairy, and other gut irritants such as garlic and onion, and has worked wonders for my intestinal health. A domino effect is that, because gluten-free foods cost a small fortune, I generally eat less than I did before starting out on FODMAP.

Naveed – the friend who once nicknamed me John Goodman – is the first to be told of my breakthrough.

"Blimey," he replies. "That's amazing work. Super proud. What changed? Fear I need to do similar!"

"All down to leaving social media," I text back. "Really. Bought me so much time to run and relax and not eat junk food to offset stress brought about from arguing with people 24/7."

It's a reply typed without second thought, but also a lightbulb moment. The time freed up to run by leaving social media has been well documented on these pages, but until now I'd not considered its effect on my eating habits. Historically, my stock response to feeling low was to munch the misery away. Those Facebook election debates were often 'complemented' with pizza or carb binges or a little pack of biscuits to dip into a cuppa. Dairy-free, gluten-free, but alas not calorie-free. Then for breakfast the next day I'd double down: a toast mountain, accompanied by anything with enough sugar to propel me through the morning.

Without those evening stresses I rarely dip into comfort food after 7pm, and my morning eats have remained consistent: a bowl of porridge and a couple of gluten-free biccies. It sounds like the most boring breakfast in the world, but put it all together with the social media escape and it's resulted in a project milestone. Toasted, naturally, with an ice cold can of Coke.

Monday 26 October

Yet another football anecdote. Apologies. I'm charging towards a loose ball during tonight's rainy six-a-side clash when I feel a sensation much like being shot in the back in the leg. Or what I assume being shot in the back of the leg feels like – I'd rather avoid having that particular sensation ticked off first-hand. Anyway, the salient point is that I've pulled my right hamstring.

I know immediately, because it's the 999th time I've done it in my esteemed (in my dreams) sporting career.

No more running for a little while then. Bugger.

Wednesday 28 October

The recommended means of recovering from a hamstring pull is 'RICE': rest, ice, compression, elevation. The actual chance of achieving any of those four things during half-term, while in sole care of two rambunctious daughters, is nil. So I've instead committed to hobbling around Weston-super-Mare with them for the day. Some physical pain aside, I'm hoping it'll take my mind off the injury.

Such hopes come to fruition. Other than an agonising hour's drive home, it's a wonderful three-person adventure, a one-day sequel to our Devon trip in August. Completely private and about nothing more than enjoying one another's company. Again, I take a few snaps but the only people they're shared with are Mrs E, Sam, and my mum.

I've been infatuated with piers since my youth. Devon has disappointingly few of these attractions protruding into its waters, so instead day trips to Brighton fostered our family's love of grabber machines, candy floss, and staring through wooden slats at a tempestuous sea. As much as I enjoyed ticking all those boxes on the Palace Pier, opened in 1899, it was the slowly decaying West Pier (built in 1866) which truly captivated me. Closed four years before my birth, I could pass a serene half-hour sitting on pebbles and staring at its collapsing pavilion and dilapidated concert hall. Often I did. Sadly, in my teenage years its form turned skeletal, before two 2003 arson attacks finished it off.

Weston's Grand Pier, opened in 1904, has had similarly sad encounters with fire, first in 1930 and more famously in 2008, caused by an electrical fault of unknown origin. Its pavilion was destroyed, and the rebuild took two years and cost £39 million. Its present-day mix of arcade machines and food outlets fall short of the majesty I afforded Brighton's West Pier, but maybe that's just age speaking. A couple of teddy bear wins and two portions of deep-fat-fried carbs later and my girls are euphoric.

The best of today's photos feature the girls on the beach, striding around in soggy sand with the tide out, the pier looming in the background like a time-honoured coastal guardian. There's a quintessential Britishness to this image. The attractions may have changed from 100 years ago, but the joys of a day at the seaside remain similar from generation to generation, season to season. Pushing coins into slots, wolfing down fast food without a care, travelling home with half a beach inside your shoe. Another memorable family day, spent in utter privacy, where the memories created will live first and foremost in my head, rather than my phone.

Saturday 31 October

No trick-or-treating to mark Halloween this year, given understandable mixing restrictions. We are able to offer the girls some form of celebration, by way of a socially distanced party at a soft-play centre in Yate. There's even a dance floor, decked out with '70s-style LED panels, where DJ Pirate Steve blasts Michael Jackson's scariest hits. I used to be terrified by the demonic laugh at the end of Thriller. My two are entirely unfazed. Or too distracted by complimentary hot dogs to care.

While the girls bounce around to Smooth Criminal on foam-based apparatus, I find a quiet-ish table and dip in and out of a BBC interview with champion swimmer Rebecca Adlington, part of a series entitled *Fair Play: The Women in Sport Show*. Adlington collected an OBE after winning the 400m and 800m freestyle swimming events at 2008's Beijing Olympics, but it led to her being told that "you look like a whale".

"I don't have any photos up of that day in my house," Adlington reveals. "[Social media] has changed my perception of memories... I stopped going to events for a long time, I just didn't want to go through the whole thing of putting a dress on and being slated for it."

Soak that in for a second or three. The most successful swimmer Great Britain has produced in 100 years deservedly got to meet the Queen in order to celebrate her achievements. Yet she can't bring herself to revisit pictures of the event because of the social media backlash sparked by her green dress. Revisiting the *Daily Mail* headline from the occasion is horrifying, and you can see why it would have been lapped up by cynics on Twitter: 'Olympic swimming champion Rebecca Adlington indulges her fetish for 'come to bed' shoes as she meets the Queen.'

[Adlington had worn silk-satin Jimmy Choos for the occasion. Who wouldn't wish to spruce themselves up to collect an OBE?]

"I found it very personal," says Adlington. "I still don't understand why anyone would send anyone [else] a nasty message online, let alone someone they've never met or don't know."

"I remember going into *I'm A Celebrity Get Me Out Of Here* [in 2013]," she continues. "My sister, Chloe, looked after my social media. I came out of the jungle and she was like, 'I can't actually believe the messages you get. I never want to see that again.' I'd never thought about the impact on my family before then."

She does have some sanguine notes to offer amid this tumultuous time.

"I haven't worn make-up since about February and have probably forgotten how to apply it," she says. "I hope that, if anything positive can come from this year, it is those things of relaxing on the way we look. As long as you feel good about yourself, that's all that matters."

Her Twitter and Facebook comments are calmer too. "[The online abuse] has levelled off," she says. "Luckily it's very rare that I have to block or report someone on social media now."

Coronavirus changing people's social media habits? Sounds promising. It's nice to think that the local politeness I experienced in May has translated to Twitter on a mass scale, even if events such as the upcoming US election are always certain to unleash verbal warfare.

If females in the public eye such as Fox, and Loveridge, and Adlington can be open-minded about the upside of Twitter, to the point of Rosie Leizrowice confidently returning after a four-year hiatus, then this male nobody probably should consider it, too.

End of month stats: October 2020

Weight: 13st 13lb
Twitter followers: 4,925 (-9)
Facebook friends: 836 (+2)
Instagram followers: 234 (NC)
Average sleep: 5h 45min
Books read: 3 – *Keith Stuart:* A Boy Made of Blocks, *Michael Williams:* On The Slow Train, *Jonathan Wilson:* Behind the Curtain
Distance run: 85km
Time running: 8h 3min
Best 5K time: 25min 25s
Best 10K time: 52min 51s
Best half marathon time: 2h 9min 51s

NOVEMBER

Sunday 1 November

Most Thursdays across September and October I've met up with the man friends have come to call "the husband" – sorry, Bethan! – to trek 5km then sink pints in our local. On Strava I've termed such occasions 'Stevening Runs'. The calories earned substantially outweigh the calories burned, but the weekly companionship has been instrumental in my mental health remaining intact as the nights draw in and new pandemic measures approach. The UK is heading back into lockdown for four weeks this Thursday.

We missed last week's Stevening Run due to my hamstring injury. Pub catch-ups are a no-no for the next four Thursdays due to the above announcement. Only one thing for it, then: decant to our local on a Sunday evening for one final pre-quarantine pint night.

There are two months of the project to go and I've hit my stride after officially stepping down from the PTA. Comfortably, Steve points out that I've mentioned social media much less during our recent pub visits in comparison to chats in January and February.

"Initially I didn't think you'd stick to it," Steve says. "The book was a good incentive but your life revolved around Facebook and Twitter. The level that you used to interact with all that was astonishing to me. But you did adjust fairly quickly, like a weight had been lifted. On Valentine's Day I knew you'd sussed it. And now you're so much more 'in the moment' when we talk about anything. You seem much more private and inward-looking, rather than – I mean this in a nice way! – searching for attention to keep your spirits up. Most importantly, you seem happy."

I'm chuffed and humbled. For four seconds.

"So now it's time to step it up a gear," says Steve.

"What do you mean?"

"Mate, you've done brilliantly. You're so much more mindful. You've proven that social media isn't the zenith of your existence. It's time to sack it off until the end of the year. I know your rules, the monthly check, looking for PTA or work stuff. But you don't need that monthly check, you're off the PTA, and you've been a journo long enough to find ways around the working requirement. So: no more Facebook, Instagram, Twitter, Strava, TikTok, Pinterest, whatever. Until 2021. You'll be fine."

I've not mentioned Pinterest in the book before as it's half a decade since I glanced at it. TikTok is this year's social media phenomenon, a video-sharing service in which users offer comedy or lip-syncing clips. In April it surpassed two billion worldwide downloads – 315 million in the year's first quarter alone. Given that its rise has tallied with my year off social media, I don't even have an account. No worries on either of those fronts.

As for the other four, Steve is right. I love the thought of tearing up the project's rulebook and abandoning Facebook, Insta, and Twitter. It'll be a real test of whether I can go without them permanently.

Strava, however, requires additional discussion.

"Okay, you're right about quitting," I reply after taking a few minutes to ponder his proposition. "No more of the big three until next year. But I need to negotiate with you on the Strava front."

"Fine. Imagine I'm representing your entire readership. Convince me and you'll convince them. Maybe."

"Running has been key to my mental health this year," I explain. "And while the occasional backslaps on Strava have been welcome, it's the numbers recorded on there which have kept me going: segments, distance, times, challenging myself to push ahead. Looking inward, rather than outwards, like you said earlier. I'm at 945km for the calendar year. I desperately want to see that total tick over the 1,000km mark. The book has been a brilliant way of tracking my mental ups and downs. That app has done the same for my physical ones, and I'd rather not lose that for two critical months."

Steve considers this for a bit, then comes back at me.

"So, I reckon you keep Strava, but only to be used as a solo enterprise. No Liking anyone else's runs or rides. No interacting if someone comments on yours. No adding photos, and no editorialisation – you have to use the default title for each workout. So even 'Stevening Run' has to be left as 'Evening Run'. You do a workout, you hit save, then step away until the next time you run."

It's a fair compromise, although I am nervous about blanking the few followers I do have for two months. But that impoliteness can be explained away in the New Year. Steve has freshened up the project in a way which should have a big impact on how I choose to return on 1 January. That date being a mere 61 days away just does not seem real.

Monday 2 November

When it comes to shutting down your Facebook and Instagram accounts there's a key difference between deactivation and deletion.

It's important I select the correct option this morning as I put Steve's new rules into practice. If I can't access Facebook and Instagram then I may as well switch them off completely until 2021. However, I would like to have the option of coming back, depending on how the next two months play out.

Deleting your account informs Facebook of your intention to leave forever. Even then you do get a cooling-off period in order to reverse your decision. Officially it's 14 days, although unconfirmed reports suggest you can still make a back-from-oblivion return up to 90 days after quitting.

No action so drastic for me. I'm taking the deactivation route, which for both Facebook and Instagram can be reversed by simply signing back in when ready. There are horror stories of users being unable to re-access accounts after years away, but at this juncture I'm only planning to take a few weeks.

This is it, then. I sign into Facebook for one last time this year, and deactivate. Within seconds I've done the same on Insta. No more PTA group, no more mid-month @ replies check.

Twitter presents an issue pertaining to work. Time to be straight with Sam Loveridge. "Hello! So long as it's cool with you, I'm giving up social media completely across November and December," I message. "As you know despite leaving Twitter in January I've still been using it occasionally for professional reasons via a semi-anonymous account. My new plan is to ditch that. I'll still access other resources and liaise with [news editor] Ben T to source screenshots and discuss potential stories."

"Sounds good to me!" replies Sam. "Not a problem." As occurs a lot in my existence, I've spent hours worrying about a theoretical life roadblock yet it's been happily circumnavigated in one conversation. You'd think I'd learn.

With professional worries waved away, I'm committed to exiting Twitter – but can't deactivate because of the book you're currently reading. I've recently been pitching it to agents in the hope of publication, and one of the key elements of that pitch is a link to my Twitter account, which has been dormant since 29 December 2019. To turn off that account would directly affect my chances of this book ever being released, as potential agents would have no means of viewing it.

How very meta and fourth-wall breaking, huh?

Instead I shall lock myself out. You may recall that I deleted Twitter on my phone and iPad long ago; it's my MacBook which is used for work checks via @wrestlingquiz. So I shall seal off that avenue. This requires the download of a free Google Chrome extension called BlockSite, whereby you can ban the use of up to six websites. I input twitter.com as a restricted site and then test it out by typing that URL into my search bar.

"No way, Jose," the screen screams back at me in super-sized font. "You put twitter.com in your BlockSites list. It's probably there for a reason."

I quite enjoy the automated scolding. Might as well use all six free slots, so as extra security measures I also add Facebook and Instagram, Pinterest and TikTok (just to placate Steve) and cpfc.org. Finally, truly, I'm a lone wolf. Alright, fine, a quarantined poodle.

Tuesday 3 November

This year's regular KonMari-ing has come up trumps. The house has been sold, subject to contract. Our first listing, immediately after lockdown was lifted in June, garnered minimal interest given my clutter evident in every photo. A more recent October one, featuring photos of a nearly empty home, has fared significantly better, and led to a concrete sale. That's common sense; but my hoarding often overrode common sense. It was unthinkable at the year's outset that I'd end up content to store, sell, or charity shop more than half my possessions.

It's changed the type of home I'm keen to find, too. No more need to house 150 Funko Pops, three wardrobes' worth of T-shirts and/or Blockbuster Video Streatham's entire back catalogue. The girls and I will make do with whatever is affordable, and continue to downsize as necessary. So long as there's space for their beds, a functioning kitchen, and – with Glasto 2021 now looking precarious – sufficient room in the garden for Tenty McTentface.

Oh, and a few records. Hold the 226th page: we've not covered that little addiction yet, have we?

Wednesday 4 November

Three years ago I fished my meagre record collection – all '80s, mostly tat – out of the attic with a view to dumping it on the local buy/sell/swap Facebook group. The same day, a resident down the road listed a grubby record player for £20, so I figured I may as well give some of it a listen first. I popped across the neighbourhood, paid for the small unit, plugged it into my home stereo, stuck on Def Leppard's *Hysteria*, and was hooked. Within days I'd become a vinyl bore, telling friends and family that it just sounded deeper and better and warmer than all other music formats. Chiefly because it does sound deeper and better and warmer than all other music formats.

You may not agree, but I know a man who does: Iain Aitchison of Longwell Records. This gem of a shop in Keynsham, five miles from Bristol, has been trumpeted noisily by names as esteemed as Stephen Merchant, and as my collection has grown I've become a regular customer. My year off social media has revealed that while you can stay in touch with friends and family away from Facebook and Twitter, football clubs or entertainment venues or retail outlets such as this are tougher to keep up with day-to-day.

With lockdown kicking in at midnight, I've dashed over to drop a few quid on spinning grooves. For Iain, and the store, there's no question of ever departing social media. The shop opened in April 2015 and he says that becoming "really solid across all platforms" over the past three years has been instrumental to its success. Ironically, this oldest school of musical formats is now reliant on contemporary word-of-mouth to keep interest high.

"I had an events guy come in with posters and leaflets, and had to tell him that people are just not interested," Iain says. "It clogs the shop up. He's not into social media and he didn't really understand. I think most shops are similar social media wise, although we do a lot more comedy stuff. That's just my personality – it surprises me that I don't get annihilated. Keyboard warriors are everywhere. But we're so lucky. Because we're independent, we can do things that HMV can't do, like a record shop dance-off or a quick second-hand sale – around 80% of what we sell is used. We've got a radio show on Keynsham's local station where we just talk bollocks once a week."

Social media has enabled this little shop that could to foster its own mini-community. "Last Record Store Day I had one guy call me out on Facebook because he ordered a record online and it never arrived," says Iain. "I gave him a full refund but he kept insisting I had to 'fulfil my contract'. Everyone bombarded him in response. We've got 5,000 followers on Instagram, and they're so loyal. Hopefully that stems from how we operate. We try to be genuine, both in real life and on social media."

That genuineness has been picked up by a variety of celebs and musicians, thrilled to endorse the store via their own social media accounts. "Paul Cooper, who played Martin Mucklowe in *This Country*, does lots of charity stuff with us," says Iain. "Joe Sims from *Broadchurch* saw us on Instagram and wanted to come down. Artists like Idles, Sleaford Mods, Mike Peters of the Alarm: they're just normal people when they pop into the shop, but to the outside world seeing it happen on social media is all quite exciting. Stephen [Merchant] has a zillion followers and still gives us occasional tweets, and there's a German karaoke king called Uwe Baltner. He's got almost two million followers, and he follows us. He wears our T-shirts in his videos. That's incredible."

Advertising is affordable, and a massive plus point of social media. "I'm about to do a sale so I've spent £30 on Facebook and £6 on Instagram," Iain says. "For that six quid they will promote our post to 30,000 people for a week. It pisses all over getting a banner up somewhere. If we sell two records we make that money back. A banner would cost £100. In the past I tried advertising in music mags and the response was awful. £50 a month, and once every six months someone would say, 'I saw you in such and such.' That's another reason why social media works for us so well."

There must be some drawback? "Yeah, I take things personally," confesses Iain. "There can be jealousy. I've got a sort-of-mate who runs a shop and he only ever Likes negative comments about us. I'm laughing at it now but it's quite naughty, isn't it? It's bullying, really. I'd rather he just called me a dickhead so we could have a conversation about it. People can be snobby about stuff we sell, too. Like the Jason Donovan records you buy…"

Busted! No Donovan for me, today – instead, £30 worth of Bruce Springsteen, Hollywood Undead, and (just to maintain my reputation for camp '80s naffness) Bananarama. Because I remain steadfast in my claim that even Love in the First Degree sounds sensational on vinyl. For once, Iain might have cause to disagree.

Saturday 7 November

Four days after US election polls opened, following a protracted set of counts in coin-toss states such as Arizona and Wisconsin, Joe Biden has been announced as the United States' next president. It marks the end of four years in which social media, Twitter in particular, was predecessor Donald Trump's dominant promotional platform – constantly used to whip his 18 gazillion (being off Twitter, I can't check the exact number) followers into a frenzy.

Except Trump isn't going anywhere, yet. Rather than accept the outcome, he's spent much of those four days making claims of electoral fraud with zero evidence, and proclaiming that he'll contest close counts. Again, no doubt, to trigger a backlash from social media channels. If there has been uproar from his Twitter followers, it's not translated into volatile action. Protests in Arizona, Nevada, and Pennsylvania have typically only drawn a few hundred people, mainly chanting and praying – as is their right.

I've tried to avoid making this book political, but it's fair to confirm that four years ago I was publicly despondent about Hillary Clinton losing out to Trump. Had this election taken place in 2019, I'd probably have spent the next 48 hours celebrating. Instead, after realising the degree to which political warfare affects my mental health, I text a couple of friends to toast Biden's victory, and crack on with the expedited search for a new house. Prioritising things I can control over events I can't, just as Paul advised seven months back.

Wednesday 11 November

After two days of non-stop viewings, I've decided on a house. Now to engage my legendary negotiation skills.

My father-in-law (ex-father-in-law? We never did clear that up, did we?) has a peerless knack for getting free add-ons when booking a holiday or buying a vehicle or even eating in a pub. "Here's your bill, sir. Please accept this selection of complimentary desserts and vat of cognac on us. Also, here's a voucher for 150% off your next bill. Our pleasure!"

In contrast, I was tasked with handling telephone negotiations for our latest second-hand car purchase, as touched on in the June chapter.

Here's how it went:

Me: "Hi there! I'm interested in the 2002 Koenigsegg CC8S [obviously it wasn't, but humour me] advertised on your website. I see it's on for £6,500. My budget is £5,000. What's the best price you can do me?"

Salesman: "£6,500."

Me: "Yep, got that. I realise that I'm not going to get you down to five grand. But we could collect today if you could maybe meet me in the middle at £5,750?"

Salesman: "You are welcome to collect today. For £6,500."

Me: "Okay. That really is a stretch for us. Sorry. Would you go to… £6,200, maybe? My wife and I can be over to pick it up in an hour."

Salesman: "Great, we'll be open in an hour. The cost of the car is £6,500."

Me: "Okay, okay, I get it. Are there any additional features or upgrades we can have at that price? A cup-holder or two, a monthly valet for the first year, an Ed Sheeran album you've had kicking round the office for a few months? I don't even like Ed Sheeran…"

Salesman: "For £6,500 I'll throw in new mats under every seat. Also, it's missing a cigarette lighter cover. You can have a new one of those too."

Me: "Deal!"

Surprisingly, my offer on the house is immediately rejected out-of-hand.

Sunday 15 November

Back to running, albeit gingerly given my hamstring knack. Today produces a landmark moment as I surpass 1,000km for the year. That's the same distance as London to Marseille, or San Diego to Albuquerque, or Alice Springs to being very thirsty for a very long time indeed. Particularly if the 1,000km takes you 319 days, as is the case here. That analogy has surprised me just as much as it has you. But still 'yay', I think?

Tuesday 17 November

Sir David Attenborough's million-followers Instagram record claimed from the very best of *Friends*, AKA Jennifer Aniston, has already been re-broken by *Harry Potter* actor Rupert Grint. For the first time this year, I don't know what to write.

Wednesday 18 November

Second offer on the potential new house rejected out of hand. Is it considered bad form to have your former father-in-law handle home-purchasing negotiations on your behalf? Just wondering. On behalf of a friend.

Friday 20 November

Third, final 'take it or leave it' offer on the house accepted. Waaaaaaaaa!

With that mid-morning boost propelling me into action, my final KonMari project involves sorting through the entirely of my book collection. This is truly a seismic event, with loaded, heavy boxes crammed into the back of the garage. Prior to ferreting all our stuff away for house viewings we didn't have wall space, or subtle furnishing touches. We just had bookshelves.

Given that I'm officially downsizing, at least 50% need to go.

If you're ever desperate to make yourself wince 100 times over in quick succession, download the Music Magpie app and price up your book collection. Actually, there's no need – I can tell you now that it's pretty much worthless. Music Magpie buys up the rejects of your entertainment collection for pennies then sells them on at a mark-up, but – because of weighty postal costs – books often aren't even worth pennies. Charity shop or rubbish bin are your two options.

The upside is that many books are only a pound or two to buy back, second-hand: which I may well do, once I'm moved and settled. So the process isn't as soul-destroying as anticipated. By lunchtime I've filled the car with four weighty boxes bound for Mercy In Action, and set aside three throwaways which I never got round to reading, to browse over a well-earned-if-I-say-so-myself bottle of Coke and packet of FODMAP-friendly Hula Hoops. Yep, I'm truly pushing the boat out snacks-wise to celebrate the house news.

The first throwaway is *Why Are You So Fat?*, a collection of the best cricketing sledges by Gershon Portnoi. It's decent, dip-in-and-out fare, with lots of tales of Australians insulting their on-field opponents. The best story concerns legendary English batsman WG Grace being bowled out first-ball in a match against an unnamed opponent. As the bowler celebrated, Grace picked up the bails and placed them back on the stumps, announcing to his conqueror, "they've come here to see me bat, not to see you bowl." The umpire then let the match continue with Grace still at the crease.

Next is *Nice Cup of Tea and a Sit Down*: a compendium of British biscuits, written with an easily digestible blend of history, trivia, and mickey-taking. I learn from authors Nicey & Wifey that the Jammie Dodger is produced at a rate of 12 biscuits per second at manufacturer Burton's South Wales factory; that the famous McVitie's Hobnob is surprisingly younger than I am, having been introduced in the mid-1980s; best of all, that the history of the humble shortcake dates back to pagan winter solstice festivals. In Scotland, large bannocks were baked with edges decorated to look like the rays of the sun, marking the return of summer – which is why to this day authentic shortbread has wavy lines around its sides.

Best – and most juvenile – of the bunch is *Rude Britain*, by Rob Bailey and Ed Hurst. As that title suggests it's a collection of Britain's 100 rudest place names, and I tell myself that I'm far too mature to laugh at real-life places such as Wetwang, Prickwillow, Crotch Crescent, and Titlington Mount. My resolve, however, crumbles at the simple-yet-effective Twatt and magnificent Hill O' Many Stanes. Pick of the place-name pile is a tiny corner of North Lanarkshire: the fabulously monikered Blairmuckhole & Forestdyke Road. Maybe I'll hang onto that book after all.

Sunday 22 November

I love a Twitter thread and a Facebook list – especially any kind of top 10. They're two elements of social media I always enjoyed amid my other online stresses, and while circuiting the village today it strikes me that we've made it to the penultimate month without sneaking one onto these pages. So I figure it's time to fix that.

You've had a year of me banging on about running, and music, so let's bring them together to form the top 10 running songs of my year in the wilderness.

Sorry-not-sorry if they're uncool. Literally done with worrying about being considered cool. And so should you be.

In reverse order…

10. Robbie Williams: No Regrets. Praised this in February, shall do so again here. A great means of channelling past grievances into running rocket fuel. If you're still doubting its ability to subvert expectations then listen out for the Pet Shop Boys and Divine Comedy on backing vocals.

9. The Weeknd: Blinding Lights. 2020's biggest selling song and, unlike in most years, deserving of every digital download. Sounds like a-ha motoring down a Californian highway at 2am. Bittersweet on a personal level as it landed just as January Girl and I cooled things off, but it still has to be on here.

8. Pink: Beautiful Trauma. My running songs are different from what you'd find on *Now That's What I Call Plantar Fasciitis*. I need a beat, sure, but some emotion in the lyric is critical too. This is Pink at her sweariest and catchiest and most amorous, finding love with a kindred screw-up amid a cocktail of drugs, sex, and laughter.

7. Manic Street Preachers: Motorcycle Emptiness. An early-'90s attack on capitalism, but even if the political lyrics don't get your feet moving, its inimitable guitar riff and pleading refrain will. 'Epic' was a forbidden word in my magazine journalism days due to overuse. But it applies here, on the Manics' best song.

6. Walk The Moon: Shut Up and Dance. A love song you can truly move your feet to, on the dance floor, mosh pit, or village pavement. Makes you re-believe in 'the one' even when you've spent years dismissing 'the one' as something that only exists in the brain of Richard Curtis. (Not knocking Richard Curtis. *About Time* is my favourite film.)

5. Taylor Swift: I Wish You Would. While the August release of *Folklore* oozes credibility, I still marginally prefer Swift's synth-driven decade-of-birth inspired record *1989*. This is its most underrated track, laced with longing and heartfelt regret, and set at the ideal tempo for a breezy 5K.

4. Pet Shop Boys: Always On My Mind. An Elvis Presley classic by way of Willie Nelson, miraculously enhanced by the addition of Neil Tennant and synths. Christmas number one when I was an impressionable eight-year-old, the best ballad of the '80s, and the best cover version of all time. Yes it is. Please don't argue, we've come so far together.

3. Eminem: Lose Yourself. Slight switch of genre here. Its unmistakable riff and heartbeat bassline have pounded through sports arenas across the globe over the past two decades, with good reason: there's no greater anthem for seizing the moment and hurdling the roadblocks of life. (Or penning a book: this has also been my recurring cure for writer's block.)

2. Linkin Park: Waiting For The End. Piano intro, rap verse, boy-band bridge, rock ballad chorus, nu-metal middle eight, climactic harmony-driven outro, tied together by a rousing begin-again lyric: just an incredible, inspiring four minutes of music, made extra poignant by lead singer Chester Bennington's 2017 suicide. Staggering.

1. Kids In Glass Houses: Matters At All. The best Welsh-indie-pop-punk song you've never heard, peaking at a scandalous number 65 in the UK charts. Again taking chances in the now rather than regretting them for the rest of your days is the theme, this time with a romantic tinge – placed over a metronomic beat, spliced to a last-orders-at-the-bar chorus. Perfect for running, and drinking, and believing that great things are around the corner. My just-one-more-mile mainstay.

Monday 23 November

Top of the Pops 2 may have just proven me wrong on yesterday's Always On My Mind analysis. The Pet Shop Boys' '80s thumper might, just might, only be the second-greatest cover version ever.

Because, on tonight's throwback episode, I discover that Sinéad O'Connor's timeless Nothing Compares 2 U, tear-jerking soundtrack to a million break-ups, isn't her original work, but that of Prince Rogers Nelson. As in, The Artist Formerly Known As. As in, Love Symbol (or 'squiggle', if you prefer). As in, *the* Prince.

How, in nearly 15 years of being on social media, did I never realise this before? Wait, you already knew and let us get all the way through to November without telling me? Well. *Well.*

Wednesday 25 November

To attend primary school in the 1980s, and at the same time be obsessed with football, meant three things:

1. You had to collect Panini stickers. ("Got. Got. Got. Neeeeeeed!")
2. You had to support Liverpool. (I was one of the few to duck this stereotype, and boy did I get stick for it.)
3. You had to despise Diego Maradona.

Maradona was the Argentine maestro whose mix of dazzling skill and dastardly cunning single-handedly (and I do mean that literally) eliminated England from the 1986 World Cup. During a combustible quarter-final held just four years after the Falklands War, Maradona infamously used an outstretched arm to fist the ball past goalkeeper Peter Shilton, then effortlessly pirouetted through a maze of white shirts to bag a second. That decider was majestic, yet in the playgrounds of London, and Lincoln, and Liverpool, the first crime of passion was not forgotten, and in the ensuing years comeuppance for Diego was widely celebrated. When he was booted out of the same competition in 1994 for returning positive drug tests a nation of now-teenagers rejoiced.

That rejoicing, however, had taken on a pantomime quality, eight years following the 'Hand of God' goal. As the calendar turned from '80s into '90s, youngsters so keen to sully Maradona's name had come to a realisation: this was the greatest footballer or our generation. Neutering his bad-boy instincts would sterilise his magic at the same time. As he continued to conjure goals and assists for Napoli and Argentina, playground games transformed: where once everyone wanted to hate 'dodgy Diego', suddenly everyone wanted to be him.

Today, those dreams are lost forever. Maradona is dead, from a heart attack, aged 60.

News reports describe palpable grief across Argentina, where for so long he turned a workaday national team into one of the world's most consistent, winning that 1986 World Cup, finishing runners-up in 1990. But his loss is one felt the globe over, and again I don't need to be on social media to see tributes pouring in. Various sites embed tweets from elite sportspeople past and present, stretching far outside of football: basketball star Magic Johnson, cricketing great Sachin Tendulkar. They're all merited. Maradona epitomised '80s football: to see him depart this earth is to see a vast chunk of our youth ebb away with him.

Shortly before bedtime I receive a text from my dad. Football was our bonding tool upon his return from Dubai. Filling in those Panini albums, reading the Sunday back pages, attending my first London-based match: Tottenham vs Monaco, testimonial for Glenn Hoddle, in February 1988. He was the first to explain that I had Maradona wrong. So while my social media ban prevents me soaking up memories of the average fan, dad's recollections go some way to making up for it.

"Actually felt quite emotional about the passing of the great Maradona," reads his text. "For me and I think many others he transcended not only the sport but national elegances. He was simply the greatest footballer that has ever played the game to date. When he achieved with a mediocre national side in '86, scoring THAT goal and THAT goal then pretty much winning the tournament on his own was amazing. The fact he was also a flawed genius added to his allure by us mere mortals. RIP Maradona."

Friday 27 November

A productive phone consultation with the school's speech and language specialist confirms November's suspicions. Little Blue is likely autistic. She may have SPD (Sensory Processing Disorder), where – for example – the brain can be overly sensitive to smell, taste, and/or touch. It could be Asperger's Syndrome, which is characterised by difficulties related to change and social interactions.

Girls mask autism well, we're informed, and the road ahead is a long one, beginning with referral to a paediatrician.

Suddenly so many of Little Blue's traits, previously pinned on the 'terrible twos', 'troublesome threes', and 'FFS fours', make sense. She's ruthlessly fussy over food, constantly wants to be naked because "my clothes itch", and baulks at going anywhere near the toilet unless actively needing to pee or poo in that exact moment. Last year her favourite toyshop had a Christmas Disco event, with a DJ bashing out festive hits – where the mix of loud noise and change from routine sent her haywire. Floods of tears and screams of terror ensued, only to be replaced with smiles and chatter 90 seconds after driving away.

Today's conversation, then, is upsetting – yet the chat is a relief too. We've consistently told the girls that being ordinary is boring. I stand by that. Little Blue has always been what friends call 'a character': quirky, kooky, stiflingly shy one minute, a mini pantomime queen the next. Now we know why. Whereas 18 months ago I'd have reacted to such news by broadcasting it on social media to invite advice and support and love, today I feel more restrained. I can parse this development privately. I, and we as a patchwork family, can cope.

Sunday 29 November

Three nights ago Steve proposed a new December on-foot challenge: either three miles', or 25 minutes', running every day. I've said yes because a. it's in the rules and b. I'm an idiot. It nixes plans for a half marathon in the year's final month because that'd require a recovery period, so I head out for my final of the project tonight, finishing in just short of two hours five minutes.

On 1 January, one half marathon this year felt like a fictional aspiration; to have managed five is 'pinch-me' territory. And probably 'punch-me' territory from your perspective, so you have my word that we're done with the running updates from here until December's climax.

Monday 30 November

Unlike *The Joshua Tree* era Bono, I've finally found what I'm looking for. Conclusive evidence of the link between materialism and social media, explaining my obsession with buying endless things I don't need, in order to curry favour on Twitter and Facebook.

The average number of Facebook friends any individual has is 338. In the opening chapter I mentioned mine being 838 – hardly sufficient to herald me the next Dwayne Johnson, but sufficient to suggest I'm not universally despised. (Yet.) However, a study by scientist Phillip Ozimek confirms that my above-average number has zero to do with popularity. Instead, as he explains: "The higher [a person's] chronic materialism, the higher their number of Facebook friends and the higher their tendency to objectificate and instrumentalize them in order to reach personal goals."

Ozimek's work, carried out at the Ruhr-University of Bochum across subjects aged 17 to 52, incorporated a 62-question survey assessing each respondent's Facebook habits (watching, impressing, acting) and materialistic attitude – for instance, being asked to respond to the statement, 'I admire people who own expensive homes, cars, and clothes,' on a scale of one to five. It found that the more materialistic someone is, the more prolific they are on social media in general: "Materialism can predict the amount of Facebook friends, social comparison, objectification and instrumentalization… these variables in turn appear as mediators predicting the frequency of Facebook use."

"Materialists use Facebook more frequently," it summarises, "because they are eager to compare themselves with other users, and have more Facebook friends, whom they can objectificate and instrumentalize."

I expected Ozimek's study to cement the link between materialism and social media use, having figured that, subconsciously, all my Funko Pop purchasing and posturing might be down to vanity. What I wasn't prepared for was learning that my addition of Facebook pals over the years – and, I now suspect, having a monthly numbers tracker in this book – came from the very same place. Racking up 800+ friends had little to do with me wanting to be close to every new colleague or long-lost schoolmate. It was a high score on a real-life arcade machine. A maddening, modern alternative to *Donkey Kong*. With me as the blundering, clueless ape. No wonder I had no one to turn to during that cancer scare.

I am, truly, embarrassed, as I write this. As much as I have been at any part of this project. I took so much offence at a few friends not attending a birthday party, yet Ozimek's study shows me up as the hypocrite of hypocrites. It's a humbling way to end the project's penultimate month, and a wake-up call as regards my own Facebook usage when I switch my account back on as the first strains of Auld Lang Syne ring out.

End of month stats: November 2020

Weight: 13st 12lb
Twitter followers: N/A
Facebook friends: N/A
Instagram followers: N/A
Average sleep: 6h 22min
Books read: 3 – David Jason: Only Fools and Stories, *Dawn French:* According to Yes, *Peter Ames Carlin:* Catch a Wave: The Rise, Fall and Redemption of The Beach Boys' Brian Wilson
Distance run: 115.6km
Time running: 11h 1min
Best 5K time: 23min 14s
Best 10K time: 56min 50s
Best half marathon time: 2h 4min 45s

DECEMBER

Tuesday 1 December

At this project's inception I hoped the year's final month would bring emphatic answers, and tie things up in resplendent bows. It was a lofty ambition for any 52-week period – let alone one which went on to be decimated by a pandemic. As a result those best intentions had to be amended, sometimes abandoned, on the fly.

Take sleep. As documented in the monthly stats, I'm still nowhere close to the recommended eight hours a night. Once it became clear that leaving social media wasn't a cure, I intended to submit myself to a clinical study which would assess breathing issues such as apnea and other nocturnal failings. But the standard NHS waiting time for the examination is 10 weeks, and it felt especially non-pertinent to request a GP referral with Covid running rife. Instead I looked into private alternatives, only to baulk at fees deep into four figures. My shambolic shuteye abilities therefore remain unresolved.

Similarly erratic was the January plan to have friend and family recommendations steer my year. On the TV and films front, this went well, just in ways that didn't feel right to crowbar into the book. The best thing I watched was superlative US show *Good Trouble*, the tale of two adoptive sisters moving to LA and trying to make their way while living in a commune – a recommendation by Amber, at our August farewell to the local toddler group. Similarly, during my Longwell Records trip in November, boss Iain insisted I check out the Britpop band Menswear's lost album *Hay Tiempo*. It didn't disappoint, and next time you put down this tome I urge you to immediately download Wait For The Sun and Tomorrow.

Unplanned travel, and socialising, was a different story. Coronavirus saw terms such as 'the rule of six' become commonplace, and brought severe curfews for pubs and restaurants. I ventured to Salisbury to see Colum, but otherwise this rule had to be annulled. When my cousin Scott invited me for a night out in Oxfordshire following my Uncle Dave's funeral, I initially said yes – but ultimately had to defer until 2021. The rules said I should go. But my instincts felt it reckless, and I figured you'd be okay with me forsaking one night out, with social distancing, and a 10pm finish.

If not, I owe you one socially distanced night out. In Oxfordshire. With a 10pm finish. Six people, max.

This tale, then, is not one which will be flawlessly sutured in 31 days' time. But isn't that life? I'm still excited about the project's final month, and not just because it contains two birthdays and one Christmas. It's time to reflect on the year and ponder the road ahead. To catch up with friends and family, even if it's just over WhatsApp. To run, and enjoy festive films, and limitless Wham listenings, and guilt-free alcohols on all of the days whose names end in '-day'.

Friday 4 December

Westonbirt Arboretum's annual Enchanted Christmas event is the one time of year when my Instagram skills advance from pathetic to passable. Set amid 15,000 trees spread across 600 hectares, it sees its firs, cedars, and pines prettily lit in a kaleidoscope of colours, then complemented by holographic displays and actors playing elves and Santa. Such scenery is a guarantee of gorgeous family snaps, which historically meant me mainlining Facebook to share whenever we sat down for steaming chips or mulled cider.

There's no such option today, and it changes the experience dramatically. I realise that in previous years my entire focus has been on finding, lining up, and completing Insta-worthy photos, rather than enjoying family moments as they unfolded. Anything that wasn't captured by a click of my phone failed to register. The revelation ties in with what I wrote about WrestleMania in April. I've consumed so much time and energy living experiences in ways which can be painted as idyllic online, I've often forgotten to actually enjoy them in the first person.

Tonight, I'm content to breathe it all in with the girls. They're enthralled, and enjoy lots of sisterly moments holding hands and sharing conspiratorial whispers which I'd have missed if glued to my phone. This type of event has always tested our different parenting methods; it's telling that Mrs E and I end it not just on speaking terms, but working together to manage Little Blue having a wild tantrum in the on-site shop when not allowed to purchase a dinosaur egg. The event goes so successfully that we're among the final few stragglers to depart, returning to a lonely car which had been surrounded upon arrival.

Leaving social media hasn't fixed an irreparable marriage. But it's made me more conscious of ways in which I was culpable for its demise, such as placing my focus elsewhere at events like this while Mrs E shepherded two tired, testy toddlers. I can't turn back the clock and become a better husband. But the metamorphic lessons learned this year will make me a better father, and more amicable ex. And hopefully Westonbirt is a tradition we can continue together, whatever the directions of our tree-less paths.

Tuesday 8 December

A positive day in this most dreadful of years. At University Hospital in Coventry, 90-year-old Margaret Keenan becomes the first person in the world to be vaccinated against coronavirus. Her shot in the arm is the first of 800,000 doses created by Pfizer which will be rolled out in the UK in the coming days. The US is also expecting to approve the injection imminently, with incoming president Joe Biden promising 100 million vaccinations in his first 100 days in office.

It's a day where social media's positive effects are inarguable – both in offering vaccine hope, and something more subtle, but similarly cheery. Images of Keenan being injected have been shared globally, with her choice of T-shirt for the occasion – a cartoon penguin in front of a snowy backdrop above the words 'Merry Christmas' – drumming up widespread joy, as demonstrated in a selection of tweets shared by numerous news sites. The shirt was created by the University Hospitals Coventry & Warwickshire Charity, with £4,000 being raised by online orders in the wake of Keenan becoming a social media trend. "We are only a small charity, but we have seen sales of the T-shirt triple and have had to order more stock," director Jo O'Sullivan tells the BBC. Super.

Friday 11 December

Most top-tier artists take two or three years to craft an album. At 5am this morning, Taylor Swift drops her second in five months. *Evermore* is a sister record to July release *Folklore*, and if there's been any social media speculation about it I've inevitably missed out.

Not that it takes long to get up to speed. *Evermore* is slightly more poppy than its summer sibling, although still woodsy and earthy and a departure from Swift's seven pre-2020 releases. Again Bon Iver guest on the wistful title track, while lead single Willow initially feels weaker than a host of others – not that this stops the girls from requesting its video on repeat via YouTube throughout the day.

The sultry Ivy is one of two standouts, a symbol of Swift's songwriting maturity, as the album's catchiest refrain accompanies its most desperate lyric. It's the tale of a female character realising she's married to one man while covered in the roots of another, where you're implored to sympathise with the narrator despite her adulterous temptations. Even better is No Body No Crime, where Swift teams with Haim – the all-sister act we encountered on these pages during Glastonbenny. Its howling sirens, vengeful harmonicas and chant-along country chorus is so disturbing, and unconventional, that Lady S leaves the room whenever it comes on: slightly problematic given my insistence that it's the album's best song. Post-9pm play only for that one, then.

Swift began the year typecast as an image-focussed pop damsel. She ends it as a prolific poet, wearing cottage-core outfits with pared-down hair, dropping folky tunes oozing melancholy and depth – some of which are only fit for post-watershed consumption. Unthinkable at the outset of 2020, but what hasn't been?

Sunday 13 December

The build-up to Christmas is a testing time for any parent. The kids are knackered from the grind of school and waking up at 5.55am each day in order to prise a crumb of chocolate from a cheap cardboard-foil monstrosity. You're exhausted from present buying, and big day planning, and one-too-many Friday night sherries. Alright, one-too-many every night sherries.

Then there's the internal dialogue. So many questions. Have you over-spoiled the kids, or under-bought? Are the school being ironic by casting your daughter as an angel in the nativity? Does she know her lines? Can they wear other items of mufti on Christmas Jumper day? Can they wear Christmas Jumpers on mufti day? There are still 12 days to go yet healthy eating has gone out the window, along with any sense of rationality. You're cranky, and temperamental, and not even the thought of 25 December pigs in blankets – the best thing about Christmas Day other than your cherubs' faces at 7.45am, though even that is a close call – can pull you back from the brink.

It's all too much. Until, amid all the December stress, your eldest asks a question which proves that you have at least got one critical element of parenting right.

"Daddy, can we watch *Home Alone*?"

Tuesday 15 December

Even after 24 years I can recall the reaction at school when the UK's biggest pop act of the '90s, Take That, split up. 13 February 1996. A day of tears and confusion and the sense that life would never be the same again. My female classmates seemed pretty upset too.

My eldest has a few years' head start on them, as Mrs E drops a pre-breakfast bombshell pertaining to Lady S's favourite band. All-girl quartet Little Mix were the first group she ever saw live, at the Birmingham NEC aged just four, and remain the one act occasionally permitted to override Swift in the car. So the news that Jesy Nelson has departed is too much for her brain to deal with.

Thankfully there's no sobbing on Lady S's part. Only questions. "Why has Jesy left?" ["To protect her mental health."] "Is she gone forever?" ["I suspect she'll be back performing someday."] "Will they get a replacement? ["Not if they've learned any lessons from the Sugababes."] "Can we listen to Power now?" ["Always."]

Actually, I was never a particular Take That fan but I do remember friends being devastated, and not knowing how to cope. So while the pressures of Twitter and Facebook have undoubtedly expedited Nelson's departure, those social media formats also have a positive role to play in enabling 'Mixers' to share both their grief, and support for the singer. She deserves it, too: it's a brave, groundbreaking move to admit to prioritising one's own mental health over fame and career opportunities. *The Independent* reports that her Instagram post doing exactly that has 1.7 million Likes. This instructive year has taught me to largely avoid judging anything on the number of hearts afforded it on social media but, in this case, that figure seems consequential.

Wednesday 16 December

Little Blue's birthday. No big party. No social media. Modest, private, chilled. Pretty much perfect.

Saturday 19 December

41. Forty-effing-one! Throughout my teens I assumed that I would wake up one birthday morning, perhaps in my early thirties, hear a noise like the clicking of a seat belt and think, 'this is it. You're a grown-up now. Happy adulting.'

That click never came. Instead I used birthdays as another means of seeking popularity and validation. Inviting out every friend under the sun and invariably trying too hard to be 'cool'. Usually, it ended miserably. On my 18th my mum went to the effort of hiring a karaoke DJ; before 10pm I'd been thrown off the equipment midway through Be My Baby for repeatedly dropping the mic, then collapsed into a urinal. My 21st climaxed in Colum and I having a punch-up on Balham High Street. Then there's my 40th, overshadowed – as previously outlined – by a few non-attendees at a party on the previous Saturday.

With a bit of introspection I now realise that day, documented at the time in one of my final posts before exiting Instagram, was a cracker. An hour browsing the local independent record store (picking up Chesney Hawkes' The One and Only on 12", a month before learning of his wondrous connection to Sue and Mel), an unhurried and edacious coffee-shop catch-up with Amber, an afternoon board gaming with the girls while yapping to Lindo and Hazel and January Girl over WhatsApp, a family meal in the evening. Why did I need more than that? Why did I let events of the weekend cloud a fantastic 40th?

I spend today effectively having a 40th do-over. Mixing restrictions prevent me coffee shopping with anyone from a different household, but I do head into Midsomer Norton to grab a couple of vinyls – Kate Nash reissue *My Best Friend Is You*, timeless Cheap Trick single I Want You to Want Me – before spending the afternoon swapping messages with close friends. Lindo meets me for an early evening can of gin in the local park, before I head to a first-rate eatery, La Campagna, with Mrs E and the girls.

It's not rock and roll. It'd barely warrant mention on Insta. Critically, it's enough. Plenty. Birthday wishes from distant friends are still welcome, and a scattering arrive during the day, but they're no longer a fundamental element of me enjoying the occasion. Being off social media barely registers. Neither does a football score which would have been a birthday wrecker in any year previous: Crystal Palace 0, Liverpool 7.

No party, no problem. No sign of that telltale seat belt click either, but I do feel like I've done a ton of growing up in the last year. Turning 40, leaving social media, navigating the girls through a pandemic: however cliched it sounds, I feel a different person at 41 to this day last year.

Whether that's reflected in these pages I'll leave you to decide. Please at least join me for a birthday Baileys while you ponder it. Cheers!

Sunday 20 December

As originally outlined in our March visit to the *Mendip Times*, a plus point of West Country living is the novel information delivered by local news. Today brings a textbook example. It's five days until Christmas, Covid numbers are rising again, half the country has had its 25 December plans curtailed by a sudden shift in government policy – and yet the top item on the Somerset Live home page is:

'The reason Bridgwater only has one "E" in its name.'

[Covid updates rank fourth, after a feature on 21 examples of bad parking across the county, and a general knowledge quiz.]

Negligent? Brilliant? A bit of both? I'm going for option B. With coronavirus dominating the global and national news (and, Mrs E reports, her Facebook feed) a bit of escapism is welcome. Even if the story itself is a bit cheeky. It offers no conclusive solution to the Bridgwater mystery, instead positing two theories. One is that under its original name of Brigg the town was gifted to the Walter of Douai during the Norman invasion, hence Brigg-Walter. The other is that it was once known as Bridge of Walter, and the E got lost via a name change to Bridg-of-Walter before later being truncated further.

Either way it's distracted me and a few thousand other Somerset residents from the pandemic for three minutes on a Sunday morning, so I can only offer our local news hounds a wave of cheers. Or, as one might say while motoring up the A38, a wavchers.

Monday 21 December

While most travel recommendations have had to be ditched in this stay-at-home year, Mrs E and I saved a special one for Christmas. For as long as we've been parents, friends have been compelling us to visit Stourhead.

Stourhead is a National Trust owned estate in Wiltshire, 10 miles south of Warminster, whose name derives from it being the source of the River Stour. Its mile-long Christmas trail is fabled for an uplifting mix of twinkly lights, fairground rides, and arts and crafts, although the latter offering is reduced this year due to the need for social distancing. Still, our fears of being ripped off at having shelled out £72 are soon dispelled. The circular tour of the grounds is a step up from both Westonbirt and another family favourite we've chosen to sit out this year, Longleat.

Highlights are plentiful. In one clearing, disco balls hang in the trees while bathed in pink light: bung some Bruno Mars on and you'd have the South West's coolest, if chilliest, dance floor. Unless you're not an Uptown Funk fan, in which case our friendship ceases here. In a larger open area, balls of flame lick at intricate carvings of five gold rings, three French hens and, yes, a pear-tree complete with partridge, an astounding visual with the added bonus of temporary warmth. Further along, a trail of sparkling hearts ends with a spotlight over which hangs giant mistletoe. Mrs E and I attempt to pass silently and awkwardly, but Lady S insists on puckering up to the camera.

I'm glad she's inherited my romantic tendencies. I probably won't be when she's 17.

The girls are captivated. Aside from the unspoken mistletoe avoidance, Mrs E and I are as laid-back together as we've been in years – to passing strangers we appear a united family. This year has brought genuine amicability. Leaving social media has been a major factor in that, as showcased on memorable nights like this and Westonbirt.

Wednesday 23 December

Back to Bristol for a festive catch-up with Lauren and Andy H. This time out they've taken me to Left Handed Giant, an independent brewhouse overlooking Bristol Harbour. Happiness comes in three forms. The excellent company. The almost-as-great Sky Above pale ale, scrumptiously malt-based with just a tease of citrus. And the in-house Proper Job pizza, slathered with sausage and jalapeños – and gluten, to form the most worthwhile of Christmas guilty pleasures.

I figure the above is sufficient for a brief, merry book entry. Until Snog Marry Avoid happens.

In Snog Marry Avoid, you're given three names and have to decide which to kiss, which to hitch, and which to run a mile from. Andy and Lauren have been bingeing *True Blood* of late, so she and I confer to offer Andy three characters from that show. His response: avoid Bill Compton, snog Sookie Stackhouse, marry Eric Northman. I'm yet to meet a *True Blood* fan, male or female, who wouldn't marry Eric Northman.

I prime three *Avengers* favourites for Lauren: Chris Hemsworth (Thor), Tom Hiddleston (Loki), and Mark Ruffalo (Hulk). As with the Glastonbenny artists list, she immediately tries to break the rules.

"There's no bad choices here. Can I not snog-marry them all?"

"No!" Andy and I answer in unison.

"I'd probably snog Chris Hemsworth. Marry Tom Hiddleston. And avoid Mark Ruffalo. But only because he's, like, the worst of the best three choices ever and you're forcing me to avoid someone…"

My turn. These guys know how much I love a festive hit, so I'm anticipating a selection along the lines of "Shane MacGowan, Mariah Carey, Emilia Clarke in *Last Christmas* garb". Except there's a glint in Lauren's eye. Mischief. Revenge. Payback for the *Avengers* conundrum. For insisting on the Ruffalo no-go.

"Facebook, Twitter, Instagram," says Lauren. "Snog, marry, avoid?"

"Ha, very good."

"No, really. After this year you're in a strong position to judge. So: Facebook, Twitter, Instagram?" Lauren is smiling wickedly now. "With consequences."

"Riiiiight…"

"Whichever you choose to avoid you have to stay away from once this year is up."

Oh shit.

"Oh shit! Permanently?"

"Let's say three months. Enough for it to be meaningful. Then it's your choice whether or not to go back."

Okay. Wow. Christ. For all my thinking aloud over the last few chapters, I've still not reached any firm conclusion over when to return, nor how frequently.

Now my hand is being forced. Still, maybe it's the kick up the backside I need. My first of three answers is blurted out before I can overthink it.

"Avoid Twitter. I've been taught some positives about it this year. But I don't miss the toxicity, the posturing, the anxiety. I'm in no rush to go back."

I'm torn on the others. At the end of a year where I started out content to bemoan Facebook and Instagram, I've mellowed at the prospect of reconnecting with both. It's a coin toss. The guys can tell. I find myself staring into my Sky Above pondering an answer for more seconds than is comfortable, even among close friends.

"Commit to Instagram," says Lauren, shattering the silence. "Facebook has too many racist uncles talking up conspiracy theories."

"Don't think Jenny Frost is permitted to steer!" I reply. "But, er, thanks. Do I not look vapid for marrying Instagram though? It's a world of pretty pictures."

"Ben, dude, you're marrying a social media network," laughs Lauren. "I'm fairly sure vapid is just *there*."

"They're all going to stab you in the back eventually, mate," adds Andy. "Marry Instagram. It's nice, and pretty, and it's not going to give you much shit."

"And snog Twitter!" says Lauren. "Because Twitter's dirty, and it's got a short memory. No long-term complications."

"Noooo!" I won't be swayed on Twitter, but I have let the guys talk me round on the other pair. "Okay. Marry Instagram, snog Facebook, avoid Twitter."

Just like that, one decision pertaining to my return is set in stone.

"Can we do my real turn now, guys? Snog Shane, marry Emilia, avoid Mariah, just because I couldn't handle the all-summer-long renditions of All I Want For Christmas Is You."

Two smiling faces are replaced by two masks of utter befuddlement.

Friday 25 December

It'd be dangerous to suggest that everyone could benefit from taking Christmas Day off social media. For the elderly, the lonely, the anxious, this can be one of the most difficult periods of the year, and I'm emphatically behind every individual doing whatever is necessary to feel supported. A personal priority today is checking in on Paul, after his challenging year of loss and reflection. The response comes quickly and cheerily. While missing his dad, he is in good spirits and looking forward to a catch-up in the new year. As am I.

For myself, Mrs E and the girls, fortunate to be ensconced in our own bubble, being off social media for the day results in the most relaxed, friction-free Christmas since doubling in number.

I'm embarrassed to say that previously we've settled into stereotypical gender roles for 25 December: Mrs E in the kitchen preparing a belly busting lunch and then handling the clean-up, while I help construct the girls' new toys and get to play Fun Dad, broadcasting our amusements on Twitter and Facebook. I'm dumbstruck and a tad ashamed by that imbalance now, and although Mrs E still kindly insists on the lunch prep, we swap roles for the afternoon. She gets the enjoyment of putting together an enormous Lego *Frozen* castle in front of *Nativity 3: Dude, Where's My Donkey?!* (yes, that's a real film – featuring David Tennant, no less), I get to oversee operation clean-up. Not just the turkey carcass and best crockery, either: I end up emptying the fridge and cupboards, effectively KonMari-ing every food item in the house. Soundtracked by Swift's *Evermore* it's peaceful and practical and a little bit cathartic. Anyone want some lime juice dated April 2019?

The evening is equally balanced and stress-free. Lady S and I make 'Happy Christmas' video messages for more than a dozen friends and family members; I send these out individually, then dispatch additional festive wishes to a mix of cousins, former work colleagues, and other distant friends who I know are likely spending the day alone. The following four hours are spent lost in conversations about kids, and festive ups and downs, and all of this year's idiosyncrasies – with most of the names mentioned in the book, and at least 20 who aren't. It's so lovely that I don't really know how to conclude this entry without sounding dopey and schmaltzy and whatever the five other dwarfs are called. So I won't try to.

Monday 28 December

Late in the day, maybe I do have an explanation for my insomnia after all.

Steve's comment about looking inward at the start of November inspired me to do exactly that. Mercifully, I don't mean via colonoscopy. Rather, I paid a mind-boggling £149 to use a health and ancestry service called 23andMe in order to trace my roots beyond South London and Exeter. My tube of saliva was packed off in mid-November, and the results are here.

It was intended as a fun way of closing out the project, but the findings are enlightening. Particularly on nocturnal habits: "Based on your genetics you are not likely to be an especially deep sleeper." Got that right. Tally it with another DNA finding – "you are likely to drink slightly more caffeine than average" – and it's little wonder I'm so crap at bedding down.

Those observations could be considered a fortunate punt, but the report as a whole is too accurate for me to write off. It's correct on my eye and hair colour, lifelong dandruff issues (sexy times!), and interminable weight struggles: "Your genetic result is associated with a 6% higher BMI on diets with more than 22 grams of saturated fat per day." Incredibly, after 41 years, it even explains my gluten intolerance. I have a variant detected in the HLA-DQA1 gene, which increases my risk of coeliac disease.

As for the ancestry statistics, I learn I'm 55.3% British & Irish, 40.1% French & German, 2.6% Broadly Northwestern European, 1.5% Scandinavian, and 0.5% Arab. Wherever my love life heads next, I won't be fooling anyone into thinking I'm Alexander Skarsgård. Particularly given the final revelation to follow. Mrs E and the girls especially enjoy this one, and it may well tally with your instincts as we bring this project to a close.

"Out of the 7,462 variants we tested, we found 260 variants in your DNA that trace back to the Neanderthals," explains the app. "Benjamin, you have more Neanderthal DNA than 79% of other customers."

Wednesday 30 December

Following up Kate's October question about the time reclaimed by leaving social media, I've put together some numbers of the year. Again sticking to the idea that I was spending 75 minutes per day on Twitter, Facebook, or Insta in 2019, I've got 27,375 minutes of my life back. That equates to 456 hours – or 19 full days.

Including the year-ending 10K planned for tomorrow I've completed 163 runs, over a total time of 118 hours and 35 minutes – just short of five days. I completed five half-marathons. My total distance for the year is 1,262km, roughly equivalent to running from my house in the west of England to Norway (north), Poland (east), or Portugal (south). I climbed 12,085 metres during those runs, the equivalent of almost nine trips up Ben Nevis. My December tally alone, thanks to Steve's run-daily challenge – tiring but incident- and injury-free – is 201.5km. All of which led to me shedding a stone and a half in weight.

I'm emphasising these stats as a reminder that I am not a distance runner. I'm 41 years old, my knees are rickety, my hamstrings are shot, and I'm still classed as 'overweight' from a BMI perspective. If you're willing to consider a programme like Couch to 5K, and can find a way of swapping social media apps for a pair of trainers for 90 minutes per week, you can rack up similar stats – far better stats! – over the next 12 months.

I read 37 books, which averages out at 0.7 per week, or 3.1 each month. I put on one pretend music festival, featuring 22 acts 'broadcast' on YouTube or

Netflix, which resulted in the donation of £120 to charity. I hosted one PlayStation-based international football tournament, playing all 51 matches.

I launched two YouTube channels. The girls' collection of silly cover versions was followed in November by my own casual acoustic project Rainstoppedplay. I've spent 22 years writing songs for fun. It's been rewarding to find a corner of the internet for them to sit, again without any pressure for traffic or validation.

Sadly, I missed more birthdays than I can possibly acknowledge here.

The extended break caused my productivity to soar. As well as my typical sports editor workload I also spent an hour each day, often much longer, writing this book. So if you're thinking of taking a similar social media hiatus, that's at least 366 hours of free time with which to make a start on *Good Trouble*, or get yourself acquainted with the entire Chvrches back catalogue.

There was even a financial benefit, thanks to the KonMari clearouts and reduction in all things materialistic. It would be grotesque to specify an exact sum, but as a general idea let's revisit some of spring's homeschooling methods. If Benjamin has 150 geeky Funko Pop figures, and he sells more than half of them during lockdown, and the average sale price is almost £9, what sum has he added to the new-house kitty for frittering away on Jason Donovan records and pink gin?

Critically, I spent so much more quality time with my two daughters, and rebuilding bridges with my ex-wife, which will potentially stand us in good stead as single parents, prioritising Lady S and Little Blue's happiness. That exact amount of time is unquantifiable. Yet it is, without doubt, the most meaningful statistic of all.

Thursday 31 December

It's almost done. The final day of a year without social media.

It became clear early on in this project that I was hoping to have set-in-stone preconceptions confirmed. Twitter was all toxic rudeness, Instagram a poseurs' parade, Facebook an infinite maze of echo chambers and conspiracy theories. No doubt all of those critiques carry a degree of truth, but they are so lacking in nuance and perspective. 12 months off social media, breathing in the experiences of Paul, and Lindo, and Sam Loveridge, and Iain Aitchison, has obliterated such closeted thinking. Social media is affected by vanity and vacuousness. But it also offers community, support, happiness, light, hope. Five values which everyone needed in a big way during this unprecedented year.

The watershed personal takeaway is that every facet of my existence prior to 2020 centred on an unending quest for validation by numbers. Relationship highs, mental health woes, anything and everything my children got up to: it was life, sure, but life as one non-stop content stream, searching for the next number-generating overshare. I wrote in January that my biggest mental health boost came from earning 230 Likes after sharing my CBT story. I am still hugely grateful for that support, but also now aware that the surge in self-esteem was temporary. My only means of drumming up confidence was moving from one high score to the next, like an impossible-to-complete videogame.

The second half of this project therefore panned out very differently to my expectations. For the first time in my adult life I felt comfortable being me, rather than a try-too-hard parody. Psoriasis, lazy eye, Adrian Mole mannerisms, the lot. Checking the Prologue and early chapters makes me wince now. The level to which I took offence at a few people no-showing a party, the weight I placed on a blue tick, my entire approach to life: I needed others to prop me up, and call me great, because I felt incapable of doing so myself. It's all there in the January and February entries: self-loathing enshrouded in the odd dad joke, because my intravenous drip of digital thumbs-up had been removed. Yet with no other social media safety net, I had to forge my own path.

A knock-on effect was that my circle of close friends changed profoundly. I can fit the number I message daily on one hand with a thumb to spare. When I had that cancer scare a year ago I had no idea who to turn to. In contrast, the big events of this year from spring onwards – the passing of my Uncle Dave, Little Blue's possible autism diagnosis, the ongoing challenges forced on us all by a pandemic – haven't triggered that same sense of isolation. I feel supported and loved unconditionally by three or four key people.

I cross my fingers that they know it's a mutual arrangement. Social media conditions us to take things at face value. Because your mate is smiling in her Insta pic, she's beautifully happy on the inside. Yet so often it's a facade. Knowing that has pushed me to check in with friends as often as possible. It may feel random, intrusive even, to message someone you've not heard from in a fortnight and simply say, "How's it going? Are you okay?" Yet on occasions this year I've sent that message and received the response, "Not great". Hopefully the ensuing conversations have provided a lift.

Growing closer to a handful of intimate friends hasn't made me care about distant ones any less. Christmas Day evening, catching up with so many good people who I'd not heard from for a year, brought much contentment. I sincerely hope those on the other end felt similar. There are dozens more I'm keen to re-establish contact with in January. The one-to-one catch-ups I had bumping into my old work colleague Kate, or hearing from Palace fan Ann-Marie, felt more authentic than any of our Facebook Likes over the years. Those initial meet-ups spawned organic conversation rather than social media small talk. It's a prototype I'd like to make permanent.

If you take anything away from this book, aside from the urge to give it a one-star review on Amazon, it's that checking on one friend or family member per weekend costs less time than a single tweet or Facebook status or Insta upload. Across a 52-week year, I'd wager 10% will reply to say they're struggling.

Whatever conversation ensues, knowing that someone is there, and someone cares, can be a difference maker. You might 'only' be giving them a brief pick-me-up. You might be saving a life.

As the minutes tick down, and this extraordinary year staggers to a close, I open my laptop and unblock Instagram and Facebook. I'm still not entirely sure how to 'return'. I want no fuss. There's a temptation to wordlessly update my profile picture on each site, but that feels vainglorious. Perhaps a simple 'Happy New Year', or a recent image of the girls, or both. With quarter of an hour to go I resolve to stop over-thinking and just trust my instinct when the clock strikes midnight.

Finally, the chimes arrive. Exactly like one year ago I watch the Big Ben celebrations on TV, while bangs and booms erupt high above our little village. In that instant I realise it's months since I even thought about the local forum. There's still a natural urge to send happy new year missives – but they're to Steve, and Sam, and Lindo, rather than half the internet. Once they're dispatched from my phone I find myself staring at the laptop screen again.

Facebook and Instagram.

Instagram and Facebook.

So many opportunities, so many people to catch up with, such a wealth of content to share, more than ever after a year away.

So much pressure, so much noise, so much that could unravel at a point where I've finally gained a degree of control over my mental health.

At 12.15am, after much pondering, instinct finally kicks in, as I'd hoped it would. I know exactly what to do.

I fold the laptop screen down over the keyboard, pour a glass of water, canter up the stairs, and climb into bed.

End of month stats: December 2020*

Weight: 13st 12lb
Twitter followers: 4,885 (-40)
Facebook friends: 830 (+4)
Instagram followers: 232 (-2)
Average sleep: 6h 20min
Books read: 4 – Tom Fletcher: The Christmasaurus, *Steve Hodge:* The Man With Maradona's Shirt, *Owen Nicholls:* Love, Unscripted, *Robbie Coltrane:* B-Road Britain
Distance run: 201.5km
Time running: 18h 19min
Best 5K time: 22min 47s
Best 10K time: 52min 16s
Best half marathon time: N/A

*Friend and follower counts taken on my return to social media – see following chapter. Twitter followers noted without signing in.

EPILOGUE

Sunday 31 January 2021

I returned to social media on Thursday 7 January. After pondering Iain Aitchison's thoughts on the necessity of using contemporary methods to market old-fashioned entertainment mediums, I accepted that some form of comeback had to happen if this book were to ever be seen by anyone other than my mum.

I was shaking with nerves, and on the verge of hyperventilating, as I signed back into Facebook first, then Instagram. I couldn't bring myself to post, and was in and out of both sites in under 10 minutes.

My first port of call on properly returning to Facebook was reading the tributes to Dave Snell, my uncle, and Barrington Burrell, Paul's dad. The stories of two very good men were heart-warming, and showcased a major, albeit bittersweet, strength of social media: a permanent memorial to lost loved ones, often packed with fond memories. That revelation felt especially poignant in the midst of a pandemic.

It took 24 hours to actually post. Instinct, and possibly cliche, did indeed kick in: on Facebook I chose to replace my profile picture with one of the girls on Weston beach, pier looming in the background. I added a few more for my first Insta post, but again Lady S and Little Blue were the focus: at Stourhead and Bude and Zeal Monachorum. The consensus is the shots were an upgrade on pre-2020 efforts. Otherwise, as intended, our highlights remained private.

As agreed during my final Bristol night with Lauren and Andy H, I am yet to return to Twitter outside of limited @wrestlingquiz use for sports editor work purposes.

In addition to returning to Facebook and Instagram, I expanded my social media horizons by joining Tinder. At 41 it was my first experience of any sort of online dating, so I expected to have those Neanderthal DNA traits confirmed by precisely zero matches.

Actually, it's been fine. For all the heartbreak that followed January Girl cooling things off, pandemic rules would have forced us to immediately 'bubble' together or spend months apart. Both of those scenarios risked more pain than gain, and so her decision turned out prescient. Tinder has enabled me to draw a line on that chapter, and converse with some good people. I seem to match exclusively with pleasant Welsh ladies who've climbed Pen y Fan, so maybe my next project will be a Londoner's tour guide to the Brecon Beacons. Less Gavin & Stacey, more Benjamin & Gracie.

Early on it felt as if this book was going to be about mental health alone. That wouldn't have been apocalyptic: the more written on this subject, by both sexes, the more someone suffering from depression, anxiety, suicidal thoughts and so on is likely to seek help. However, I wanted some light on these pages to go with the darkness.

Initially I sought inspiration from comic failings: DJing the PTA disco, my unfortunate Salisbury incident. Yet as I settled into life without social media, the real highs came naturally, through family. Our week in Devon was wonderful. Christmas was the best we've ever had as a foursome, despite Mrs E and I splitting 18 months beforehand. That experience has enabled me to prioritise sensibly since reactivating Facebook and Insta. My only other two posts for the month were the announcement of this book, and a celebratory gin photo the following day. I never went back to any of the Facebook groups axed in the Prologue, and have continued to run, and prioritise old-fashioned bookworming over time on my mobile. Indeed, my most recent read was Piers Morgan's *Wake Up*: a very different take on 2020 to this one.

Morgan's book is intensely political. While my leftward leanings crept into these pages, I wanted this one to be the opposite of that. My intent was to give an idea of what life felt like without social media, wherever you stand. Liberal, conservative, green, fifty shades of grey: underneath our beliefs we're all human, all susceptible to depression and anxiety, for which social media is so often a trigger.

Leaving social media also made me more insular in terms of digesting news. Selfish, even: choosing to focus on my mental health, and daughters' upbringings, rather than the issues of the day. That won't be for everyone, but it proved healthy for us as a family. I enjoyed feeling disconnected from whatever brouhaha accompanied the US election. However, the Black Lives Matter movement provides an example of the challenge faced going forwards. I want to be involved in campaigns for equality and parity – but without finding myself caught up in Facebook warfare. I've not missed falling out with neighbours on the local group. It's going to be a delicate balancing act.

Morgan goes into much more on the above in his book. He's true to the changes he spoke about back in May: the text regularly criticises "illiberal liberalism", but it also takes Donald Trump and the UK government to task over their approach to the pandemic. His days of riling up his followers over vegan sausage rolls really do seem to be done.

As for Trump, my observation regarding non-volatile reaction to his election defeat proved premature. 15 days before Joe Biden was sworn in as US president, five people, including a police officer, died as protestors stormed the Capitol Building. In response, Trump tweeted in apparent support of the rioters, calling them "great patriots" and telling the world to "remember this day forever". He was banned from Twitter permanently on 8 January.

When I started putting pen to paper – or rather, fingertip to keyboard – the notion of a global pandemic felt limited to history books and movies such as *Contagion*. As Covid-19 spread, it became clear that every diary entry could be committed to updating the horrendous developments in China, then Italy, then across the entire globe. After careful deliberation I chose not to take that route, instead focussing on the day-to-day minutiae of raising two children, mental health battles, and trying to find pockets of joy in a desperately troubling period. The pandemic was a daily concern for us, as all families, so if at times this book painted it as a background character, please rest assured that wasn't the case in reality. My sympathies go out to all who lost loved ones, and those still struggling with Long Covid.

On 21 January, Michael and Emily Eavis announced the cancellation of the 2021 Glastonbury Festival. It was the correct call, and this time around my reaction was rational, measured, and calm.

One year ago today I was getting over January Girl by attending 'Farewell EU' drinks with Lauren and Andy H. Unaware of the manner in which Covid-19 would decimate 2020, and in need of a mental health boost, it remains a very fond memory. However, the first part of that sentence is the reason we can't emulate it: after a brief taste of freedom in December, public socialising is again banned. Instead, I make do with some WhatsApp reminiscing before heading out for a lazy lope in the rain with Steve.

Those same restrictions meant H-Buzz couldn't have a birthday party this year. But I did at least remember the date without Facebook assistance, enabling Little Blue to deliver a present and card to her front door. Progress, of sorts. That's what I'm looking for day to day, week to week, month to month, on the back of this project. Progress, of sorts.

"Cheers for everything, mate," I wheeze at Steve as we slow to the end of our drizzly gallop and pose for a snap together – which this time he does permit me to share on Strava.

"Pleasure, dude," Steve replies. "Just stick to everything you've learned. Use social media for what makes you happy. If that's just to promote the book and track running times, so be it. No big, divisive political rants. No photo galleries of Avon Valley. And, bloody hell, no falling in love with women you've only known for six weeks."

"Alright mate. Will do, on the first two. Will try, on the last one but, well, you've met me right? Thank you."

I mean those last two words wholeheartedly. Steve had no idea what he was getting into on popping over to mine for *Avengers: Endgame* 392 days ago. Neither of us did. He's been an inspiration, and a confidante, and above all a most dependable friend.

"You're welcome, Benji boy."

"Actually, I do have one last favour to ask. Social-media related, natch."

"Okay…"

"After all those years of waiting, and after the 13 months we've just had, and all our Thursday night runs… is there any chance, pretty please, that you can *finally* accept my goddamn Facebook friend request?"

"Ha. Nope!"

ACKNOWLEDGEMENTS

Committing a year to planning and writing and editing a book was the most ludicrous decision of my professional life, but also the most rewarding and fulfilling. As such, I owe a thousand F-words and a million thank yous to Olivia McLennan, who spent two decades insisting I was good enough. I guess now we find out whether she was right. Even if she wasn't, I am forever grateful to her for inspiring me to take the plunge.

Thanks also to Liv's husband Colum Cavanagh, for everything – other than the Salisbury vomiting incident.

Pitching a book is harder than writing one and while ultimately it was necessary to self-publish, I am indebted to Becky Thomas at Johnson & Alcock for her positive, tailored feedback. Thanks to Melanie Marshall for cutting and tweaking with diligence and honesty, and Andrew Leung for the Glastonbenny poster and cover design.

To Steve Angell, what do I say? The poor bloke turned up at my house one night to watch *Avengers: Endgame* and ended up cast as my wingman, to the surprise of us both. Mate, it's been a pleasure to drink with you and run with you and set the world to rights with you. Massive thanks, too, to Bethan Angell for repeatedly letting me borrow her bearded boy on a whim.

The early months of this project were written in a fog of heartbreak and mental health calamity, to the point that I almost abandoned it numerous times in February and March. I owe so much to Hazel Freear, Andy Hartup, Lauren O'Callaghan, and Andy Sherwood for steering me through.

That said, the winter weeks with January Girl propelled me over the starting line, and offered a tantalising glimpse at drive-in-movie romance. Cheers, JG, for the tunes, belief, encouragement and so very many laughs.

Many friends went above and beyond in this most unconventional year, particularly once they discovered the project. Katie 'Lindo' Castle and Sam Wise offered unconditional support on a daily basis, while Amber Chivers was a treasure trove of book and TV recommendations. Massive thanks to them, and all the mummy and daddy mates who've kept me going over the last eight years. That list begins with Lou Carter, Hannah Hillier, Anna Holbrook, Filippa Ross, Leanne Vincent-Norgate, Amelia Welham, and Curt Wise, but there are so many more too.

Massive love to Paul Burrell for transforming my perspective by way of our April chats, and to Rob Goodwin, Naveed Khan, Ann-Marie McDonald, and Anna Woodcock, for their enthusiasm and feedback. Up the Palace!

Cheers to Rich Ellershaw and Rowena Smith for combing over my first draft so willingly and thoroughly. Along similar lines, I bow down to Sophie Mason for suggesting some key last-last-last-minute changes which transformed the book for the better.

Thanks to my PTA pals and the staff at Lady S and Little Blue's school, in particular RN, AT, and AW.

Props to all at GamesRadar, especially Sam Loveridge for keeping me in gainful (and enjoyable) employment throughout the process of writing this book, and Rachel Weber, for rescuing me at E3 2012.

Thanks to Jen for bravely permitting me to include her Facebook messages in the June chapter.

Thanks to LR for limitless advice, kindness, and gin fizz.

Thanks to Iain Aitchison, Tim Beerh, Louise Blain, Alby Bowers, Kath Brice, Mel Chalfont-Griffin, Bethany Chalmers, David Chalmers, Tim Clark, Toni Duncan, Matt Elliott, Emily Graham, Fran Harvey, Nathan Irvine, James Jarvis, Sarah Jordan, Rosie Leizrowice, Helen Lewis, Al Linley-Munro, Louise

Marchant, Stefan McGarry, Sarah Montrose, Carly Nair, Rohit Kumar Neralla, Gemma Parker, Joel Snape, Kim Snell, Scott Snell, Kate Stothard, Helen Webber, Amber White, and Chris White.

Heartfelt thanks to the many Facebook friends who welcomed me back in January with all manner of kind thoughts, and support for the book. The response was overwhelming, and a total perspective changer compared to how I felt sat in that doctor's surgery 13 months beforehand. My gratitude and love to every last one of you.

I cannot thank Mrs E enough for freeing up so much time for me to write, even as the spectre of divorce hovered over us.

Frances Wilson: Everything I am I owe to you. Love you, Mum.

Donna Wilson-Marlow, Marc Ashmore, Dean Ashmore, Harry Ashmore: I adored writing about the council estates, the box rooms, the boot sales, the Dawlish days, because they reminded me of you so very much. I would not swap our upbringing for anyone's. It made us 'us'.

Much love to Graham Spencer, and my extended family: Gary Marlow, Bea Lopez De La Manzanara, April Xin, Ian Ashmore, Diana Hodges, Philip Hodges, Simon Hodges, and Donna Haines.

Thanks to Lady S and Little Blue, for being my everything.

Paint the skyline ten thousand colours
But I only need two, you can whitewash the others

SOURCE NOTES

PROLOGUE

How to charge your phone at Glastonbury, ee.co.uk (17 May 2019)

Facebook explains why it shows who ignored your event, Ashley Carman, The Verge (27 March 2018)

JANUARY

8: *Salmon Fishing in the Yemen*, dir. by Lasse Hallström (Lionsgate UK, 2011)

21: *Eleanor Oliphant is Completely Fine*, Gail Honeyman (HarperCollins, 2017)

25: China coronavirus: UK tests come back negative, BBC News (25 January 2020)

26: US basketball legend Kobe Bryant dies in helicopter crash, BBC News (26 January 2020)

26: Kobe Bryant has died in a helicopter crash, TMZ (26 January 2020)

27: Gianna Bryant: young basketball talent killed alongside father, BBC News (27 January 2020)

FEBRUARY

2: *How to Change the World*, Jean-Paul Flintoff (MacMillan, 2012)

3: Searches for JLo and Shakira spike on PHub following Super Bowl halftime performance, Pornhub press release (3 February 2020)

4: Tracy Brabin: MP tweets tongue-in-cheek retort…, BBC News (4 February 2020)

4: "Hello, sorry I don't have time…", Tracy Brabin, Twitter (4 January 2020)

11: 1 Year Without Social Media, Rohit Kumar Neralla, Noteworthy (11 February 2019)

16: Samaritans' media guidelines for reporting suicide, Samaritans (accessed 16 February 2020)

16: "Anything… we can literally choose to be anything…", Caroline Flack, Instagram (5 December 2019)

20: Male suicide: 'His death was the biggest piece in the jigsaw', BBC News (28 March 2018)

20: Suicide statistics report, Samaritans (September 2019)

24: *Rocketman*, dir. by Dexter Fletcher (Paramount Pictures, 2019)

29: More than 750,000 sign petition for 'Caroline's Law' launched by South Shields man after death of TV presenter Caroline Flack, Sarah Sinclair, The Shields Gazette (20 February 2020)

29: How petitions work, UK Government & Parliament (accessed 29 February 2020)

MARCH

4: *Mendip Times* Volume 15 Issue 9 (Mendip Times Limited, February 2020)

4: *Mendip Times* Volume 15 Issue 10 (Mendip Times Limited, March 2020)

10: Glastonbury and Hay festival organisers press on despite coronavirus fears, Mark Brown, *The Guardian* (8 March 2020)

12: "So, after much consideration…", Emily Eavis, Instagram (12 March 2020)

14: Visual guide: how the novichok suspects made their way to Salisbury, Cath Levett / Finbarr Sheehy / Pete Guest / Lydia Smears, *The Guardian* (5 September 2018)

15: Match of the Day, Jim White, *The Sunday Telegraph* (15 March 2020)

17: Coronavirus confirmed as pandemic by World Health Organization, BBC News (11 March 2020)

17: UEFA postpones Euro 2020 by 12 months, UEFA (17 March 2020)

17: Euro 2020: host cities and stadiums, UEFA (accessed 17 March 2020)

20: How proper carb-loading can help you crush your next race, Dimity McDowell, *Runner's World* (21 October 2019)

20: The right way to carb load before a race, Dimity McDowell, *Australian Women's Health* (15 June 2018)

20: The perfect pre-running breakfast, Alice Palmer, *Runner's World* (17 April 2018)

20: On-the-run fuelling for half-marathon runners, Nicola Joyce, Run Windsor (18 August 2017)

23: PE with Joe, *The Body Coach TV*, YouTube (23 March 2020)

23: The lady without the lamp, BBC News (11 May 2010)

26: *Grace's World*, YouTube (accessed 26 March 2020)

26: *Come Play With Me*, YouTube (accessed 26 March 2020)

APRIL

7: NHS Active, Strava (7 April 2020)

11: What is the KonMari method?, konmari.com (accessed 11 April 2020)

12: Coronavirus: Boris Johnson 'says it could have gone either way', BBC News (12 April 2020)

28: Roughly how many books have you read over the last 12 months?, YouGov (7 March 2019)

28: *Step By Step: The Life in My Journeys*, Simon Reeve (Hodder & Stoughton, 2018)

28: How to read more: read everywhere, Joel Snape, Live Hard (April 2017)

28: When is a nation not a nation?, Joshua Keating, The *Guardian* (20 July 2018)

30: Why do we pay more attention to negative news than positive news?, Stuart Soroka, LSA (25 May 2015)

MAY

6: *How to Grow Old: A Middle-Aged Man Moaning*, John Bishop (Ebury Press, 2019)

11: Interview: Piers Morgan on coronavirus and turning against Trump, Decca Aitkenhead, *Sunday Times* (9 May 2020)

14: Caroline Flack: Govt trying to avoid debating petitions calling for stricter media laws, campaigners allege, Gemma Peplow, Sky News (14 May 2020)

16: *102 Minutes*, Jim Dwyer & Kevin Flynn (Arrow, 2005)

16: *Notes From A Big Country*, Bill Bryson (Doubleday, 1998)

23: Stardom wrestler Hana Kimura passes away, Vatsal Rathod, Sportskeeda (23 May 2020)

23: Netflix halts release of new 'Terrace House' episodes after star Hana Kimura's death, Daniel Levine, Popculture (23 May 2020)

23: Hana Kimura passes away at 22 years old, Dave Meltzer, F4W Online (22 May 2020)

29: The ten weirdest things to do at Glastonbury, Mark Beaumont, NME (20 June 2017)

31: "They killed him right in front of cup foods...", Darnella Frazier, Facebook (26 May 2020)

31: 'World needed to see,' says woman who took video of man dying under officer's knee, Chao Xiong / Paul Walsh, *Star Tribune* (26 May 2020)

31: 17-year-old who recorded George Floyd's murder, Darnella Frazier, says she is traumatized, Ime Ekpo, The Source (29 May 2020)

31: May 31 George Floyd protest news, Amir Vera Daniella Diaz / James Griffiths / Jenni Marsh / Laura Smith-Spark / Fernando Alfonso III / Jessie Yeung / Steve George, CNN (31 May 2020)

31: Italy reacts to death of George Floyd, Margaret Kovick, Wanted in Milan (29 May 2020)

31: Anti-racism protesters around the world demand justice for George Floyd, Nadine White, Huffington Post (31 May 2020)

31: Peaceful protesters lament violence at George Floyd demonstrations, but understand the rage behind it, Alia Dastagir / Tyler Davis / Carol Hunter, *USA Today* (31 May 2020)

31: George Floyd's killing touches a nerve with Africans who know police brutality at home and abroad, Yomi Kazeem, Quartz Africa (1 June 2020)

JUNE

3: Quechua customer reviews, Decathlon (accessed 3 June 2020)

3: Quechua customer reviews, Amazon (accessed 3 June 2020)

13: Glastonbury festival 2019 tickets: how much money should I take and how do I get more?, Liam Trim, Somerset Live (27 September 2018)

25: In pictures: a hand-written playlist from an Ultimate Power night, Clare Zerny, Kentishtowner (26 July 2013)

26: Haim: why we fired our agent over equal pay, Hannah Flint, *Grazia* (13 June 2018)

26: George Floyd death: Three police reform plans compared, BBC News (17 June 2020)

28: Yoga for complete beginners: 20-minute home yoga workout, *Yoga with Adriene*, YouTube (18 November 2013)

JULY

1: OPM outs Quantic Dream's Beyond, Ellen Page mentioned in leaked shot, VG247 (4 June 2012)

5: 木村花さん母が告白　娘が明かしていた「テラスハウス」の"やらせ", *Shukan Bunshun* (accessed 5 July 2020)

5: July 6 2020 Observer Newsletter: outbreak forces WWE to make changes, F4W Online (accessed 5 July 2020)

6: Fifa v PES: the history of gaming's greatest rivalry, Ben Wilson, *The Guardian* (26 June 2020)

10: World Cup lots draw 1990, Mare Footage, YouTube (26 February 2012)

11: *Adrian Mole: The Prostrate Years*, Sue Townsend (Michael Joseph, 2009)

12: Top 10 most popular Ukrainian foods, Corina Onet, Chef's Pencil (8 May 2019)

12: Katy Perry Hot 'n' Cold Ukrainian Polka band, luca782, YouTube (24 March 2009)

12: Il Mondo, Jimmy Fontana (RCA, April 1965)

29: Premier League star Wilfried Zaha says he's 'scared' to open Instagram due to number of racist messages, Matias Grez / Darren Lewis / Zayn Nabbi, CNN (29 July 2020)

31: Grow your own rainbow activity, WaterAid (accessed 31 July 2020)

31: After the storm: one year on from Cyclone Idai, Oxfam International (accessed 31 July 2020)

31: Cyclone Idai – delivering aid by motorbike and canoe, Oxfam GB, YouTube (8 May 2019)

31: 5 problems with 'sustainable' palm oil, Greenpeace (1 November 2019)

31: Plastic pollution, Greenpeace (accessed 31 July 2020)

AUGUST

5: Your race reimagined, Great North Run (accessed 5 August 2020)

9: Secret Diary of a Call Girl's Billie Piper and Lucy Prebble have reunited for new TV drama I Hate Suzie, Benji Wilson, *Sunday Times* (6 August 2020)

19: Five years since we reopened Dawlish, Network Rail (4 April 2019)

19: Second phase of £80 million project to strengthen sea defences at Dawlish approved, ITV News (18 August 2020)

19: *Britain's Scenic Railways*, Julian Holland / David Spaven (Times Books, 2012)

19: *The South Devon Railway*, RH Gregory (The Oakwood Press, 1982)

19: The black swans, Dawlish Town Council (accessed 19 August 2020)

29: Chadwick Boseman: Black Panther star dies of cancer aged 43, BBC News (29 August 2020)

29: "Chadwick came to the White House to work with kids when he was playing Jackie Robinson…", Barack Obama, Twitter (29 August 2020)

SEPTEMBER

5: Mike Tyson learns that Street Fighter 2's Balrog was based on him, Matthew Byrd, Den of Geek (18 July 2019)

13: History of the Great North Run, NewcastleGateshead (accessed 13 September 2020)

13: Great North Run results and statistics, NewcastleGateshead (accessed 13 September 2020)

13: Kosgei breaks half marathon record at Great North Run as Farah wins sixth title, PA Media, *The Guardian* (8 September 2019)

13: Paula Radcliffe worried her career will be overshadowed by poo, James Ingham, Daily Star (23 April 2017)

18: *Twitchhiker: How One Man Travelled the World by Twitter*, Paul Smith (Summersdale, 2010)

18: Twitter's doubling of character count from 140 to 280 had little impact on length of tweets, Sarah Perez, TechCrunch (30 October 2018)

22: *Coal Black Mornings*, Brett Anderson (Little, Brown, 2018)

25: Sir David Attenborough breaks Jennifer Aniston's Instagram record, BBC News (24 September 2020)

25: "Hello Instagram, David Attenborough has spent a lifetime travelling…", David Attenborough, Instagram (24 September 2020)

28: Virtual Great North Run, Graham Bee, Strava (13 September 2020)

30: *Within the White Lines: How the Beautiful Game Saved my Life*, Ruth Fox (Inspirational, 2018)

OCTOBER

1: US computer and video gamers from 2006-2020 by gender, J Clement, Statista (accessed 1 October 2020)

2: Trump hospitalized following Covid diagnosis as ex-aide Kellyanne Conway tests positive – as it happened, Lois Beckett / Joan E Greve / Martin Belam, *The Guardian* (2 October 2020)

6: Trump Covid: President downplays virus on leaving hospital, BBC News (6 October 2020)

6: Trump says he's 'FEELING GREAT, has NO coronavirus symptoms and is looking forward to the debate next Thursday', Emily Goodin, Mail Online, (6 October 2020)

6: "Flu season is coming up…", Donald Trump, Twitter (6 October 2020)

11: *Lost: Pilot – Part 1*, dir. by JJ Abrams (Buena Vista Television, 2004)

18: Brighton and Crystal Palace get set for latest bout in the oddest of rivalries, Dominic Fifield, *The Guardian* (27 November 2017)

18: The M23 derby: the spicy story behind the fierce Crystal Palace and Brighton rivalry, Jack Porter, The Sportsman (8 March 2019)

20: Four years without social media, Rosie Leizrowice, rosieleizrowice.com (11 June 2020)

28: History of the West Pier, West Pier Trust (accessed 28 October 2020)

28: Fire hit pier reopens after £39 million facelift, *The Telegraph* (22 October 2010)

28: 6 things you didn't know about the Grand Pier, Grand Pier Weston-super-Mare (accessed 28 October 2020)

31: *Fair Play: The Women in Sport Show* – Rebecca Adlington, BBC Radio Scotland (29 October 2020)

31: Rebecca Adlington: Former Olympic champion on online abuse and body image problems, Heather Dewar, BBC Scotland (30 October 2020)

31: Olympic swimming champion Rebecca Adlington indulges her fetish for 'come to bed' shoes as she meets the Queen, Deborah Arthurs, Mail Online (3 June 2009)

NOVEMBER

1: TikTok reaches 2 billion downloads, Ashley Carman, The Verge (29 April 2020)

2: Want to delete your Facebook account? It'll take 30 days, Dalvin Brown, *USA Today* (4 October 2018)

2: Support – get answers for BlockSite frequently asked questions, BlockSite (accessed 2 November 2020)

7: Joe Biden wins US election after four tumultuous years of Trump presidency, Lauren Gambino, *The Guardian* (7 November 2020)

7: Why are we STILL waiting? Protesters gather in Pennsylvania, Georgia, Arizona and Nevada where thousands of votes are left to count as the election fiasco enters day FIVE, Matthew Wright, Mail Online (7 November 2020)

17: Rupert Grint breaks Sir David Attenborough's Instagram record, BBC News (17 November 2020)

20: *Why Are You So Fat?*, Gershon Portnoi (Simon & Schuster UK, 2010)

20: *Nice Cup of Tea and a Sit Down*, Nicey & Wifey (Sphere, 2005)

20: *Rude Britain: The 100 Rudest Place Names in Britain*, Rob Bailey & Ed Hurst (Boxtree, 2005)

25: World Cup '94: After Second Test, Maradona Is Out of World Cup, Sam Howe Verhovek, *New York Times* (1 July 1994)

25: Remembering Diego Maradona: 'The world has lost a legend', Associated Press, ABC News (25 November 2020)

25: Diego Maradona: Latest tributes and live news as football mourns an icon, Malik Ouzia, *Evening Standard* (25 November 2020)

30: 53 Incredible Facebook Statistics and Facts, Kit Smith, Brandwatch (1 June 2019)

30: Materialists on Facebook: the self-regulatory role of social comparisons and the objectification of Facebook friends, Phillip Ozimek / Fiona Baer / Jens Förster, US National Library of Medicine (20 November 2017)

DECEMBER

4: About us, The Friends of Westonbirt Arboretum (accessed 4 December 2020)

8: Covid vaccine: UK woman becomes first in world to receive Pfizer jab, Jessica Murray, *The Guardian* (8 December 2020)

8: Margaret Keenan: T-shirt gives charity a boost, BBC News (9 December 2020)

8: Biden promises 100 Million vaccine shots in 100 Days, but shortage worries Rise, Sheryl Gay Stolberg / Sharon LaFraniere, *New York Times* (8 December 2020)

15: Little Mix: Jesy Nelson leaves band after it 'took a toll on her mental health', Sky News (14 December 2020)

15: Fans praise Jesy Nelson for prioritising her mental health after leaving Little Mix, Annabel Nugent, *The Independent* (15 December 2020)

15: 'To all my Mixers, the last nine years…', Jesy Nelson, Instagram (14 December 2020)

20: The reason Bridgwater only has one 'E' in its name, Ross Millen, Somerset Live (12 December 2020)

EPILOGUE

Wake Up: Why the world has gone nuts, Piers Morgan (HarperCollins, 2020)

US Capitol riots: Everything we know about what happened when Trump's supporters stormed Washington, Ben Riley-Smith / Rozina Sabur / Nick Allen, *The Telegraph* (23 January 2021)

Trump calls his Capitol mob 'GREAT PATRIOTS' and claims they rioted because election was 'viciously stolen' - then tells them 'Go home with love…', Geoff Earle / Nikki Schwab / Emily Goodin / Katelyn Caralle / Kayla Brantley, Mail Online (6 January 2021)

'These are the things and events that happen…', Donald Trump, Twitter (6 January 2021)

Permanent suspension of @realDonaldTrump, Twitter Inc (8 January 2021)

Twitter boss: Trump ban is 'right' but 'dangerous', James Clayton (14 January 2021)

Glastonbury 2021 cancelled due to coronavirus pandemic, Will Richards, *NME* (21 January 2021)

'Thank you for all of your support and all the incredibly kind offers…', Emily Eavis, Instagram (21 January 2021)

Printed in Great Britain
by Amazon